£6.99 7Q

Library of
Davidson College

JUDGEMENT IN THE COMMUNITY

JUDGEMENT IN THE COMMUNITY

A STUDY OF THE RELATIONSHIP BETWEEN
ESCHATOLOGY AND ECCLESIOLOGY IN PAUL

BY

CALVIN J. ROETZEL

LEIDEN
E. J. BRILL
1972

ISBN 90 04 03409 9

Copyright 1972 by E. J. Brill, Leiden, Netherlands

All rights reserved. No part of this book may be reproduced or translated in any form, by print, photoprint, microfilm, microfiche or any other means without written permission from the publisher

PRINTED IN BELGIUM

To Caroline

CONTENTS

Preface ix
Abbreviations x

   I. The Problem and the Present State of Research . . . 1

  II. Background of Judgment 14

 III. Judgment Terminology, Form, and Themes in Paul's Letters 68

 IV. The Church and Judgment 109

  V. Conclusion 177

Selected Bibliography 181

Indexes 197

PREFACE

This book was presented in a somewhat different form to the Graduate School of Arts and Sciences of Duke University as a doctoral dissertation. It grew out of an original interest in the Fourth Gospel stimulated by a much admired and respected teacher at Perkins School of Theology, Professor Fred Gealy. But, as is often the case in graduate school, a study takes sudden and unexpected turns. An examination of *krisis* in the Fourth Gospel led to a study of *krisis* in a seminar on Romans with Professor Price. Through my work with him, whose advice and scholarly competence I greatly respect, I became convinced that the present project might more usefully serve the scholarly dialogue.

While it is impossible to name all of the teachers, family and friends who contributed directly to the completion of this work, I would be exceedingly ungrateful if I did not name Professors James L. Price who guided me in my dissertation research and writing, D. Moody Smith, Jr. for his stimulating comments and suggestions, W.F. Stinespring for numerous assists with Hebrew and Aramaic materials, and Ernst Käsemann for his many courtesies to me while I was at Tübingen. Lest it be suspected that I am trading on the good names of these respected scholars, let me hasten to absolve them of the mistakes in copy and judgment in this book which are my own.

I would also like to thank the Danforth Foundation whose generous assistance relieved me of financial worry in 1966-68 during my graduate study and the writing of this dissertation. Thanks are due Macalester College for giving me leave which made the revision of my dissertation possible, the editors of E.J. Brill for accepting this work for publication, and Dr. Scott Bartchy for the generous offer of the resources of the Disciples Institute in Tübingen. Last but not least, thanks to my wife whose contribution is acknowledged in the dedication of this book. Her support, patience, supportive love, and sense of humor helped me apply to this work Paul's insight about the provisional nature of all human achievements.

Tübingen, Germany
June 22, 1971   C.J.R.

ABBREVIATIONS

BT	Babylonian Talmud
CD	The Cairo Damascus Document
LXX	The Septuagint
MR	Midrash Rabbah
MT	The Masoretic Text, from *Biblia Hebraica*, edited by R. Kittel.
I QH	(The number stands for the cave in which the manuscript was found. "Q" represents "Qumran," and the following letter is the initial letter of the Hebrew title.) *hôdayôt* (thanksgivings) The Thanksgiving Psalms
I QM	*milḥāmāh* (war) The War Scroll
I QpHab	*pešer* Habakkuk (interpretation of Habakkuk) The Habbakuk Commentary
I QS	*sérek hay-yáḥad* (order of community) The Manual of Discipline
RSV	*The Holy Bible*, Revised Standard Version

CHAPTER ONE

THE PROBLEM AND THE PRESENT STATE OF RESEARCH

The concept of judgment is a major theme in Paul's theology. The sheer number of judicial references in his letters would support this statement; however, more significant than the number of allusions to judgment are the questions their interpretation raises and the theological importance of the various answers.

In the past the discussion of judgment in Paul's letters has polarized around Roman Catholic and Protestant theological positions concerning justification by faith. While allowing for the importance of this doctrine for an understanding of Paul's conception of judgment, Roman Catholic scholars have insisted strongly on the importance of works for salvation.[1] Scholars in the Reformed tradition, on the other hand, have usually interpreted Paul's view of judgment as a corollary of his doctrine of justification by faith.[2] At least one recent work offers some prospect of bridging the gap between these two positions.[3] However, the work poses an issue which it fails to resolve satisfactorily, namely, the relationship of Paul's doctrine of recompense to his doctrine of grace. In summary, we may say that Protestant studies have attempted to reconcile the apparent conflict between judgment and justification by faith in Paul's letters, and Roman Catholic scholars have been content to deny that such a conflict exists.

In the most recent studies[4] the discussion of these issues seems to have reached an impasse. If this stalemate is to be broken, New Testament scholars must attempt to see more clearly than they have the relationship of judgment to other major themes of Paul's letters. It is also important to view judgment in the light of the particular purposes of Paul's letters as well as its relation to ancient Jewish

---

[1] *Infra*, pp. 2-3.
[2] *Infra*, pp. 3-8.
[3] *Infra*, pp. 7-8.
[4] Lieselotte Mattern, *Das Verständnis des Gerichtes bei Paulus* (Abhandlungen zur Theologie des Alten und Neuen Testaments, vol. XLVII; Zürich/Stuttgart : Zwingli Verlag, 1966). Richard Campbell Devor, "The Concept of Judgment in the Epistles of Paul" (unpublished Ph. D. dissertation, Drew University, 1959).

and early Christian conceptions. It is at this point that this writer hopes to make a contribution.

This study is divided into four parts : (1) The Old Testament, apocalyptic, and rabbinic background of judgment, (2) the judgment vocabulary, form, and themes of Paul's letters, (3) judgment and the church, and (4) a summary and new directions.

As an introduction, a survey of recent scholarly work on the subject will be given.

P. Stanislas Lyonnet, S.J., cogently presents the Roman Catholic position on the relationship of judgment and faith in the Pauline letters. While acknowledging that for Paul no work of man contributes to his justification, he asserts that this justification requires from him the accomplishment of works. The Christian's life is to be full of good works; these works are the deeds of man which God works in him and they are not solely the gift of God.[1] Lyonnet chides his "separated brothers."

> C'est cette compénétration de l'activité divine et de l'activité humaine, compénétration mystérieuse assurément, mais combien Paulinienne, que beaucoup de nos frères séparés semblent avoir le plus de peine à admettre, à la suite d'ailleurs de Luther.[2]

Lyonnet notes that Luther's commentary on Romans draws heavily from Augustine's juxtaposition of the law of works and the law of faith. Drawing from Augustine, Luther distinguishes between those living by these different laws by their confidence, or lack of it, in man's own powers. The persons living by the law of works say, "I have done what is commanded." The Christian living by the law of faith says, "Give what you command."[3] For Luther, therefore, "le chrétien s'identifie donc au pécheur, incapable d'observer la Loi, aspirant à une justice toujours à acquérir, 'pro acquirenda suspirat'."[4] Lyonnet claims that Luther, haunted by the danger of succumbing to pride, has neglected an important Augustinian emphasis which is found in *de Spiritu et Littera* :

> Par la loi des œuvres Dieu dit : Fais ce que je commande (fac quod iubeo); par celle de la foi, on dit à Dieu : Donne ce que tu commandes (da quod iubes).

---

[1] "Gratuité de la justification et gratuité du salut," in *Analecta Biblica*, XVII-XVIII (2 vols.; Studiorum Paulinorum Congressus Internationalis Cathlolicus; Rome : Pontificio Instituto Biblico, 1963), I, 106.

[2] *Ibid.*, p. 109.

[3] *Ibid.*

[4] *Ibid.*

> Car, si la Loi commande, c'est pour rappeler à la foi ce qu'elle doit faire. Celui qui reçoit un ordre, s'il ne peut encore l'accomplir, doit savoir ce qu'il a à demander (si nondum potest, sciat quid petat).[1]

According to Lyonnet, Luther knows man only as sinful and impotent whereas Augustine sees two possibilities :

> ... mais s'il le peut et l'accomplit en obéissant à la Loi (si autem continuo potest et obedienter facit), il doit savoir également en vertu de quel donateur il le peut (debet etiam scire quo donante possit).[2]

Lyonnet then concludes that if justification is absolutely free and the demands may be fulfilled by faith alone then the parenetic demands are not founded on the Christian existence. Nothing is required of a Christian except faith. The author concludes : " ...bien au contraire, c'est en affirmant cette réalité de l'être chrétien, que l'on fonde le plus sûrement en dernière analyse l'absolue gratuité du salut." [3]

In light of the statements above Lyonnet's understanding of Paul's doctrine of judgment is clear. Paul's statement in Romans 2 : 4-6 that man is judged "according to his works" is no concession to the Jewish doctrine of justification by works. Justification by faith and judgment according to works are in Lyonnet's mind far from contradictory. Since they deal with different dimensions of experience, how could they be contradictory? In Lyonnet's words—

> ... le premier concerne exclusivement le passage de l'état de péché à l'état de grâce,—en termes pauliniens, de l'homme sans l'Esprit à l'homme en possession de l'Esprit ..., le second principe concerne exclusivement le jugement eschatologique. Il s'ensuit donc que Paul ne se représente pas exactement de la même façon la gratuité du salut et celle de la justification.[4]

While Lyonnet makes an interesting analysis of Luther's use of Augustine, he brings little evidence forward to support his statement against his "separated brothers."

From among Prostestant scholars Herbert Braun may be selected as author of one of the older studies on judgment in Paul.[5] Braun attempts

---

[1] *Ibid.*, pp. 109-110.

[2] *Ibid.*, p. 110.

[3] *Ibid.*

[4] *Ibid.*, p. 106. See P. Stanislas Lyonnet, S.J., "Justification, jugement, rédemption, principalement dans l'épître aux Romains," *Recherches Bibliques*, V (1960), 166-184; P. Joseph Huby, *Saint Paul Épître aux Romains* (rev. ed.; Verbum Salutis, vol. X; Paris : Beauchesne, 1957).

[5] *Gerichtsgedanke und Rechtfertigungslehre bei Paulus* (Untersuchungen zum Neuen Testament, vol. XIX; Leipzig : J.C. Hinrichs'sche Buchhandlung, 1930).

to understand the relationship of judgment and righteousness in the Pauline epistles.[1] Though the concepts are separated terminologically,[2] he argues that they belong together theologically.[3] Paul, in fact, bases a radicalized form of judgment on his doctrine of righteousness. This judgment goes beyond reward for good deeds and punishment for sinful works. Through his act of salvation God fulfills what he requires in the judgment.[4] God's righteousness residing in the Christian completes the judgment demand on the Christian.[5] The unique thing about Paul's doctrine of judgment is the coupling of the strong judgment norm with a great confidence in the favorable outcome for Christians.[6] This confidence is not based on the expectation of a judgment in which sin is overlooked but rather on the belief that God's righteousness will actually mould Christians to the will which is revealed at the judgment.[7] Through submission to the gift of righteousness one actually performs what is required. Therefore, the reward which is received in the judgment is what one is due.[8]

In this connection Braun observes that Paul is unconcerned with the question of motive for one's action (I Cor. 9:16, 23, 27). The basis for this lack of concern on the part of the apostle lies in his conviction that the power ($\pi\nu\epsilon\hat{\upsilon}\mu\alpha$) to perform righteous acts was more important than the proper starting-point for behavior.[9] Here Braun touches an important issue for our study, but he fails to see the implications of this insight for further interpretation of Paul's theology.

Braun argues that Paul borrowed his judgment ideas from his Jewish background, but that he radically altered their application.[10] For example, the object of the judgment is now the Christian people rather than the heathen nations.[11] No longer does God show partiality to the

---

[1] *Ibid.*, pp. 32-33.
[2] Braun, *Gerichtsgedanke*, pp. 78-79.
[3] *Ibid.*, p. 92.
[4] *Ibid.*, p. 98.
[5] *Ibid.*, p. 61.
[6] *Ibid.*, p. 63.
[7] *Ibid.*, p. 95.
[8] *Ibid.*, p. 98.
[9] *Ibid.*, p. 94.
[10] *Ibid.*, p. 44. Braun observes that Paul speaks of judgment over the Christians about sixty times versus barely twenty times over the non-Christians.
[11] *Ibid.*, p. 50.

chosen people.¹ Furthermore, the severity of the judgment is softened.² Finally, Paul no longer sets reward and works, or sin and punishment in a *quid pro quo* relationship.³

Although Braun argues that Paul alters the Jewish materials which he borrows to conform to his Christian outlook, at some points Paul failed fully to assimilate these materials. Certain atomistic tendencies remain from Paul's background although these do not dominate his theological understanding of judgment.⁴ Some parenetic sections in Paul's letters reveal undigested Jewish and Hellenistic materials which Paul has not fully assimilated into his theological outlook.⁵ After making this point Braun asks rhetorically, "Sollte aber ein gelegentlicher Rückfall in den Tenor jüdischer Paränese uns wundern bei einem Mann, der die erste Hälfte seines Lebens wie kein anderer in den Voraussetzungen jüdischer Soteriologie gelebt hat?" ⁶

Braun's study is significant because it views Paul's doctrine of judgment in relationship to an important motif other than justification by faith. Moreover, in Braun's study Paul alters but does not repudiate his background as a Jew. Nevertheless, the study is incomplete at other points. Braun fails to see the corporate nature of both judgment and righteousness in Paul's thought. He likewise fails to notice the degree to which the eschatological tension in Paul's thought affects his discussion of judgment and righteousness.

More recently, Lieselotte Mattern has given an excellent statement of the classical Reformed understanding of judgment in Paul.⁷ Miss Mattern's work treats judgment in light of the doctrine of justification by faith and is divided into two parts: Section One deals with the possibility of the Christian experiencing the judgment of condemnation. Section Two treats the passages in which the Christian is judged in a more limited sense.

In the first section of her treatment, Miss Mattern views Paul's statements in juxtaposition to the judgment concepts of "late Judaism." The Jewish materials, according to Miss Mattern, serve Paul as a

---

¹ *Ibid.*, p. 33. After charting Paul's juridical and soteriological terms, Braun concludes that Paul is less interested in reprisal than in salvation.

² *Ibid.*, p. 58.

³ *Ibid.*, p. 51.

⁴ *Ibid.*, pp. 96-97. Braun cites Rom. 2:6-11, I Cor. 6:9-10.

⁵ *Ibid.*, p. 97.

⁶ Mattern, *Verständnis*.

negative example of the kind of judgment from which Christians are delivered. Since Christians have been and will be justified *sola gratia*, the last judgment of condemnation does not apply to them. As Miss Mattern says, "Paulus hält das sola gratia der Rechtfertigung heute und im Endgericht ohne Abstriche durch." [1] This freedom from the judgment remains in spite of the presence of sin in the Christian. Only if the Christian ceases to be a Christian is he liable to the judgment of condemnation.[2]

In Section Two of her book, Miss Mattern treats the specific passages which deal with the judgment of the Christian in a more limited sense. The last judgment, according to Miss Mattern, makes a sharp distinction between the believer and the unbeliever, between the saved and the damned. But, in a more limited sense, the relative goodness of the works of the Christian will be decided. It is not the good works which will justify the Christian because the works of the Christian are only a way of participating in the work of God. The Christian as a fellow-worker with God exercises his responsibility at different levels of achievement and it is the degree of the Christian's participation in the work of God that is judged. Thus it is not the sin of the Christian which demands a judgment but his good works must be taken seriously. Thus, Miss Mattern concludes, Paul's doctrine of judgment fits quite well with his doctrine of righteousness *sola gratia*.[3]

We can be grateful for Miss Mattern's clear, careful, and tightly reasoned treatment of the role of judgment in Pauline theology. A number of questions can be raised, however, about her presentation. Her tendency to make justification by faith normative is thoroughly Lutheran in outlook, but one may ask whether or not it is thoroughly Pauline. Paul's views are set in sharp opposition to the thought of contemporary Judaism, and isolated from his background. It is tacitly assumed that all of the judgment passages in Paul's letters can be understood through the principle of justification by faith. But this assumption overlooks the probability that Paul's purposes in writing were more complex and varied. Using justification by faith uniformly as the norm for interpreting Paul's thought, Miss Mattern's work inevitably focuses on the individual, virtually excluding the corporate dimension in Paul's thought. Her approach necessarily eliminates any possibility of understanding

---

[1] *Ibid.*, p. 213.
[2] *Ibid.*, pp. 212-215.
[3] *Ibid.*, pp. 212-215

Paul's doctrine of judgment in relationship to his understanding of salvation history. Finally, Miss Mattern's emphasis on individual salvation by faith tends to relax the eschatological tension in Paul which this study will attempt to show is a very significant factor in Paul's doctrine of judgment.

In his Drew University dissertation, "The Concept of Judgment in the Epistles of Paul," Richard Campbell Devor takes a position similar to that of Miss Mattern. He sharply distinguishes Paul the Christian, justified by grace, from Paul the Jew, justified by works. In the summary of his position, he says:

> What, then, judgment according to works meant for the Christian ... was not an incomprehensible throwback to Judaism, nor a hopeless paradox, nor even manifest proof of his justification by faith, although it was that. The ultimate solution to the problem of justification by faith and judgment according to works ... was that the works brought forth by faith, were determinative of the position of the redeemed within the Kingdom of God.[1]

One could fault Devor's work at the same points where we have criticized Miss Mattern's study.

Floyd V. Filson's position falls midway between that of Mattern and Braun. In his doctoral dissertation, *St. Paul's Conception of Recompense*,[2] Filson argues that even after becoming a Christian, Paul still retained some of his Pharisaic beliefs. Paul, according to Filson, kept his Pharisaic belief that God holds man accountable for his life, and rewards him for keeping the law while punishing him for disobedience.[3] After a careful study of the judgment passages in Paul's letters Filson attempts to refute the thesis of Gillis Petersson Wetter that the principle of reward had no significance for Paul as a Christian. While the recompense principle is important to Paul, according to Filson, the kerygma enables him to face the judgment in confidence though realizing that he is never beyond the possibility of final rejection.[4]

In Chapter X of his work, Filson attempts to show how Paul's "recompense principle" and his doctrine of grace are related.[5] He claims

---

[1] Devor, "Concept of Judgment," p. 524.
[2] Floyd V. Filson, *St. Paul's Conception of Recompense*, herausgegeben von Hans Windisch (Untersuchungen zum Neuen Testament, vol. XXI; Leipzig: J.C. Hinrichs'sche Buchhandlung, 1931).
[3] *Ibid.*, p. 8.
[4] *Ibid.*, pp. 92-97.
[5] *Ibid.*, pp. 126-132.

that "Paul held the two lines of thought together at the same time and without any feeling of inconsistency." [1]

Filson's work is an important one because it seeks to understand Paul in conjunction with rather than in isolation from his background. Filson, however, is not absolutely consistent on this point. In his "Apendix II. Paul and Luther," Filson notes that "Luther's experiences at the time of entering the monastery and the time of breaking with the Roman Catholic Church show no signs of absolute break with the past as do those of Paul." [2] In spite of Filson's effort, generally speaking, to see Paul in light of his background, his work suffers from some of the same weaknesses we have seen in the studies of Miss Mattern and Herbert Braun. Filson tends to see Paul's thought of the individual in isolation from his comprehension of the broad movements of salvation history and the church. Consequently, Paul's doctrine of judgment sounds highly individualistic in Filson's interpretation. This interpretation in turn makes Paul's ethics appear atomistic.

While the works cited above constitute the major scholarly treatments of judgment in the Pauline Epistles, a number of scholars have presented shorter interpretations. Some scholars have argued that the judgment concepts in Paul's letters cling to his argument as relics of his Jewish background which he was never able to assimilate with his Christian understanding of grace.[3] Maurice Goguel, however, objects that it is unfair to expect Paul to present a closely reasoned, logically developed theological treatise. Certain conflicting concepts, he argues, may have lain side by side in the apostle's theology without arousing any feeling of uneasiness.[4]

The great majority of scholars, however, feel that for Paul justifica-

---

[1] *Ibid.*, p. 129.

[2] *Ibid.*, p. 144.

[3] Wilhelm Bousset, *Der Erste Brief an die Korinther*, herausgegeben von Johannes Weiss (Die Schriften des Neuen Testaments, vol. II; Göttingen : Vandenhoeck & Ruprecht, 1908), pp. 84-85. "Trotz aller Predigt von Glaube und Gnade kennt er den evangelischen Gerichtsgedanken in seinem ganzen Ernst." *Ibid.*, p. 94. William Wrede, *Paul*, trans. Edward Lummis (London : Philip Green, 1907), p. 136, argues that Paul was never able completely to discard his Jewish belief in judgment.

[4] Maurice Goguel, "Le caractère, à la fois actuel et futur, du salut dans la théologie paulinienne," *The Background of the New Testament and Its Eschatology : In Honour of Charles Harold Dodd*, ed. W.D. Davies and David Daube (Cambridge : At the University Press, 1956), p. 336.

tion by faith and God's righteous judgment are not conflicting concepts. They argue that Paul views faith as a positive response to God's justifying act; judgment tests one's stewardship of the salvific deed, or preserves the decision character of faith. Faith is a positive appropriation of God's gift; judgment measures the responsible use of the gift.[1]

The above survey shows that with few exceptions scholars have consistently discussed judgment in relationship to justification by faith. This has remained true in spite of the fact that a significant number of Paul's references to judgment occur in contexts where faith is not mentioned,[2] that an increasing number of scholars question the assump-

---

[1] Emanuel Hirsch, "Das Gericht Gottes," *Zeitschrift für systematische Theologie*, I (1923), 225, says that "Er sagt beides, dass wir das Unterpfand des Geistes schon empfangen haben, und dass wir dem Gericht noch entgegengehen." Paul Althaus, *Die Letzten Dinge* (6th ed.; Gütersloh : Carl Bertelsmann Verlag, 1956), pp. 193-196. Joseph Bonsirven, *L'Évangile de Paul* (Paris : Éditions Montaigne, 1948), p. 205. According to Bonsirven, Paul believed in justification by faith "...mai foi qui n'exclut pas les œuvres, ni avant, ni pendant, ni après la justification." Richard Kabisch, *Die Eschatologie des Paulus* (Göttingen : Vandenhoeck & Ruprecht, 1893), p. 254. Kabisch believed that there was no ressurrection except for the Christians ; therefore, commenting on II Cor. 5:10 he says, "Doch ist dabei nicht die Frage, ob σωτηρία oder ἀπώλεια, da die σωτηρία ihnen sicher ist... sondern nur, ob grössere oder geringere δόξα." Archibald Robinson and Alfred Plummer, *A Critical and Exegetical Commentary on the First Epistle of St. Paul to the Corinthians* (The International Critical Commentary; New York : Charles Scribner's Sons, 1916), pp. 159-160. Jean Héring, *Le Royaume de Dieu et sa Venue* (Paris : Libraire Felix Alcan, 1937), p. 252, says, at the judgment "Il ne s'agit que du rang et du rôle à remplir parmi les 'sauvés'." Adolf Schlatter, *Der Glauben in Neuen Testament* (4th ed.; Stuttgart, Calwer Vereinsbuchhandlung, 1927), p. 382. Hans Lietzmann, *The Beginnings of the Christian Church*, trans. Bertram Lee Wolf (3rd ed. rev. London : The Lutterworth Press, 1953), p. 123, says, "The Last Judgment decides whether the Christian has really been justified in the spirit by faith, or whether he has remained in the flesh as a sinner. This is not casuistical legalism... but, it is the final and crucial question as to what dominates the Christian life."

On the relationship of faith and works see : William Sanday and Arthur C. Headlam, *A Critical and Exegetical Commentary on the Epistle to the Romans* (The International Critical Commentary; New York : Charles Scribner's Sons, 1895), p. 57. Heinrich Schlier, *Der Brief an die Galater* (Kritisch-exegetischer Kommentar über das Neue Testament; Göttingen : Vandenhoeck & Ruprecht, 1949), pp. 195-196. Ernst Lohmeyer, *Die Briefe an die Philipper, an die Kolosser, und an Philemon* (9th ed.; Kritisch-exegetischer Kommentar über das Neuen Testament ; Göttingen: Vandenhoeck & Ruprecht, 1930), p. 101. Robert Henry Charles, *A Critical History of the Doctrine of the Future Life* (London : Adam and Charles Black, 1899), p. 398.

[2] Davies, *Paul*, p. 222, observes that it "is only in those Epistles, namely, Galatians and Romans, where Paul is consciously presenting the claims of his Gospel over against those of Judaism that Justification by Faith is emphasized." Where Paul speaks of

tion that justification by faith is the central theme of Paul's letters,[1] and that many scholars believe that the major thrust of Paul's theology is corporate rather than individualistic.[2]

This study will take place in a context which has been formed largely by the works of four men : Albert Schweitzer, William David Davies, Johannes Munck, and Hans Joachim Schoeps. The works of all of these men raise some incisive questions about the traditional interpretation that has been put on the relationship of judgment and justification by faith in Paul's letters.

In 1931 Albert Schweitzer published his significant study, *The Mysticism of Paul the Apostle*.[3] At least two hypotheses dominate Schweitzers work. First, he believed that it was possible to separate Hellenistic from Semitic concepts of mysticism in first-century Judaism. Second, he believed that one could distinguish between apocalyptic Judaism and Pharisaism in the first century. Consequently Schweitzer argued that Paul's thought was rooted in Jewish apocalypticism and was the culmination of it. Schweitzer emphasized the cosmic significance of Jesus' death and resurrection; moreover, he insisted that the "in Christ" motif was normative for understanding Paul. Consequently, in Schweitzer's understanding of Paul the customary emphasis on justification by faith as the center of Paul's theology was displaced.[4]

---

judgment in I Cor. 3:10-16, 4:1-5, 5:1-8, 6:1-11, 10:1-12, 11:27-32, II Cor. 5:10, and in II Thess. 2:1-12, there is no mention of justification by faith.

[1] More recently Käsemann and Stendahl have argued persuasively that justification by faith deals less with the introspective conscience than with the inclusion of the Gentiles in the true Israel. Krister Stendahl, "The Apostle Paul and the Introspective Conscience of the West," *Harvard Theological Review*, XXIX (1963), 199-215, reprinted in S.H. Miller and G. Ernest Wright (eds.), *Ecumenical Dialogue at Harvard* (Cambridge, Mass. : Belknap Press of Harvard University Press, 1964), pp. 236-256; Ernst Käsemann, "God's Righteousness in Paul," trans. Wilfred F. Bunge, in *The Bultmann School of Biblical Interpretation : New Directions*? (Journal for Theology and the Church, vol. I; New York : Harper Torchbooks, 1965), pp. 100-110.

[2] Howard Clark Kee, Franklin W. Young, Karlfried Froehlich, *Understanding the New Testament* (2d ed.; Englewood Cliffs, N.J.: Prentice Hall, Inc., 1965), pp. 193-194; Russell Philip Shedd, *Man in Community : A Study of St. Paul's Application of Old Testament and Early Jewish Conceptions of Human Solidarity* (London : The Epworth Press, 1958); cf. *infra*, pp. 11-13.

[3] Albert Schweitzer, *The Mysticism of Paul the Apostle*, trans. William Montgomery (New York : The Macmillan Co., 1955).

[4] Schweitzer, *Mysticism*, p. 225, called the "doctrine of righteousness by faith" "a subsidiary crater" in Paul's thought.

Schweitzer's work shifted the emphasis in Paul's theology away from a preoccupation with individual salvation and a concern with inward motive to participation in God's salvation events.[1]

Although Schweitzer's work explains too simply the influence of Paul's background on his thought, and draws too sharply the line between Jewish apocalypticism and Pharisaism,[2] nevertheless, his work did much to question the tendency to view Paul in opposition to Judaism and in highly individualistic terms. Although Schweitzer's work can be faulted at some points, it has informed the work of most Pauline scholars since his time.

The works of William David Davies have shown both the strengths and weaknesses of Schweitzer's book.[3] Davies has shown that the lines between Palestinian and Hellenistic Judaism were not as distinct as Schweitzer had believed, and that Schweitzer was right to see Paul in light of his background rather than in juxtaposition against it. Davies questioned Schweitzer's tendency to see apocalyptic thought and Pharisaism as separate entities,[4] but he has agreed with Schweitzer that justification by faith is less than the heart of Pauline theology. Davies argues that—

> ... even if we could accurately characterize Rabbinic Judaism as entirely a religion of works we must deprecate that approach to our problem which exaggerates the antithesis between Pauline Christianity as a religion of Faith and the Spirit and Rabbinic Judaism as a religion of obedience and the Torah, and which has elevated the doctrine of Justification by Faith to the primary place in Paul's thought. In some contexts justification is merely one metaphor among many others employed by Paul to describe his deliverance through Christ, and we are not justified in petrifying a metaphor into a dogma.[5]

---

[1] *Ibid.*, pp. 101-140.

[2] See William David Davies, "Paul and Judaism" in *The Bible and Modern Scholarship*, ed. J. Philip Hyatt (Nashville : The Abingdon Press, 1965), pp. 178-186, reprinted in William David Davies, *Paul and Rabbinic Judaism* (2d ed.; New York : Harper Torchbooks, 1967), pp. vii-xv; Robert C. Tannehill, *Dying and Rising with Christ* (Beiheft zur Zeitschrift für die neutestamentliche Wissenschaft und die Kunde der Älteren Kirche, vol. XXXII; Berlin : Töpelmann, 1967), p. 5.

[3] William David Davies, *Christian Origins and Judaism* (Philadelphia : The Westminster Press, 1962), pp. 19-30; Davies, *Paul;* Charles Harold Dodd, *The Bible and the Greeks* (London : Hodder & Stoughton, 1935); Erwin Ramsdell Goodenough, *Jewish Symbols in the Graeco-Roman Period* (12 vols.; New York : Pantheon Books, 1953-1965).

[4] Davies, *Paul*, p. xi.

[5] Davies, *Paul*, pp. 221-222.

Half apologetically, Davies adds :

> It will, of course, be understood that when we relegate the doctrine of Justification by Faith to the periphery and not to the centre of Paul's thought, we do not thereby belittle its profound truth or its significance for Christian theology; we merely assign it to that proper place where it can be viewed in true perspective in its relation to the Pauline teaching as a whole. It is a simplification and even a falsification of the complexity of Paul's thought to pin down Justification by Faith as its quintessence.[1]

In 1954 Johannes Munck's major contribution to Pauline scholarship appeared.[2] In a caveat against the Tübingen School, Munck views Paul in light of *Heilsgeschichte*. Paul understood his call not as an individual's conversion only but as an eschatological event. The completion of God's *Heilsplan*, according to Munck, depended on the fulfillment of his eschatological function. As is readily apparent, Munck argues that Paul is writing less about salvation as an individual experience than about God's entire work of salvation which encompasses all mankind as well as the whole of history.

Hans Joachim Schoeps's equally significant work appeared five years after Munck's.[3] The pivotal section of Schoeps's work is his chapter on eschatology (chapter III). Schoeps agrees basically with Schweitzer that more weight should be given to eschatology in interpreting Paul than is customarily given. According to Schoeps, only the conviction that the eschaton had already begun with the death of Jesus differentiated Paul from the first-century apocalyptists :

> We should misunderstand the apostle's letters as a whole, and the governing consciousness from which they sprang, if we failed to recognize that Paul only lives, writes, and preaches in the unshakeable conviction that his generation represents the last generation of mankind.[4]

Although Schoeps radically disagrees with Munck's understanding of

---

[1] *Ibid.*, p. 222.

[2] Johannes Munck, *Paulus und die Heilsgeschichte* (Aarsskrift for Aarhus Universitet, vol. XXVI; Aarhus : Universitets forlaget, 1954), English trans. *Paul and the Salvation of Mankind*, trans. Frank Clarke (Richmond, Va.: John Knox Press, 1959).

[3] Hans Joachim Schoeps, *Paulus : Die Theologie des Apostles im Lichte der jüdischen Religiongeschichte* (Tübingen : J.C.B. Mohr, 1959), English trans. *Paul : The Theology of the Apostle in the Light of Jewish Religious History*, trans. Harold Knight (Philadelphia : The Westminster Press, 1961).

[4] Schoeps, *Paul*, p. 102.

Paul at many places,[1] it is significant that, like Munck, he sees eschatology as the key to understanding Paul's thought.[2]

Though this sketch does not include all of the recent studies of Paul which are significant, it may serve to delineate the context of Pauline scholarship in which this study is placed. The most recent studies on judgment in the Pauline Epistles have failed to appropriate the insights of the scholars mentioned above. Thus one of the significant motifs of Paul's thought has not received the attention it merits.

---

[1] See Chapter II (pp. 51-87), where Schoeps argues against Munck that Paul was rooted in the primitive *Gemeinde*.

[2] Owing to the continuing significance and general acquaintance with these works, it is unnecessary to give a full review here. The significance of these works for this study, however, could not be overlooked.

CHAPTER TWO

BACKGROUND OF JUDGMENT

In this chapter we shall investigate the background of Paul's understanding of judgment. This consideration will be divided into four parts: (1) the prophetic understanding of judgment, (2) the apocalyptic background (3) judgment in the Qumran texts, and (4) judgment in the rabbinic materials.[1] It is readily acknowledged that the lines between these various categories are often blurred, and that there is some interplay between them; nevertheless, while realizing the complexity of the period from which the sources are derived, such distinctions are useful for an orderly discussion. It should be added that all of these materials are relevant, we believe, for understanding Paul. While they do not explain Paul's doctrine of judgment, they illumine the thought of this unique and highly original person.

---

[1] Philo's concept of judgment differs noticeably from Paul's and, therefore, is omitted.
   Although division and separation into equal opposites is a common theme in Philo as among the Stoics, his understanding of judgment differs markedly from that which we see in Paul. Sometimes, but not consistently, Philo associates judgment with the dividing act of the Logos; however, this separation is not always called *krisis*. The word *krisis* is not a prominent one even in such a treatise as "On Rewards and Punishments," in *Philo*, trans. F.H. Colson (10 vols.; The Loeb Classical Library; Cambridge, Mass.: Harvard University Press, 1939), VIII, 365ff. Where *krine* is used in this treatise it appears in a wholly positive sense: "When He judges that there are some worthy of salvation, men of peaceful disposition who cherish brotherly affection and goodly fellowship in whom envy has either found no room at all or has entered only to take its departure" (*ibid.*, p. 391). In the discussion of the curses which are euphemistically called loss of reason there is no mention of judgment (*ibid.*, pp. 393 ff.). Philo is careful to purge God of negative emotions. Not once does Philo suggest that God condemns the wicked. The Old Testament references to the anger of God are rationalized ("On the Unchangeablness of God," in *ibid.*, p. 21). God's regret for having made man is allegorized. It appears that for Philo *krisis* has its classical Greek meaning: "sifting" or "parting" (Homer, *The Iliad*, trans. A.T. Murray [2 vols.; The Loeb Classical Library; Cambridge, Mass.: Harvard University Press, 1960]). It is easy to see that judgment for Philo lacks the same moral seriousness that it has for the apocalyptic writers and for Paul.

A. Judgment in the Literary Prophets

When we consider judgment in the literary prophets, we notice at once how deeply their thought is rooted in Israel's rich theological tradition. Both God's creation and the covenant figure prominently in prophetic thought, if not always explicitly, at least implicitly. Within their heritage the moral seriousness of the judgment, for example, was directly related to the concept of the covenant. As Walther Eichrodt notes, the Elohistic history

> ... kept alive a constant feeling for the terrifying seriousness of judgment as the means by which the holy God protected his covenant from those who despised it; and therefore they were awake to the danger of falling prey to that relentless divine vengeance which continually threatened the nation whenever it proved slack or faithless in service.[1]

Thus we see that the memory of the curse which Yahweh laid on disobedient mankind (Gen. 3:14-19) continued to have great significance for Israel's faith.

Along with Israel's emphasis on the covenantal demand went a corresponding delight in the joys of the creation. Prosperity and wealth were seen as a sign of God's favor. This enjoyment of the creation could exist side by side with the emphasis on the moral seriousness of judgment without any sense of contradiction. As a consequence, great social gaps could exist between rich and poor without stirring the rich to works of compassion. Thus the stage was set for the message of the early literary prophets.[2]

One must grasp the rich meaning of the key terms the prophets used in order fully to appreciate their message of judgment. An exhaustive word study is not possible within the scope of this investigation; therefore, we shall confine our list to the most significant words and phrases which cluster around the judgment pronouncements.

1. שפט in the most ancient Old Testament traditions means "to rule," "to counsel,"[3] or "to judge." The executive, counseling, and judicial functions of this word are inseparable. It is clear in I Samuel 8 that the king is also the judge. In II Samuel 15:4 Absalom's lament,

---

[1] Walther Eichrodt, *Theology of the Old Testament*, trans. J.A. Baker (2 vols.; The Old Testament Library; Philadelphia : The Westminster Press, 1961), I, 462-463.

[2] Eichrodt, *Theology*, I, 464.

[3] I am indebted to Dr. William F. Stinespring for this suggestion.

"Oh, that I were שֹׁפֵט in the land," is simultaneously a desire to be judge and king. In II Samuel 15:6 the people of the land come "to the king for judgment [advice?]." This unity of function is also seen in I Samuel 8:20. The people say, "Our king will *judge* us." [1] In Judges the statement that "so and so" "judged Israel" means that the person ruled a tribe, and served as its military leader, champion, counselor, deliverer and judge (Judges 2:16).

Lindblom properly notes that the noun form מִשְׁפָּט also had a very broad application. It included all obligations whether religious or moral, as well as ethical obedience and proper attitude.[2]

We see then that שפט and its cognates had positive as well as negative connotations. To say that God is judge means Israel's conduct is given great moral seriousness; the people who violate the covenant with God can expect punishment. On the other hand, the oppressed can look to the judge for freedom from their oppressors and relief from their affliction. Very often the emphasis on God's chastisement of his refactory people was minimized, and his uplifting of the weak and the oppressed was emphasized and interpreted to mean that God showed special favoritism toward Israel. Eichrodt says

> ... so long as the minds of the mass of the people were dominated by the conviction that for all their shortcomings they represented a nation pleasing to God ... God's judicial authority occupied less of their attention than his maintenance of the rights of the covenant people.[3]

These observations help us to understand why for the literary prophets God's right to condemn and destroy was anchored in his sovereign authority over his creation. God is at once counselor, judge, and king of Israel.

2. צדקה is also an important word for our consideration. According to Eichrodt any attempt to define the concept of divine righteousness is hampered by our inability to know the original root meaning of צדק.[4] When the term is applied to God it often carries forensic connotations; however, the word includes vastly more than a sense of distributive justice.

---

[1] Emphasis added.
[2] Johannes Lindblom, *Prophecy in Ancient Israel* (Philadelphia: The Westminster Press, 1965), p. 348.
[3] Eichrodt, *Theology*, I, 243.
[4] *Ibid.*, p. 240.

Ernst Käsemann rightly says:

> From the beginning it should also be noted that in the sphere of the Old Testament and Judaism righteousness means primarily not a personal, ethical quality, but a relationship. Originally it meant loyalty to the community, and in a trial referred to the restored "status" of the member of the community who had been declared innocent.[1]

Righteousness, then, designates behavior which is true to and responsible for the claims of a relationship.[2] It was believed that God kept his word by safeguarding the community against outside foes. Israel's victories were therefore proofs of God's righteousness (Judges 5:11, 1 Sam. 12:7). Furthermore, Yahweh safeguarded the life of his community by protecting it from the internal perversion of משפט.

As can be seen from the description above, the relationship between משפט and צדקה is a very close one. The terms are not, however, synonymous. צדקה is the more basic term theologically because it is God's righteousness which guarantees his משפט. As we have noted in the above discussion of שפט, the conviction that God always acts in the best interest of his people allows for perversion. God's covenant relationship can be accepted, some may assume, without accepting the accompanying responsibilities.

It was at this point that literary prophecy interpreted God's righteousness in a new way. The succor which God gives his people was connected with his awful judgment on the covenant breaker. God preserves his righteousness by destroying those who violate his covenant.[3]

It is interesting to note that in the exilic and post-exilic periods צדקה is understood more and more to designate the obligation Yahweh imposes upon himself to guarantee his covenant. צדקה is associated with Yahweh's promise to assure Israel's future, and to defend its cause. Consequently, צדקה becomes practically synonymous with help, salvation or deliverance.[4] No more, as in pre-exilic times, do we hear of God destroying the covenant breaker to preserve his צדקה.

3. דין appears only ten times in the literary prophets;[5] nevertheless,

---

[1] "God's Righteousness in Paul," pp. 271 ff. See Rudolf Bultmann's response to Käsemann: "ΔΙΚΑΙΟΣΥΝΗ ΘΕΟΥ," *Journal of Biblical Literature*, LXXXIII (1964), 12-15.

[2] See Eichrodt, *Theology*, I, 240.

[3] Eichrodt, *Theology*, I, 245.

[4] Lindblom, *Prophecy*, p. 382.

[5] Jeremiah 5:28 (twice), 21:12, 22:16 (twice), 30:13 (twice); Isaiah 3:13, 10:12; Zechariah 3:7.

the word merits consideration. This technically legal term for lawsuit is applied to God only in Isaiah 3:13. In the Jeremiah references the word refers to a lawsuit on behalf of the defenseless poor. It is clear in all of these ten references that דין has a more restricted meaning than does שפט. דין applies more narrowly to the judicial *process*. משפט may designate the legal process but its meaning transcends the forensic connotation to include the relationship of Yahweh with the accused.[1]

4. חמה. זעם. חרון אף, חרון are all used by the literary prophets in some connection with judgment. God's anger is an inward burning (חרון and חמה) which is blown or snorted (used with רוח and אף), or foams and boils, or breaks forth to consume the disobedient. Anthony Tyrell Hanson errs when he suggests that wrath is missing in Amos but is present in Hosea (e.g., 11:8-9).[2] While it is true that the term "wrath" does not appear in Amos, there are copious references to fire (אש) which will consume his wayward peoples (1:4, 7, 10, 12, 14; 2:1, 5, etc.). Surely in these contexts fire is synonymous with wrath.

The manifestation of God's wrath is closely related to a breach of the covenant in the pre-exilic prophets.[3] Although the pre-exilic prophets make little use of the term ברית, still the breach of the covenant stands behind almost all of the prophetic denunciations,[4] whether of the cult,[5] or of society,[6] or of political alliances,[7] or of idol worship. The fact that the term does not appear frequently—although it does appear in some important contexts (e.g., Jer. 11:1 ff., 31:31 ff., etc.)—is not the decisive factor, because the covenant concept is implicit in so many of the judgment proclamations.

The prophets constantly announce that since the people have forgotten Yahweh and have spurned his love, God will pour out his wrath upon them. Yahweh hesitates to punish his refractory people. He sends mis-

---

[1] Gerhard Kittel, *Theological Dictionary of the New Testament*, trans. Geoffrey W. Bromiley (Grand Rapids : Wm. B. Eerdmans Publishing Co., 1964), III, 924.

[2] *The Wrath of the Lamb* (London : SPCK, 1957), p. 6.

[3] Eichrodt, *Theology*, I, 465. Amos, 2:9-11, 3:2; Hosea 11:1-6; Isaiah 1:2, 5:1 f., 17:10; Jeremiah 2:1-3, 31:1-3; Ezekiel 16:4-14, as cited by Johannes Fichtner, "ὀργή" in *Theologisches Wörterbuch zum Neuen Testament*, ed. Gerhard Kittel (Stuttgart : W. Kohlhammer Verlag, 1954), V, 404. Cf. Eichrodt, *Theology*, I, 259.

[4] Hosea 5:10, 8:5, 13:16; Isaiah 9:11; Jeremiah 4:4, 17:4; Ezekiel 5:13, 7:3, 20:8, as cited by Fichtner, ὀργή, p. 404.

[5] Amos 5:21-27; Hosea 6:6; Isaiah 1:10-17; Jeremiah 6:20, 7:21-28, as cited *ibid*.

[6] Amos 7:10-12; Isaiah 1:15-17; Micah 3; Jeremiah 5:28.

[7] Hosea 5:13, 7:11; Isaiah 30:1-5, 31:1-3; Jeremiah 2:35-37; Ezekiel 16:23.

fortune to warn his erring children to repent and be restored. He gives Israel time to repent. He tries to educate his wayward childern in right paths, but when all of these fail Yahweh pours out his wrath in judgment (Amos 4:6-11; Isa. 9:11; Jer. 4:4; etc.).

This wrath was not an arbitrary act of God, but his legitimate reaction to Israel's offense against his holiness and to her violation of the covenant. This judgment was not sinister in its intention but rather, according to the prophets, God's wrath was his retributive justice.[1]

Some understanding of wrath as God's displeasure apparently had long been a part of Israel's religious thought. The new factor which emerged in pre-exilic prophecy was that wrath no longer was interpreted as a temporary misfortune but as inescapable eschatological doom.[2] Hence, according to Amos, the Day of Yahweh would not be a day when Israel would be vindicated but a day when she would be humiliated and shamed (5:18 ff.).

It is perhaps an overstatement to say with Eichrodt that the concept of God's wrath against Israel ended with Deutero-Isaiah.[3] It is true, however, that Israel's general outlook was much more hopeful after the exile. God's wrath from the exile on was increasingly focused on the heathen and the unfaithful in the community.[4]

5. Any preliminary study on judgment would be incomplete without at least a brief mention of the phrase יום יהוה. Judging from Amos, the Day of Yahweh was traditionally viewed in a very positive light. In 5:18 Amos says : הוי המתאוים את יום יהוה. The hithpael form of אוה means to desire or to long for something. Most likely, Israel longed for the Day of Yahweh because it promised to be a day when God's elect would be vindicated. It would be a day of great joy and happiness. It would be a day of light (5:20).

Arvid S. Kapelrud argues that since Amos mentions the Day of Yahweh in connection with cultic acts, the Day of Yahweh was a day of cultic celebration, or great rejoicing, of libations, and sacrifices (cf. Hos. 9:1 ff.).[5] More specifically, Sigmund O.P. Mowinckel believes the Day of Yahweh was the day of the celebration of the throne ascension of Yahweh, or a part of the New Year festival in the fall.[6]

---

[1] Eichrodt, *Theology*, I, 262-263.

[2] *Ibid.*, 267.

[3] *Ibid.*, p. 269.

[4] Psalms 9:17 f., 56:8, 79:6-8, 7:7, 11:5 f., 28:4, 94:2, etc.

[5] *Central Ideas in Amos* (Oslo : Oslo University Press, 1961), pp. 73-74.

[6] *Psalmenstudien II; Das Thronbesteigungsfest Jahwäs und der Ursprung der Eschatologie* (Kristiana : Dybwad, 1922-24), pp. 190-202.

Two elements in the festival are relevant to our study : (1) The idea of judgment which was associated with the festival. Perhaps this minor theme harks back to a pre-Yahwistic time. We may see some hint of this theme in Psalms 82:1 : "God has taken his place in the divine council; in the midst of the gods he holds judgment.". In a similar way, Mowinckel notes, the council of the gods in Assyria-Babylonia exercises judgment during the New Year festival.[1] (2) The coming of Yahweh which was associated with the festival. It was believed that Yahweh would come on the last day of the festival and take power over Israel and the neighboring peoples. His coming would herald a day of joy and light.[2]

If this description is accurate, then the use Amos makes of the tradition is striking. He expands and emphasizes the relatively minor role given to judgment to award it the major if not exclusive role in the festival. Consequently, Yahweh's coming will mean gloom and darkness, not joy and light.

6. ריב is often associated with a judgment pronouncement in the literary prophets. George Ernest Wright sees a basic lawsuit (ריב) pattern in the works of the pre-exilic prophets.[3] Isaiah 1:2-3, for example, he believes conforms to this pattern :

> Hear, O heavens, and give ear, O earth
> for the Lord has spoken :
> Sons have I reared and brought up,
> but they have rebelled against me.
> The ox knows its owner,
> and the ass its master's crib;
> but Israel does not know,
> my people does not understand.

Wright believes this pattern developed out of the judgment motif in the New Year festival. Yahweh, Lord of the covenant, calls the vassal to trial for breaking the covenant. He summons heaven and earth as witnesses. Whether one can agree with Wright that the lawsuit pattern runs throughout the writings of the pre-exilic prophets, one finds it difficult to dispute his claim that Micah 6:3-5 describes a lawsuit. Micah 6:1 suggests a courtroom scene :

> Arise, plead your case before the mountains,
> and let the hills hear your voice.[4]

---

[1] Mowinckel, *Psalmenstudien II*, pp. 160 ff.

[2] Kapelrud, *Central Ideas*, p. 74.

[3] "The Lawsuit of God," in *Israel's Prophetic Heritage*, ed. B.W. Anderson and W. Harrelson (New York : Harper & Brothers, 1962), pp. 26-27.

[4] Amos 3:9, 13 etc. also seem to suggest a trial.

From the word studies above it seems apparent that judgment had various positive as well as negative connotations before the pre-exilic prophets. The message of doom of these prophets undermined the sham security Israel had constructed through misappropriation of the covenant traditions. Only occasionally in the pre-exilic prophets do the positive aspects of judgment shine through. In the exilic and post-exilic prophets, however, we witness a renewed emphasis on the vindication of Israel through God's judgment.

We gain insight into the prophetic message of judgment not only through a word study but also through an investigation of the literary forms the prophets used. Claus Westermann sees two basic forms of judgment speech in the prophetic books: (1) the speech addressed to individuals within the nation, and (2) the speech addressed to the entire nation.

The speeches addressed to individuals contain the following parts:
   a. Summons to hear
   b. Accusation
   c. Introduction to the announcement of the sentence by the formula "therefore"
   d. Announcement of judgment.[1]

Amos 7:16-17 contains this type of judgment speech:
   a. Summons to hear: "Now, therefore, hear the word of the Lord."
   b. Accusation: "You say, 'Do not prophesy....'"
   c. Message formula: "Therefore, thus says the Lord:"
   d. Announcement: "Your wife shall be a harlot in the city, and your sons and your daughters ..., and your land .... You yourself...."[2]

The speech addressed to the entire nation originated with Amos. Westermann notes that all of the prophetic announcements in the books of Kings are addressed to individuals, and never to whole nations of individuals.[3] On the other hand, in Jeremiah the judgment speeches are no longer addressed to individuals but only to the nation as a whole. What is new in Amos, for example, is not the note of judgment, but the fact that judgment is pronounced on the entire nation. As Westermann says:

---

[1] *Basic Forms of Prophetic Speech*, trans. Hugh Clayton White (Philadelphia: The Westminster Press, 1967), p. 131.

[2] *Ibid.*, p. 131. Similar instances can be seen in Isaiah 7:13; 22:16; 37:23,24, 29; Jeremiah 22:15, 17; 28:13, 15b; 29:25; 36:29; 29:21, 23.

[3] *Ibid.*, p. 137.

> The sins of the nation as a whole, as the transgressions of "the corporate personality," had acquired such a significance that the commission of the prophet to intervene as the messenger from the court of God in case of a transgression (particulary of the King) is no longer sufficient. The accusation must now be brought against the entire nation and the judicial decision of God announced to all the people.[1]

Since the prophetic judgment was addressed to a "corporate personality," and since a number of misdeeds were involved, the accusation was expanded. The expansion included a general description of the sins of the people followed by an adumbration of the specific offense. For example, we see in Amos 2:1:

> General accusation : "For three transgressions of Moab, and for four ...."
> Development : "... because he burned to lime the bones of the king of Edom." [2]

A similar bifurcation took place in the announcement. The first part dealt with the intervention of God and the second part dealt with the punishment. We see this development in Hosea 13:8 :

> Intervention : "I will fall upon them like a bear robbed of her cubs, I will tear open their breast."
> Punishment : "And there I will devour them like a lion, as a wild beast would rend them." [3]

In Amos and Ezekiel especially this expansion gave the judgment speeches more flexibility and latitude for greatly expanding the units. Westermann's work helps us see the creative way the literary prophets used existing forms for their bold enterprise. It is obvious that the prophets used this pregnant form not only as a framework for presenting their message, but also as a means of their message.[4]

Westermann notes that after the exile the judgment form declines in use. It disappears from the Deuteronomic version of Jeremiah's prophesies and from the Chronicler's version of the earlier prophetic utterances. Haggai and Zechariah no longer use the judgment form of the eighth and seventh centuries B.C. but instead use the forms more closely associated with salvation prophecy. Perhaps after the prophecy of God's

---

[1] *Ibid.*, p. 138.

[2] Other examples cited by Westermann, *Ibid.*, p. 171 : Isaiah 8:5-8, 9:7-11, 17-20; 22:8b-14; 28:7-13; 29:13-14; 30:12-14, 15-17.

[3] *Ibid.*, pp. 170-171.

[4] Westermann (*ibid.*, p. 210) believes that other judgment forms stand in close relationship to the judgment speech. He mentions such forms as the judicial procedure, the disputation, the parable, the lament, etc.

judgment was fulfilled in the exile, the form was no longer needed. Westermann observes that after the exile the announcement of judgment was replaced by the call to repentance, and a conditional announcement of salvation was substituted for the unconditional announcement of judgment. Even the proclamation of the pre-exilic prophets was interpreted as a call to repentance. Westermann concludes that

> ... so far as we know, there were no more unconditional announcements of judgment from the time of the exile on. It did not return until the proclamation of Jesus in the woes of Chorazin, Bethsaida, and Capernaum (Matt. 11:20-24; Luke 10:13-15), and the announcement of the fall of the city of Jerusalem in Luke, ch. 21.[1]

Westermann's study supports our earlier conclusion from the word studies that judgment as woe was more and more exchanged for salvation prophecy after the exile, and that God's condemnation was shifted either to the other nations or to certain sinful individuals or apostate practices of groups within the community.

When we seek to summarize the contributions of the pre-exilic prophets at least three issues face us. Is there hope in the pre-exilic prophets ? What is the place of eschatology in the pre-exilic prophets ? And, what is distinctive in the thought of each prophet ?

In response to the first question, few scholars would disagree with the statement that the primary message of the pre-exilic prophets was one of doom. Are the positive notes, then, secondary additions ? Many scholars feel the prophets would not have weakened their message of judgment by promising salvation. On the other hand, Erling Hammershaimb has argued that the alternation between judgment and salvation was a part of the Near Eastern understanding of history and that, therefore, the positive statements are original.[2] Both positions present some difficulties. If the first argument is based only on the *a priori* psychological improbability of a prophet's attempt to combine positive and negative statements, then it is difficult to establish. At the same time Hammershaimb's schema is also an *a priori* imported from a selective use of extra-Israelite material.

What other evidence can be brought to bear on this question ? It would seem likely that prophecies which foresee the exile and Israel's return are later additions. Helmer Ringgren notes, however, that some

---

[1] Westermann, *Basic Forms of Prophetic Speech*, p. 210. Westermann obviously overlooks John the Baptist.

[2] *Amos* (Copenhagen : Nyt nordisk forlag, 1946), pp. 136-137.

of the messianic prophecies do not presuppose the end of the Davidic dynasty. The term "Messiah," Ringgren believes, was not at this time an eschatological *terminus technicus*. Rather, it designated the Israelite king. Only in later Judaism did the word acquire its eschatological meaning.[1]

Other studies seem to confirm the genuineness of the concept of the remnant.[2] This evidence, however, is ambiguous. Amos 3:12 and 9:8 f. may be additions. Amos 3:12 clearly interrupts the text and 9:8 f. is a part of the ending of the book which Ringgren believes is secondary.[3] If these passages are removed as seondary additions, it is doubtful if it can be said that Amos held the idea of a remnant.[4] Hosea does not speak of the returning remnant at all. Jeremiah presents so complex a textual picture that it is impossible to evaluate every relevant passage in this study. It can be said, however, that the remnant concept for Jeremiah was not an entirely hopeful sign. In bitter mockery he speaks of the horrors of war, death, and devastation which the remnant will witness (21:7). To be among the spared, he says, will be a fate almost worse than death. Although Lindblom believes Isaiah was the first prophet to see the remnant as an object of faith, he insists that Isaiah's "primary thought was the destruction of the nation." [5]

When considering the individual books, one is almost compelled to agree with William F. Stinespring that Hosea is a prophet of doom. It seems clear from his study that the more hopeful passages are later additions.[6] Likewise, Amos 9:11-13 harmonizes so poorly with the preceding section and with the rest of the book of Amos that it probably should been seen as an addition.[7]

It does appear, however, that Amos holds out some hope of deliverance. Such invitations as "Seek me and live" (5:4), "Seek good, and not evil, that you may live" (5:15), and "Hate evil, and love good, and establish justice in the gate; it may be that the Lord, the God of hosts,

---

[1] *Israelite Religion*, trans. David Green (Philadelphia : The Fortress Press, 1966), p.258.

[2] E.W. Heaton, " The Root š'r and the Doctrine of the Remnant," *Journal of Theological Studies*, III (1952), 27 ff.

[3] Ringgren, *Israelite Religion*, p. 258.

[4] Lindblom, *Prophecy*, p. 363.

[5] *Ibid.*, p. 369.

[6] " Hosea, Prophet of Doom," *Crozer Quarterly*, XXVII (1950), 200-207.

[7] Ringgren, *Israelite Religion*, p. 261.

will be gracious to the remnant of Joseph" (5:15), seem to harbor some hope for a healthy response and good outcome. In 4:6-12 Amos seems to hope that Yahweh will give Israel the opportunity to repent again as he has given her the opportunity in the past.

Though there do seem to be some genuine flickers of hope in the message of Amos they remain only flickers. The overwhelming preponderance of his message is one of doom.[1] In what are probably the last lines of the original book of Amos only a dismal fate is expected:

> Behold the eyes of the Lord God
> are upon the sinful kingdom,
> and I will destroy it from the
> surface of the ground [9:8].

While Micah entertained some hope for the lower classes, his message was very similar to that of Amos and Hosea. As Lindblom says

> ... by and by it became clear to him that the religious and moral decay was general and radical. Judgment and destruction alone remained. Samaria would be destroyed by a terrible earthquake. Jerusalem with its temple would be laid in ruins. The land would be conquered by enemies and the population deported into a foreign country. Thus the end had come upon Israel. It had no future to hope for.[2]

Although Isaiah's message included the concept of the remnant as a future reality, it was dominated by the threat of the end of the nation. During the Syro-Ephraimitic war Isaiah voiced some hope, but this positive element does not dominate his thought.[3] In most essential respects Zephaniah's message agrees with Isaiah's. So whether one accepts some or all of the positive statements in the pre-exilic prophets as original or later additions, one would not hesitate to say that doom was certainly the dominating feature of these books. It seems likely, however, that Paul and his contemporaries read these books in something near the same form in which they now rest, and would have simply taken the integrity of the books for granted. Nevertheless, even with the retention of admittedly positive elements the dark threat of judgment looms on the horizon.

Through calling attention to the dark side of God's judgment, the pre-exilic prophets sought to destroy the false security of Israel. The

---

[1] Lindblom, *Prophecy*, p. 363.
[2] *Ibid.*, p. 365.
[3] *Ibid.*, p. 369.

words of Yahweh which Israel thought would be for her comfort would be spewed out as blazing fire (Amos 2:5). The prophets called the popular hope for a Golden Age a dangerous illusion if it did not rouse men to obedience.[1] Amos ruthlessly attacked the cultic salvation hope in which men had isolated themselves thus becoming insensitive to Yahweh's radical demand (5:21-24). Israel's religion had become a comfort-religion with its own priesthood of *shalom* prophets. All of the pre-exilic prophets were dedicated to a remorseless exposure of this phantasy-religion. Until this task was complete it would have been premature to speak to men of hope.

Inevitably the question intrudes : Is there an eschatology in the pre-exilic prophets ?[2] If eschatology is narrowly described as a doctrine of last things or the creation of a "new heaven and a new earth," then there is no eschatology in the pre-exilic prophets. If, however, one allows for a broader view—a view of history as goal-directed—then one can agree with von Rad that the message of the pre-exilic prophets is eschatological.[3] Even though the imminent events about which the prophets speak are *within* history, they are of such a final and absolute nature that they transcend history. As von Rad says, "the new age that is coming can no longer be understood as the continuation of previous history." [4] Johannes Grønbaek more precisely calls the eschatology of the prophets an eschatology of judgment with a certain "conclusive aspect".[5] The judgment, he says, is absolute and final. God's efforts to win back his wayward people have been in vain, and therefore, since "the people have not repented... Yahweh will exterminate his people." [6] Ringgren is quite correct, therefore, when he says, "The eschatology of the prophets from the very beginning is an eschatology not of salvation but of judgment," i.e., of condemnation.[7] The eighth-century prophets introduced a

---

[1] See Gerhard von Rad, *Old Testament Theology*, trans. D.M.G. Stalker (2 vols.; New York : Harper & Row, 1965), II, 169 ff.

[2] Johannes Lindblom, "Gibt es eine Eschatologie bei den alttestamentlichen Propheten ?" *Studia Theologica*, VI (1952), 79 ff.; T.C. Vriezen, "Prophecy and Eschatology," *Supplements to Vetus Testament*, I (1953), 199 ff.

[3] Von Rad, *Old Testament Theology*, II, 129.

[4] *Ibid.*

[5] " Zur Frage der Eschatologie in der Verkundigung der Gerichtspropheten," *Svensk exegetisk ärsbok*, XXIV (1953), 10-11.

[6] *Ibid.*

[7] Ringgren, *Israelite Religion*, p. 260.

new element into Israel's religion. The future acts of God, and not merely the past ones, are the decisive events for the community of Israel. This future element, according to von Rad, ultimately formed the basis of apocalyptic thought.[1] We see this tendency to assign the judgment to a future, trans-historical occurrence in many of the post-exilic and exilic prophets (e.g., Ezekiel). In this case, however, the more typical thought of judgment as condemnation is replaced by an element of hope. As Walther Eichrodt says, Ezekiel focused not on the exile as judgment but on a "final purifying judgment in which God would purify his favoured people from all impure elements in order to establish his sovereignty in them." [2] Zechariah and Haggai join Ezekiel in exalting the judgment to a place transcending time and space.

Coupled with Ezekiel's understanding of a future judgment, trans-historical in character, was his emphasis on the judgment of each individual. Every man is answerable for himself in the judgment, and to every man is offered the possibility of escape from the destruction associated with the judgment if he will repent. It should be noted, however, that the corporate judgment is not replaced by Ezekiel, but only amended. Now, God's hostile judgment is directed more and more toward the Gentiles or the *massa perditionis*, and judgment again means vindication for Israel although individual Israelites may still suffer purging. This hostile judgment on the pagan nations was seen as Yahweh's response to the Gentile rebellion against Yahweh which in turn came to be equated with their persecution of Israel (Ez. 25; 37:26; Isa. 47:1 ff.; Micah 7:7 ff.; Obad. 9 ff.).[3]

The separate approaches of this study converge to support each other. As we noted in the word study, wrath and judgment are applied less and less in a threatening way to Israel in the post-exilic prophets. We noted in section two of this division that in post-exilic Judaism the judgment form fell into disuse. Now we have seen in our survey of the books themselves that the exile is the dividing line between the time when the prophets understood condemnatory judgment in a final unqualified sense on Israel and the time when it was applied for the most part to the Gentiles and the evil in the community and shifted into the future. We shall see how this development is reflected in the following sections of this chapter.

---

[1] Von Rad, *Old Testament Theology*, II, 185-186.
[2] Eichrodt, *Theology*, I, 467.
[3] *Ibid.*, p. 468.

B. Apocalyptic Background of Judgment

It is not possible within the scope of this study to consider all of the writings which are grouped under the heading "Apocalyptic Literature," nor is it possible to enter the heated and unresolved debate over what properly constitutes apocalyptic literature. Our investigation will be limited to certain books with a very strong eschatological outlook which for the sake of convenience we shall rather arbitrarily call "Apocalyptic Literature." For our purposes the selection will be made from a larger list of books which David Syme Russell includes in his discussion of the apocalyptic outlook.[1] The representative works which we shall consider are: I Enoch, II Baruch, IV Ezra, Jubilees, and the Psalms of Solomon. A closely related consideration of judgment in the Qumran materials will follow.

Before outlining the most salient points of apocalyptic judgment thought we should briefly note the relationship of the prophetic to the apocalyptic understanding of judgment. Even a cursory reading of the prophetic and the apocalyptic writings will reveal certain differences as well as likenesses.[2] In the prophetic books, for example, God's triumph is expected in the present world order; in the apocalyptic writings (with the possible exception of Daniel) God's victory lies beyond history.[3] In the apocalyptic materials demonic powers and principalities as well as flesh and blood are the enemy of God. In the prophetic writtings God battles primarily against flesh and blood.[4] The apocalyptic battles are of cosmic proportions; the prophetic battles are international.[5]

This distinction between prophetic and apocalyptic writings is perhaps a necessary one; however, it needs qualification. While making certain alterations,[6] apocalyptic materials share certain themes and vocabulary with the prophetic books.[7] Moreover, as we noted above, even though the events about which the prophet speaks are *within*

---

[1] *The Method and Message of Jewish Apocalyptic* (Philadelphia : The Westminster Press, 1964), pp. 36-39, includes these among others.

[2] Robert Henry Charles, *Eschatology, The Doctrine of a Future Life in Israel, Judaism, and Christianity* (3rd ed.; New York : Schocken Books, 1963), pp. 177 ff.

[3] Russell, *Method*, p. 205.

[4] *Ibid.*

[5] *Ibid.*

[6] *Ibid.*, p. 270.

[7] *Ibid.*, p. 265.

history, in prophetic as well as apocalyptic books they are of such a final and absolute nature that they transcend history.[1] Russell basically agrees:

> The apocalyptists differ from the prophets in their interpretation of the end of history and in looking beyond history for the fulfilment of their "mighty acts" in an age in many respects different from that in which men now live. But basically they express the same beliefs and share the same tradition, finding the ultimate meaning of history in the working out of the divine purpose.[2]

In a significant study of the relationship of prophetic and apocalyptic thought, Thomas Walter Manson argues that apocalyptic is an attempt to rationalize and to systematize the predicative side of prophecy, and that the other side of the systematizing process is the scribal treatment of the Law which ultimately produces the Mishnah.[3] Manson sees *ta logia* of God as the common denominator of apocalypticism and rabbinism. *Logion* which stands for an oracle of divine demand and divine promise ultimately splits, forming the apocalyptic and rabbinic traditions.[4] These two movements, in effect, replace prophecy. While Manson's work too neatly separates apocalypticism and rabbinism, its great contribution is the light it throws on the relationship between apocalyptic and prophetic thought. Such a relationship will become evident in our consideration of some of the same judgment themes and terminology in the apocalyptic books which we noted above in the prophetic writings.

1. While the use of the term משפט (Grk. κρίσις) in the apocalyptic *Denkweise* resembles that of the prophetic, it goes beyond the prophetic understanding. The apocalyptic writers like the post-exilic prophets apply judgment as condemnation primarily to the pagan world, and they generally interpret judgment in a corporate sense. This corporate judgment is indiscriminate, falling alike on Jews, Gentiles, fallen angels, shepherds, apostates, kings, rich and mighty. But, the outcome is clearly delineated: the Gentiles face condemnation; the Jews can expect vindication. Even the neutral nations which are spared condemnation

---

[1] Von Rad, *Old Testament Theology*, II, 129.

[2] Russell, *Method*, p. 205.

[3] "Reflections on Apocalyptic," in *Aux sources de la tradition chrétienne, Mélanges offerts à M. Maurice Goguel* (Bibliothèque Théologique; Neuchâtel, Paris: Delachaux & Niestlé S.A., 1950), p. 142.

[4] *Ibid.*, see diagram on p. 145.

(II Baruch 68:5) must serve and do homage to the people of God (I Enoch 91:14; 9:30, 33, 35; cf. 91-104, and the Psalms of Solomon). Generally speaking, however, the Gentiles are condemned *qua* Gentiles. The righteous under command from Yahweh will assist in their destruction; the Jews cut down their past oppressors with the sword (I Enoch 91:12). In Jubilees 24:28-30 the Gentiles are driven out of Palestine, and the angels destroy them. On the Day of Judgment God will smite the earth and it will swallow up the Gentiles (I Enoch 90:18). The Messiah will assist in punishing the Gentiles (Psalms of Solomon 17:17), and those who survive will become his slaves (Psalms of Solomon 17:32 ff.). Russell notes that the

> ... contrast between "the righteous" and "the wicked" is essentially the contrast between the Jewish nation and the other nations of the earth... The fate which was reserved, in certain writings, for the sworn enemies of Israel is now meted out to all Gentiles. That fate is eternal torment or else annihilation. Either way they have no share at all in the blessings of the messianic kingdom.[1]

In the same manner I Enoch speaks of the judgment of the mighty and the powerful (62:9-13), the judgment of the fallen angels and shepherds which are all cast into a "fiery abyss" (90:20-27).

The Jews (except for the apostates), on the other hand, can look forward to their vindication at the judgment. While others perish, their names will be preserved before the Lord of Hosts (I Enoch 104:1). The mighty will fall but the elect will be saved (I Enoch 62:13). Israel may experience punishment in the judgment but the chastisement is administered for corrective purposes, not for destruction:

> Thy chastisement is upon us as (upon) a first born, only-begotten son,
> To turn back the obedient soul from folly (that is wrought) in ignorance
> May God cleanse Israel against the day of mercy and blessing
>   (Psalms of Solomon 18:3-6; cf. II Baruch 13:9-10).[2]

Our investigation so far supports Russell's observation that during the inter-testamental period

> ... the eschatology of Judaism in general and of apocalyptic in particular

---

[1] Russell, *Method*, p. 301. Cf. I Enoch 50:2-5, where the righteous triumph and the Gentiles repent and are saved. This, however, is the exception rather than the rule.

[2] Unless otherwise noted all translations of the apocalyptic materials are from Robert Henry Charles, *The Apocrypha and Pseudepigrapha of the Old Testament* (2 vols.; Oxford: At the Clarendon Press, 1913).

was primarily concerned with the salvation of Israel as the people of God. Some of these writers interpreted their beliefs about the last things in terms of the fate of the individual souls after death, but in the main their eschatological hopes were predominantly nationalistic .... In a number of apocalyptic books a distinction is made between "the righteous" and "the wicked" on purely ethical grounds without any reference to nation or race (e.g., I Enoch 91-108); but *for the most part* the tendency is to identify "the righteous" with Israel and "the wicked" with the Gentiles.[1]

George Foot Moore has claimed that "Jewish eschatology is the ultimate step in the individualization of religion... [because] Everyman is finally judged individually, and saved or damned by his own deeds." [2] To be sure we do see certain individualizing tendencies in apocalyptic literature. I Enoch mentions the weighing of good against bad deeds (104:13, 61:8). IV Ezra says that each man must answer for himself before the divine tribunal (7:104 f.). The prevailing context, however, is corporate, not individualistic. Even in these isolated instances where the individual comes into focus it appears that he typifies the community or is paradigmatic of it. What H. Wheeler Robinson says of Ezekiel is true of the apocalyptic materials as well: "The individualizing development takes place within the matrix of a social relation to God." [3]

Unlike the prophets, however, some apocalyptists ascribed to the community a share in the ruling and judicial functions of the coming Kingdom. The prophets on the other hand see Yahweh as the sole arbiter of the eschatological crisis. I Enoch 1:9 says

> And behold! He cometh with ten thousands of [His] holy ones
> To execute judgment upon all,
>   And to destroy [all] the ungodly:
> And to convict all flesh of all the works of their ungodliness which they have committed.
> And of all the hard things which ungoldly sinners [have spoken] against them.[4]

---

[1] Russell, *Method*, p. 297.

[2] *Judaism in the First Centuries of the Christian Era: The Age of the Tannaim* (3 vols.; Cambridge : Harvard University Press, 1946), II, 377. See also Rudolf Bultmann, *History and Eschatology* (The Gifford Lectures, 1955; Edinburgh : The University Press, 1957), p. 31, who says, " In the apocalyptic view the individual is responsible for himself only."

[3] "The Hebrew Conception of Corporate Personality," *Werden und Wesen des Alten Testaments* herausgegeben von Paul Volz, Friedrich Stummer, und Johannes Hempel (Zeitschrift für die alttestamentliche Wissenschaft, Beiheft, LXVI; Berlin : Verlag von Alfred Töpelmann, 1936), p. 54. See Moore, *Judaism*, II, 94-95; Davies, *Paul*, p. 83.

[4] "And I saw till a great sword was given to the sheep, and the sheep proceeded

Israel also experiences a pedagogical judgment in the present in order that salvation may come on the final eschatological Day. This judgment is merely preparatory to the final accounting and does not represent as in Paul an invasion of the present by the final eschatological Day itself (I Enoch 104:1; Psalms of Solomon 18:3-6).

2. צדקה or δικαιοσύνη is a fundamental term for Jewish apocalyptic as well as prophetic thought. This word connotes God's power to create and sustain his covenant people as well as his power to destroy the covenant violator. In order properly to understand the concept of righteousness in apocalyptic thought one must view it in its vital and dynamic relationship with the covenant concept.

While the term ברית (Grk. διαθήκη) does not frequently appear in the apocalyptic literature it does occupy a more prominent place in apocalyptic than in rabbinic literature. The Psalms of Solomon refer to the covenant made with the fathers:

> For Thou didst choose the seed of Abraham before all the nations
> And didst set Thy name upon us, O Lord,
> And Thou wilt not reject (us) for ever.
> Thou madest *a covenant with our fathers* concerning us;
> And we hope in Thee, when our soul turneth (unto Thee)
> (9:17-18; emphasis added).

In II Baruch, Israel is admonished to remember "the law and Zion, and the holy land and your brethren, and the covenant of your fathers" (84:8). Jubilees, likewise, sees the covenant in relationship to the patriarchs (15:11, 15, 17, 18, 22, 26), and attributes the apocalyptic struggle to Israel's neglect of the covenant:

> And they shall strive one with another, the young with the old, and the old with the young, the poor with the rich, the lowly with the great, and the beggar with the prince, on account of the law and the covenant; for they have forgotten commandment, and covenant, etc. (23:19).

Except in Jubilees 15:26 and 15:33-34 where "covenant" is a synonym of circumcision, ברית designates a relationship which God initiated with Israel usually through the patriarchs.

Although the word "covenant" appears rather infrequently in the

---

against all the beasts of the field to slay them" (I Enoch 90:19).

In I Enoch 90:30 the sheep rule as well as judge: "... and I saw all the sheep which had been left and all the beasts on earth, and all the birds of heaven, falling down and doing homage to those sheep and making petition to and obeying them in everything." (Cf. I Enoch 47:3; 94; 102:2, etc.).

prophetic writings this observation does not contradict our earlier claim that the apocalyptic writings developed from the prophetic understanding. Eichrodt believes that the prophets deliberately avoided using the term because it

> ... had long become too fixed as a relationship established once for all, a statutory institution, and no longer did justice to *the vital, personal quality of the divine human relationship*. And this, for the prophets, was the thing that mattered. For them election was only the beginning of permanent intercourse, the reality of which delivered from constant fresh decision for God.[1]

Although one might disagree with Eichrodt's claim that the prophets deliberately avoided the term [2] ברית, one can scarcely object to his claim that the prophets sought to reclaim the rich theological meaning the word earlier symbolized. In light of other developments in Judaism,[3] we may witness a similar recovery attempt in the apocalyptic writings. At least we can say that the concept of covenant which we see in the apocalyptic materials is very similar to that of the prophetic writings. As in the prophetic writings, so also here God's judgment is his righteous action aimed at protecting his covenant by destroying those who violate it.

While the Torah occupies a less significant place in apocalyptic literature than in the rabbinic materials, there remains in the apocalyptic materials an acute consciousness of the intimate relationship between the Torah and the covenant (II Baruch 84:4). Charles thought that " the messianic expectation tends to eclipse the supremacy of the law" [4] in the apocalyptic writings but it is more accurate to say that the centrality of the Torah is displaced rather than eclipsed.

Although the righteous man conceived as one who keeps all of the ordinances is less prominent in the apocalyptic writings than in rabbinic thought, this persuasion remains to some degree.[5] In I Enoch 106:

---

[1] Eichrodt, *Theology*, I, 374.

[2] ברית occurs in Isaiah 12 times, Jeremiah 21 times, Ezekiel 17 times, Hosea 5 times, Amos once, Zechariah twice, and Malachi 6 times. One might note also the frequent use of חסד in the prophets for covenant loyalty and thus expressing this same vital, affective union of purpose—Yahweh's and Israel's.

[3] *Infra*, pp. 46-48.

[4] Charles, *Eschatology*, p. 23.

[5] Against Dietrich Rössler, *Gesetz und Geschichte, Untersuchungen zur Theologie der jüdischen Apokalytpik und der pharisäischen Orthodoxie* (*Neukirchen : Neukirchen Verlag*, 1960), p. 139, who says that in the apocalyptic writings righteousness never depends on the fulfillment of all the laws and ordinances, but that men are separated into righteous and unrighteous categories by their fundamental position for or against the Torah.

14 sin is understood as a transgression of the Law : "And behold they commit sin and transgress the Law..." Similarly in I Enoch 5:4 sin appears as a failure to keep the commandments : "But ye--ye have not stood fast, nor done the commandments of the Lord." A like understanding prevails in II Baruch 51:3, 5 where those who are "justified in My Law" are elevated in the judgment over those who "do not keep the Law." In II Baruch 77:1-4 the exile is seen as punishment for breaking the Law. Even Gentiles shall suffer torture because "receiving precepts they yet kept them not" (IV Ezra 7:22; cf. I Enoch 99:2). Likewise, in Jubilees 2:27 a Sabbath-breaker dies. Elsewhere, the righteous appear as those "who have been saved by their works" (II Baruch 51:7).

Thus while righteousness is conceived as keeping all of the ordinances in parts of the apocalyptic literature, one must hasten to add that this is not the dominant emphasis. More common are references to the Law as an entity to which the righteous man makes a positive response. Man's basic attitude toward the Law determines his place in the judgment. In I Enoch 60:6 punishment is visited on those "who worship not the righteous Law." II Baruch speaks of men whose thoughts shall burn in fire because they "remembered not the Law of the Mighty One," and whose meditations shall be tried in the flames because "My Law they knew not by reason of their pride" (48:40). Likewise, Adam and his kin suffer corporate extinction because they have forsaken the Law (II Baruch 48:42 f.). The Law will requite the transgressors on the Last Day (II Baruch 48:47).

By the same token, the unrighteous are those who despise the Law and face condemnation at the judgment : "Therefore ask no more concerning the multitude of them that perish; for having received liberty they despised the Most High; scorned his Law and forsook his ways" (IV Ezra 8:56). Defiance of the Law is coupled with the failure to recognize God and both offenses receive the same punishment : "For all who failed to recognize me in their life time...and all who defied my Law... these must be brought to know after death by torment" (IV Ezra 9:10 f.).

In summary, unrighteousness is understood as despising, rejecting, or transgressing the Law, but righteousness is seen as obeying the Law, responding affirmatively to the Law, or bringing forth the fruit of the Law (I Enoch 108:1; IV Ezra 9:31). Therefore, God's reward comes to those who respect the Law. Long life is promised to those who keep the Law (Jubilees 23:26-28). Zion's consolation follows her remembrance of the Law (II Baruch 44:7). The world to come will be given to those who preserve the truth of the Law (II Baruch 44:15). In the eschatological trials God protects those who have the fruits of the Law in their hearts (II Baruch 32:1, 5).

The belief that the righteous will be vindicated in the judgment was related to a yet more significant theme—that God himself will be vindicated. Since apocalyptic is not primarily anthropocentric but theocentric in emphasis, the task of judgment is to reveal and to establish the sovereignty of God and his right action as much as it is to vindicate the righteousness of his people.[1] In IV Ezra and II Baruch the destruction of Jerusalem stands in the foreground,[2] but the question of Israel's misfortune is tied to the larger question of God's righteousness. Why, the people ask, do we suffer and our enemies prosper? IV Ezra, for example, raises the poignant cry:

> Why is Israel given over to the heathen for reproach,
>   thy beloved people to godless tribes given up?
> The Law of our fathers has been brought to destruction ...
> We indeed are not worthy to obtain mercy;
>   but what will he do for his own name whereby we are called
>
> (4:23, 25).

Baruch asks Yahweh, "[I]f Thou destroyest Thy city and deliverest up Thy land to those that hate us, how shall the name of Israel be again remembered? Or how shall one speak of Thy praises?" (II Baruch 3:5)

Again the author of II Baruch asks, "How long will that which is corruptible remain, And how long will the time of the mortals be prospered?... Command therefore in mercy and accomplish all that Thou saidst Thou wouldst bring, that Thy might may be made known to those who think that Thy longsuffering is weakness" (II Baruch 21:19f.; cf. IV Ezra 3:33 f.; 4:23-30; 6:55-59; 8:37-40).

---

[1] Russell, *Method*, p. 101, says, "the suffering of the righteous and the moral government of the universe (cf. I Enoch 91-104; Pss. of Solomon; II Baruch; II Esdras; Apoc. of Abraham, etc.) are the constant concern of these men who judge history and the end of history in terms of a holy and righteous God." Martin Noth, *The Laws in the Pentateuch and Other Studies*, trans. D.R. Ap-Thomas (Edinburgh, London : Oliver & Boyd, 1966), p. 214, agrees : "What (according to apocalyptic) gives world history its final unity amidst all its variety of different phenomena, and indeed its significance, is the fact that it stands face to face with the kingship of God, which is to pronounce judgment upon the whole history."

[2] Otto Plöger, "Das 4. Esrabuch," *Die Religion in Geschichte und Gegenwart* (6 vols.; 3rd ed.; Tübingen : J.C.B. Mohr [Paul Siebeck], 1958), II, 697-699.

In the references above the writers raise the question of the justice of God in the face of historical events which seem to negate God's justice. These authors, however, are not content merely to raise the issue of God's sovereignty; they also defend his justice which will one day be established in his righteous judgment. Baruch tells the exiles that he has given them the words of the epistle : "...that ye may be comforted regarding the evils which have come upon you, and... that ye may justify His judgment which he has decreed against you" (II Baruch 78:5). I Enoch voices a similar concern : "...for righteous is the judgment of God; for to the faithful he will give faithfulness in the habitation of upright paths" (I Enoch 108:13; cf. 50:4). IV Ezra also defends God's righteous judgment. Realizing the limitations of his own understanding (4:1-11, 12-21, 22-32, 6:2b, 6; 7:32-34), Ezra feels condemned for judging God (7:17), and hears the call to give thanks for his place among the righteous instead of doubting God's just judgment (IV Ezra 8:37-40, 46-62).

> (And yet) I will justify Thee, O God, in uprightness of heart,
> For in Thy judgments is Thy righteousness (displayed), O God.
> For Thou hast rendered to the sinners according to their deeds,
>   Yea according to their sins, which were very wicked.
> Thou hast uncovered their sins, that Thy judgment might be manifest;
> God is a righteous judge,
>   And He is no respecter of persons (2:16-18).

In the Psalms of Solomon the princes and mighty of the earth are called to attest to the righteousness of God's judgment (2:36-40). The righteous gratefully rejoice in the righteousness of God's judgment (3:3-4), and the unrighteous fear the righteous judgment (4:28-29). The writer lauds God's judgments which have been just "since the creation of heaven and earth" (8:7b-8), and which are just in the present as well : "Behold now, O God, Thou hast shown us Thy judgment in Thy righteousness" (8:25). God's judgment which is visited on Israel is just (8:30, 38-40), and his judgment which falls on "every nation" is just (9:2-3). God's just and chastening judgment brings " good pleasure " to Israel, but destruction to the wrongdoer. The psalmist can write in confident praise, "Faithful is the Lord in all His judgments which He doeth upon the earth" (17:12).

This survey of the concept of righteousness in apocalyptic shows that this literature is not, as is often claimed, writings of despair but books of hope. Russell rightly says : "Behind the eschatological hopes of the apocalyptists was the deep set conviction that the righteousness of God would at last be vindicated, that good would be rewarded and wickedness punished." [1] The apocalyptists looked forward to the time when the promises made to ancient Israel would be fulfilled and God's righteousness would be vindicated.[2]

3. The concept of wrath is closely tied to the righteousness of God and his judgment on the covenant breaker. In Jubilees 36:10 God's wrath falls justly on those who devise evil against the brother:

> But on the day of turbulence and execration and indignation and anger, with flaming devouring fire as He burnt Sodom so likewise will He burn his land and his city and all that is his, and he shall be blotted out of the book of the discipline of the children of men, and not be recorded in the book of life, but in that which is appointed to destruction. And he shall depart into eternal execration; so that their condemnation may be always renewed in hate and in execration and in wrath and in torment and in indignation and in plagues and in disease for ever.

Wrath, like judgment and righteousness, has primarily a corporate application in the apocalyptic materials. To the elect as a group comes the promise that they will not die of the divine "anger or wrath, but they will complete the number of the days of their life" (I Enoch 5:9). By contrast the evil are condemned as a body for they "have not been steadfast, nor done the commandments of the Lord... And the years of your life shall perish, And the years of your destruction shall be multiplied in eternal execration and ye shall find no mercy" (I Enoch 5:4 f.). I Enoch implores God to "destroy from the earth the flesh which has aroused Thy wrath, but the flesh of righteousness establish as a plant of the eternal seed" (I Enoch 84:6; cf. 84:4, 103:7 ff.). The seer predicts that the community of the heathen will "be cast into a judgment of fire and shall perish in wrath" (I Enoch 92:9). Likewise the fellowship of sinners " shall be cast into a furnace of fire" (I Enoch 98:3), and "in the fire shall they burn" (I Enoch 108:3). Those who afflict the righteous are singled out for special woe (I Enoch 100:7).

Although God's wrath falls on mankind in the present it is but a preliminary manifestation of the outpouring of wrath which will come at the final judgment (I Enoch 84:1). Wrath falls on unrighteousness in the *hic et nunc* but it is only when transgressions and blasphemy have run their full course that "the holy Lord will come forth with wrath and chastisement to execute judgment on earth" (I Enoch 91:7). II Baruch, likewise, records the lament: "What, therefore, is our strength that we

---

[1] Russell, *Method*, p. 101.
[2] *Ibid.*, pp. 17-18.

should bear Thy wrath, or what are we that we should endure Thy judgment ? " (48:17; cf. II Baruch 64:4). It is erroneous to suggest, however, that we see the same eschatological tension here that we see in Paul between the now and not yet. Although the writer sees the fall of Zion in the reign of Manasseh as a sign of God's wrath, this visitation is merely preparatory to the great Day of Wrath. The writer looks forward to the day when Zion will be rebuilt and God's wrath will be poured out on the nations (II Baruch 68:5-8). The punishment which God administers in the present is aimed at preparing Israel to stand in the final Judgment. Paul's letters, on the other hand, trumpet the announcement that the eschatological Day of Wrath and redemption is already present. No longer is the manifestation of God's wrath a preliminary sign of the last Day; the Day itself has dawned.

4. יום or ἡμέρα as in the prophetic literature, is germane to our study of judgment in apocalyptic thought. In the apocalyptic books the Day of Judgment has a double meaning. It simultaneously promises punishment for evil and reward for righteousness. This double nature is sometimes characteristic of the prophetic Day of the Lord as well, although, as we noted above, the salvation aspect of the Day is either unuttered or muted by the pre-exilic prophets in order to challenge Israel's comfort-religion. Elsewhere, however, the day of Yahweh's vengeance on the evildoers is also the day of his vindication of the righteous : [1]

> For a day of vengeance was in my heart,
> And my year of redemption had come.
> I looked, but there was none to help,
> I looked in amazement, but there was none to uphold;
> So my own arm helped me,
> And my fury upheld me
>
> (Isa. 63:4, 5; cf. Joel 2:21).

On that Day the heathen nations will be destroyed but Yahweh's people will be comforted.[2] Von Rad correctly observes that for the post-exilic prophets the Day of Yahweh meant destruction for the pagans but for Israel it promised protection (Zech. 12:1 ff.), purification (Mal. 3:2),

---

[1] H. Wheeler Robinson, *Inspiration and Revelation in the Old Testament* (Oxford : At the Clarendon Press, 1946), p. 137.

[2] Ladislav Černy̆, *The Day of Yahweh and Some Relevant Problems* (Prague : Universita Karlova, University Karlovy, 1948), p. 106.

cleansing (Zech. 13:1 f.), the gift of the Spirit (Joel 3; Zech. 12:10), etc.[1] Much the same pattern emerges in the apocalyptic thought.[2]

Miss Mattern denies the dual nature of this judgment in apocalyptic thought. The righteous, she argues, do not stand before the Last Judgment. Apocalyptic, final judgment, according to her view, is identical with destruction; therefore, the righteous who are promised salvation cannot stand before this judgment.[3] From the allusion to separation at death in I Enoch,[4] she concludes that already before this Day of Judgment humanity is divided into two categories—righteous and sinners; therefore, a final separation is not needed.[5] The judgment, then, only executes the verdict which has already been set.[6] According to her view, an ultimate judgment is really no longer necessary. Rather, it is only necessary that there be a reward sometime or other.[7] Consequently, the Last Judgment does not apply so much to the righteous as it does to the heathen who are separated for destruction.[8]

According to Miss Mattern the punishment for the sins of the righteous takes place in a preliminary judgment, perhaps immediately after

---

[1] Gerhard von Rad, "ἡμέρα," in *Theological Dictionary of the New Testament*, trans. Geoffrey W. Bromiley (Grand Rapids, Mich.: Wm. B. Eerdmans Publishing Company, 1965), II, 945.

[2] When Yahweh is revealed on the throne of judgment—
"... then shall the Most High say to the nations that have
been raised [from the dead] :
Look now and consider whom ye have denied, whom ye have not served,
whose commandments ye have despised.
Look, now, before [you] :
here delight and refreshment,
there fire and torments !"
Thus shall he speak unto them in the Day of Judgment,
for thus shall the Day of Judgment be :
[A Day] whereon is neither sun, nor moon, nor stars :
neither clouds, nor thunder, nor lightning ....
save only the splendour of the brightness of the Most High,
whereby all shall be destined to see what has been determined (for them)
(IV Ezra 39-44; cf. I Enoch 38 : 1 ff.; 45:6; 50:4 f.; Psalms of Solomon 8:7b-8; 9:2-3:9; 15:13-15; II Baruch 30:1-5, etc.).

[3] Mattern, *Verständnis*, p. 29.

[4] *Ibid.*, p. 26. Miss Mattern believes that I Enoch 22 could just as well be describing an earlier judgment, one which takes place at death perhaps.

[5] *Ibid.*, p. 24.
[6] *Ibid.*, p. 23.
[7] *Ibid.*, p. 27.
[8] *Ibid.*

death, and this is the only definitive Judgment the righteous endure. The final, future Day of Judgment does not deal with the sin of the righteous, but only with the destruction of the wicked. She admits that the sin of Israel is mentioned in a thoroughly apocalyptic context in II Baruch 1:2 ff.; however, she interprets this reference to sin to refer to a judgment which is now executed over Israel (present tense). She concludes, therefore, that the final judgment in the apocalyptic literature has only one function: to destroy the wicked. She applies the same development to Paul. The Last Judgment in the Pauline letters does not apply to the Christians, but only those who reject Christ. The Christians have already, perhaps at death, undergone an individualistic, preliminary judgment. The final corporate judgment applies only to the damned.

It is obvious that Miss Mattern's argument avoids the dual nature of the Last Judgment. Two objections can be raised to her view. (1) It is clear that contrary to Miss Mattern's view, certain apocalyptic books do refer to a decision made regarding the righteous at the Last Judgment.[1] (2) Paul Volz is surely correct when he says that in the apocalyptic literature we do not see different levels of judgment but rather "ein mehraktiges Gerichtsdrama, und die einzelnen Akte haben samt und sonders den gleichen Zweck, die Erlösung zu schaffen."[2] Volz rightly calls a double judgment such as Miss Mattern constructs "eine künstliche Bildung der späteren Reflexion."[3] What we see in the apocalyptic materials is not two judgments, but two aspects of one apocalyptic Day. This eschatological Day promises salvation to the righteous but condemnation to the sinner.

We see in the above discussion certain recurring themes that support Manson's claim that the predicative element in prophetic thought influenced the development of the apocalyptic vocabulary and outlook. The double nature of the judgment, the way the future Day impinges on the present, the justification of God's righteous judgment, and the close relationship of judgment and God's covenant loyalty are familiar to both the apocalyptic and the prophetic writers. Apocalyptic thinkers, however, in contrast to the prophets tend to conceive of the final judgment in ahistorical terms.

---

[1] E.g., I Enoch 104:13; 61:8.

[2] *Die Eschatologie der jüdischen Gemeinde im neutestamentlichen Zeitalter* (2d ed.; Tübingen J.C.B. Mohr, 1934), p. 274.

[3] *Ibid.*, p. 273.

Also in contrast to the prophetic pronouncement, the apocalyptic judgment passages apparently assume no definite form. Their aim is not to issue Yahweh's judgment pronouncement but to assure the elect of their future vindication if they remain steadfast in faith and suffering. Moreover, in contrast to Paul,[1] there is no hortatory element attached to the judgment references. II Baruch 30:1-5 is typical of the apocalyptic judgment allusions:

> And it shall come to pass at that time that the treasures will be opened in which is preserved the number of the souls of the righteous, and they shall come forth, and a multitude of Souls shall be seen together in one assemblage of one thought, and the first shall rejoice and the last shall not be grieved. For they know that the time has come of which it is said, that it is the condemnation of the times. But the souls of the wicked, when they behold all these things, shall then waste away the more. For they shall know that their torment has come and their perdition has arrived.[2]

C. Judgment in the Qumran Scrolls

Whereas this treatment overlaps the preceding section to some degree, the Qumran materials contain such a large mass of congenial data that they merit special consideration. The relevance of the Qumran scrolls for this study is obvious when one recalls their pervasive eschatological preoccupation.[3] While recognizing this uniform coloring, it is

---

[1] *Infra*, pp. 118-122.

[2] Cf. IV Ezra 7:31-44; II Baruch 85:13-15; 41:3-4; 42:1-2; Jub. 15:33-34; I Enoch 91:14-17; 68:2-3; 80:8, etc.

[3] While some might accuse Dupont-Sommer of committing the "all fallacy," his statement is probably correct that "all the Qumran commentaries are dominated by eschatological preoccupation" (André Dupont-Sommer, *The Essene Writings from Qumran*, trans. G. Vermes [Oxford : Basil Blackwell, 1961], p. 311). Kurt Schubert, *The Dead Sea Community*, trans. John W. Doberstein (London : Adam & Charles Black, 1959), pp. 88-89, says that in "the community of Qumran, which believed that it was itself living in the last days... nothing happened which was without eschatological purpose." Herbert Braun, *Qumran und das Neue Testament* (2 vols.; Tübingen : J.C.B. Mohr, 1966), II, 266, calls the Qumran texts "apokalyptische Literatur." Most strikingly, Richard Patrick Crosland Hanson calls the Qumran community, "a cooled-down apocalyptic sect" similar in aims and ideals to the apocalyptic sects seen elsewhere ("Qumran and the Essenes," in *A Guide to the Scrolls*, ed. Alfred Robert Clare Leany [London : S.C.M. Press], p. 64). For excellent treatments of this material see also Frank Moore Cross, Jr., *The Ancient Library of Qumran and Modern Biblical Studies* (rev. ed.; The Haskell Lectures, 1956-1957; New York : Anchor Books, 1961), and Helmer Ringgren, *The Faith of Qumran*, trans. Emilie T. Sander (Philadelphia : Fortress Press, 1963).

necessary to be aware of the great variety of eschatological shadings in the scrolls themselves.[1] The Qumran texts, like the apocalyptic books considered in the preceding section, come from different times and from different authors or circles. Consequently, here, as was the case earlier, it is necessary to speak only of the prevailing trends because there is no logically developed system of eschatology in the scrolls. [2] As in the above sections, here also we shall study the judgment terminology and form of the Qumran texts in light of the preceding investigation.

1. As was the case in the preceding section, so here the judgment has a double character. For the covenanters the impending judgment promised vindication, but for the unfaithful Jews punishment, and for the Gentiles destruction. The double character of the judgment comes clear in the use of a word shared with the prophets: "Visitation" (פקודה). God's visitation may portend punishment for evildoers or vindication of the righteous.

In the Manual of Discipline (I QS) 4:6-8, for example, "Visitation" has a positive meaning; the good is rewarded:

> And as for the Visitation (ופקודת) of all who walk in this (Spirit), it consists of healing and abundance of bliss, with length of days and fruitfulness, and all blessings without end, and eternal joy in perpetual life, and the glorious crown and garment of honour in everlasting light.

In 4:11-14, however, the Visitation has a negative tone. Those who walk in the spirit of perversity can only expect punishment and destruction:

> And as for the Visitation (ופקודת) of all who walk in this (Spirit), it consists of an abundance of blows administered by all the angels of destruction in the everlasting Pit by the furious wrath of the God of vengeance, or unending dread and shame without end, and of the disgrace of destruction by the fire of the regions of darkness. And all their times from age to age are in most sorrowful chagrin and bitterest misfortune, in calamities of darkness till they are destroyed with none of them surviving or escaping.

Shorter references to this dual character of the Visitation appear else-

---

[1] Millar Burrows, *More light on the Dead Sea Scrolls* (New York: The Viking Press, 1958), p. 273, says there is no "rigid standard of uniformity in belief, ritual, or organization" in the scrolls. Cf. Otto A. Piper, "The 'Book of Mysteries' (Qumran 27), A Study in Eschatology," *Journal of Religion*, XXXVIII (1958), 95-106; Harold Henry Rowley, *Jewish Apocalyptic and the Dead Sea Scrolls* (London: The Athlone Press, 1957).

[2] Burrows, *More Light*, p. 342.

where in the Manual of Discipline. The Teacher of Righteousness taught about "the Visitation with which they are smitten together with the times when they are blessed" (3:14). The Creator allotted to man "two Spirits that he should walk in them until the time of His Visitation" (3:18; cf. 4:26). Only in 4:8b-19 is the Visitation described as entirely negative; however, this reference may be influenced by 4:11-14 where the Visitation of vengeance is contrasted with the Visitation of deliverance in 4:6-8.

The Hymn Scroll (I QH) likewise refers to the double character of the Visitation "bringing gladness unto them, together with < > all the blows that smite them" (1:17).

In the Damascus Document (CD) one reference to the Visitation is purely negative (7:20 f.), while a second reference has a dual character: the poor of the flock "will be delivered at the time of the Visitation, but the rest will be put to the sword " (19:10).

With one or possibly two exceptions, we see that פקודה has a dual meaning : [1] it means vindication for the righteous and damnation for the wicked. This linking of the positive and negative elements in the description of the judgment is similar to the dual emphasis we noticed in our earlier discussion of the apocalyptic materials. This observation, we believe, gives additional support for our position against the claim of Miss Mattern that the final judgment in Jewish apocalyptic means exclusively damnation.[2]

It is noteworthy that in the Qumran scrolls the community figures prominently in the judgment. The community exercises judgment in both the present and the future, and the community believes that it will stand before the great Judge on the eschatological Day.

We see a strange anomaly in the Qumran community. Acutely conscious of the presence of sin in its members (I QS 10:11-13), the community exercised a stern judgment hoping thereby to keep its members unspotted from the world. This discipline of the community is referred to as the "trials and judgments destined to condemn all those who transgress a precept" (I QS 5:6). The Manual of Discipline provides a long

---

[1] It should be noted that this same consistency does not hold with other forms of פקד. In the perfect this word can mean to examine (10 times), to appoint (3 times), to enforce (twice), to attend, etc.

[2] *Supra*, pp. 39-40. Cf. Jean Daniélou, "Eschatologie Sadocite et eschatologie Chrétienne," in *Les manuscrits de la Mer Morte* (Paris : Presses Universitaires de France, 1957), pp. 115-116, who supports the position taken here.

list of penalties for specified offenses which come before the community for judgment. Anyone who lies about his income faces a year's suspension from the community (6:25). A similar sentence is pronounced on a brother who is disrespectful of another, or who seeks to exact justice with his own hand (6:26 f.). Final excommunication or possibly death [1] could be inflicted for blasphemy (6:27-7:2). Likewise, he who speaks in anger shall be put in solitary confinement, fined for a year and " excluded from the pure thing of the Many" (7:3). A sizeable list of crimes with the appropriate penalties follows.[2] In all of the instances mentioned above (except possibly blasphemy) the judgment has two purposes: (1) to maintain the integrity of the community and (2) to save the individual. The community used the judgment to ready itself for the eschatological Day.

The community of the elect, it was believed, would also participate in the future judgment of the world. The interpreter of Habakkuk (I QpHab) says, "God will judge all the nations by the hand of His elect" (5:4). The War Scroll (I QM) opens with a long list of nations destined to fall before God's elect in the final eschatological battle (1:1-2). These nations stand in fear of the judgment of God's elect (I QH 4:25 f.; cf. I QH 6:26, 29). Elsewhere it is said that God will judge and destroy every idolatrous nation (I QpHab 12:14, 13:3).

References to the apostate Jews who persecute the Dead Sea sect are especially vituperative. The elect will also participate in the judgment of these erring brothers. Apostate Jews will be forced to atone for their persecution of the sect through punishment inflicted by the elect community (I QpHab 5:4). Again the thought appears that God will assist the community in its judgment. His wrath will burn the Jerusalem priests and Levites in eternal destruction (I QS 2:15). The accomplices of the Wicked Priest [3] are singled out for a fiery judgment for insulting and outraging the elect of God (I QpHab 10:13). God will declare the Wicked Priest guilty before the elect and will punish them with sulphurous fire (I QpHab 10:3).[4] Perverse Jews who act disrespectfully toward "matters revealed" shall suffer

---

[1] Dupont-Sommer, *Essene Writings*, p. 87, n. 2.

[2] For other instances see 7:4-25; 8:20-27; 9:1-23.

[3] Dupont-Sommer, *Essene Writings*, pp. 351-357, thinks this was Hyrcanus II through whom impure sacrifices were offered by ill-prepared priests.

[4] I. e., from before the Tribunal before which all mankind is tried at the end of time.

eternal destruction and have no remnant (I QS 5:12; cf. I QH 3:27). All those who attack the Teacher of Righteousness will be declared guilty at the Last Judgment (I QH 7:12). Unlike the apocalyptic books examined earlier, the judgment of eternal damnation is not confined to the heathen nations. Judgment upon apostate Jews is sometimes described in more vitriolic terms than those used to depict the judgment of the Gentile nations.

Although the Qumran texts speak frequently of the judgment of destruction, other passages speak in a hopeful way of the judgment. The righteous remnant will atone for the sins of the apostate Jews and the wider world. The commentator on Habakkuk says that the righteous community will "be accepted as expiation for the earth" (8:10). In still other cases the suffering in the judgment is said to have redemptive powers (I QpHab 5:4).

It is very clear that in the Qumran texts the elect community itself will face a future judgment. This judgment will be the time of vindication of the holy remnant. God, the Habakkuk commentator writes, will deliver the covenant community "from the House of Judgment" (I QpHab 8:1-2). The covenanter feels certain that God will vindicate his righteousness at the final judgment (I QS 11:2, 5, 10, 12, 13). The principal emphasis of The Hymn Scroll (I QH) is on the present suffering of the righteous and their confidence in the future triumph of their cause (e.g., 7:6-25).

2. משפט as in the apocalyptic writings is closely tied to צדקה. We note here, for example, as in our study of the Psalms of Solomon,[1] an argument for God's righteousness, a vindication of his judgments. The initiate confesses, "just (צדיק) is God who has fulfilled His judgment against us and our fathers" (I QS 1:26). The author of the Manual of Discipline calls on God "to justify Thy judgment of truth in the midst of the sons of men" (I QS 11:14). The psalmist believed that his suffering was a means through which God might be "glorified in the judgment of the wicked" (I QH 2:24). One covenanter exclaims to God, "faithful is Thy judgment over us" (CD 20:30; my translation).

The very close relationship between God's righteousness and his covenant receives an even greater emphasis in the Qumran materials than in the apocalyptic writings. The copious references to the covenant in the Scrolls [2] stand in marked contrast to the paucity of allusions to

---

[1] *Supra*, pp. 36-37.
[2] There are forty-two references in the Damascus Document alone. Karl Georg Kuhn, *Konkordanz zu den Qumrantexten* (Göttingen : Vandenhoeck & Ruprecht, 1960), p. 37.

the covenant in the rabbinic materials. While ברית usually means "ordinance" in the rabbinic materials,[1] in the Qumran texts the word connotes a variety of rich theological meanings. Moreover, the covenant concept plays a much more prominent role in the Qumran scrolls collectively than in the earlier known books of the Apocrypha and Pseudepigrapha which we have examined, although the two bodies of material do share some of the same meanings.

In the Qumran texts the covenant is "of God" (I QpHab 2:4; I QS 5:8; 5:11, 18, 19, 22, etc.), and hence is eternal (I QM 17:3; I QS 4:22, etc.). The sect taught that God concluded the covenant "with our fathers" (I QM 13:7; 14:8 CD 1:4; 4:9; 6:2), and that he protected the covenant (I QM 14:4). He continued to keep the believer in the covenant (I QH 2:22; 7:8; 7:10; 7:20; 15:14). God, in other words, initiates and sustains the covenant by his continual action.

The concept of the righteous remnant is closely associated with the covenant concept. From the beginning to the end of holy history God has saved and will always save a remnant (CD 2:6 f., etc.). The Qumran community understood itself as this remnant alone remaining faithful to the covenant of God (I QS 5:3; CD 1:4). Thus to enter the community was in many instances equated with entering the covenant (I QS 1:16, 18, 20, 24; 2:10; 2:12; 5:20; 6:15, etc.).

No remnant of the evil ones will be preserved (CD 2:6 f.). These evil ones are those outside the community who "do not know his covenant" (I QS 5:19), who transgress his covenant (CD 1:20), or who in the past "forsook the covenant" (CD 5:11). Those Jews who do not enter the new covenant or renewed covenant relationship in the Dead Sea Community are called apostates who have followed "the Man of the Lie" (CD 20:12).

The tendency of the sectarians to view the covenant as signifying the gracious and sustaining relationship of God with his community, certainly places them within the ancient Israelite tradition. As within this tradition, Qumran's concept of the covenant—like Torah, grace, forgiveness, etc.— is understood in a corporate context. To be sure, the Hymn Scroll does stress individual election; [2] however, even in these psalms as in the canonical ones we see a strong corporate consciousness. Indeed, the psalmist sees himself in light of the community itself. He

---

[1] *Infra*, p. 62-63.
[2] Schubert, *The Dead Sea Community*, p. 84.

calls himself a "banner for the elect of righteousness" (I QH 2:13). He lives and prays for the sake of the community. Dupont-Sommer underscores this point:

> The Qumran documents constantly return to the idea of "community": the corresponding Hebrew word, *yahad*, is used in these texts with a characteristic frequency, and is the exact equivalent of the Greek *koinonia* employed by Philo and Josephus. The sect is not only called the "Council of the Community", but also the "Institution of the Community", the "Community of God", the "Community of the Eternal Covenant", the "Covenant of the Community", the "Covenant of the Eternal Community". Among the brethren, everything was held in common: in the Rule (VI, 2-3) we read:
>
> And they shall eat in common, bless in common, and deliberate in common.[1]

The covenant is bound indissolubly with the corporate image in the Qumran texts. The Law by which the community organizes its life is, like the remnant, a reality closely tied to the covenant relationship (CD 4:6-9; 19:1, etc.).

The covenant community at Qumran, like that of the apocalyptic books, is to order its life by the Law, and by this Law it will be judged. Those who despise the Torah as interpreted and expanded by the sectarians draw down on themselves the condemnation of God and/or excommunication from the community (CD 7:9; 8:19; 1:5; Ms. "B" of CD 1:31-32; I QpHab 1:11; 5:12). Those who sin against the Law are expelled from the community (I QS 8:22). Conversely whoever enters the covenant community is converted to the Law (I QS 5:8; CD 15:7b-9; 16:2). The Angel of Hostility departs from man when he is converted "to the Law of Moses" (CD 16:5), but after being converted to the Law of Moses apostasy is a horrendous deed (CD 15:12). Man's eternal destiny is shaped by his decision for or against the Law.

The outlook sketched above resembles that which we saw in the apocalyptic section of this study.[2] It should be noted, however, that here we have a strong parallel emphasis on performing the precepts of the Law. Those who observe the Law (I QpHab 7:11; 8:1) are the same as those who practice the Law (I QpHab 12:4 f.). Community members are to keep faithfully every maxim of the Law (I QS 9:9), and to strive to act according to the spirit of the Law (CD 6:14). The just are those who faithfully "observe the Law" (I QpHab 8:1). Men of the community are distinguished by their works and ranked according to their understanding of the Law (I QS 5:21; 6:18; 6:22).

---

[1] Dupont-Sommer, *Essene Writings*, p. 44.
[2] *Supra*, pp. 33-35.

In spite of this strong emphasis on doing the requirements of the Law, the principal if not the "sole aim of Torah study was the detection of the will of God."[1] This aim is evident in the opening verses of the Manual of Discipline: "He shall seek God... and in ... order to do what is good and right before Him, as He commanded through Moses and through all of his servants the prophets (1:2-3; cf. 8:15 f.).

The Torah is understood in an eschatological context in the Qumran texts. A sense of impending judgment hovers over the community. The righteous and the sinners are soon to be separated. Repentance and amendment of life are urgently needed. The repentance, we can see, was not understood as a simple return to the old Mosaic Law.[2] Long parenetic sections regularly appear in various Qumran texts which certainly go beyond the Law and the Prophets.[3] It has been suggested that the "*halaka*, as we know it from CD, is closely akin to traditional rabbinic *halaka*."[4] It should be noted, however, that since the parenetic materials in the Qumran texts are set in an eschatological context this tone is different from the parenesis in the rabbinic materials. In the rabbinic writings the parenetic sections are made up of moral maxims that apply the Law to daily life; in the Qumran texts the parenesis is much more of an emergency ethic which guides the community in its life under the shadow of the impending judgment. It is the sanction of this future deed of God and his retributive justice more than the fear of transgressing the Torah and suffering the community's opprobrium which forms the organizing center of the Qumran materials.

We can omit a discussion of wrath in the Qumran materials at this point since in the discussion below[5] we shall see that the same general characteristics of wrath in the apocalyptic materials appear in the Qumran texts.

The form of the judgment pronouncement at Qumran is irregular. Usually the pronouncement is terse and straightforward with no introduction or conclusion. For example, the Habakkuk commentator

---

[1] Preben Wernberg-Møller (trans. and ed.), *The Manual of Discipline* (Leiden : E.J. Brill, 1957), p. 13.

[2] Braun, *Qumran*, II, 270.

[3] See CD 10:14-18 which deals with Sabbath observance; I QM 2:1-14:16 which describes battle procedures; I QS 5:1-7:25 which deals with the rule of the Community, etc. Mattern, *Verständnis*, p. 29, is in error when she says that parenesis plays no significant role in apocalyptic literature.

[4] Wernberg-Møller (trans. and ed.), *Manual*, p. 20.

[5] *Infra*, pp. 82-83.

announces that the accomplices of the Wicked Priest will "come to the judgment of fire for having insulted and outraged the elect of God" (I QpHab 10:13). Similarly, in 12:14 the interpreter declares that the idols of the nations "will not deliver them on the Day of Judgment." The Manual of Discipline speaks of the perverse ones who "have treated with insolence matters revealed that wrath might rise unto Judgment and Vengeance be exercised by the curses of the Covenant, and solemn judgment be fulfilled against them unto eternal destruction, leaving no remnant" (I QS 5:12; cf. I QpHab 13:3; I QS 1:26; 2:15; QH 7:12, etc.). Even in the longer judgment passages (I QS 10:16b-21) we see this same straightforward promise of reward for the suffering, poor, righteous and the blunt threat of eschatological torment for the rich, mighty, strong, and pagan Gentiles as well as the apostate Jews.

In the community judgments we see the same direct relationship between the offense and the penalty with no introduction or conclusion. In I QS 7:5, for example, it is written that "Anyone who spits into the midst of the session of the Many shall be fined for thirty days." It is therefore safe to conclude that no judgment form comparable to that used by the pre-exilic Prophets or by Paul [1] is employed by either the Qumran or the apocalyptic writers.

In summary, it can be said that the community plays an increasingly prominent role in the judgment procedure in the Qumran materials, and that the unrighteousness of the covenant member is contrasted with the righteousness of God. Paradoxically, an equally strong emphasis on the purification of the community emerges. The covenant also gains in importance in the Qumran texts. Like the apocalyptic and prophetic writings the Qumran materials contain a strong *heilsgeschichtliche* orientation. Qumran's desire for an uncorrupted priesthood,[2] and for the day when pure offerings would be substituted for the polluted sacrifices in Jerusalem [3] and the correct interpretation of scripture for error [4] shows that the community was more than a future-

---

[1] *Infra,* pp. 91-94.

[2] Braun, *Qumran,* II, 267.

[3] E.g., Manual of Discipline, 4:25.

[4] Dupont-Sommer, *Essene Writings,* pp. 257-258, notes that "The great number and diversity of commentaries discovered or indirectly attested at Qumran leads us to assume that the Essenes worked not only on one or other of the biblical books, but almost all of them."

oriented, apocalyptic sect. The Dead Sea community obviously believed that it was recovering a religious heritage that had been lost.[1]

D. Judgment in the Rabbinic Materials

Increasingly it is being recognized that it is not as important to attempt to find literary parallels to Paul's writings as it is to try to uncover the religious culture and outlook of the world Paul would have known.[2] This approach is especially apt in any consideration of the rabbinic materials whose literary deposit though late was based on a pervasive oral tradition surely as early as Paul's day. In order to try to reconstruct an accurate picture of the rabbinic understanding of judgment we shall limit our consideration to the earlier materials, giving special weight to the sources dated before the death of Akiba (A.D. 132). We readily grant that uncertainty about the dates of the traditions and the integrity of the texts makes our finding tentative. While we are not able to make an exhaustive survey and analysis of these materials within the scope of this study, we shall attempt to select representative passages.[3]

Those to whom justification by faith is normative for comprehending Paul quite understandably claim that Paul rejected his Pharisaic

---

[1] *Ibid.*, p. 255, charges that the Qumran community prostituted the scriptures in the interest of an eschatological obsession. The commentaries on Habakkuk, Nahum, Isaiah, etc. do contain evidence that the Qumran scholars sought to discover the secrets of the divine books which allude to the cataclysmic events soon to come. It is unfair, however, to expect the covenanters to practice a form of "objective interpretation" which evolved only in the modern period. Moreover, although in many cases the Qumran interpretation did misconstrue the intent of the original writer as we would understand him, it remains an open question whether the spirit of the tradition was violated. The same emphasis on the fulfillment of God's Old Testament promises prevails in the Habakkuk Commentary, for example, that we see in the Gospel of Matthew (Braun, *Qumran*, II, 323). Is it in order then to ask if in some measure the Qumran interpretations are not true to the Old Testament promise?

[2] Robin Scroggs, *The Last Adam* (Philadelphia : The Fortress Press, 1966), pp. 16-17.

[3] Davies, *Paul*, pp. 3-4, issues a warning to scholars using these sources. One should recognize, according to Davies, that the extant rabbinic materials come from a wing of the Pharisean party, that of Johanan ben Zakkai which had almost completely triumphed over the rest of the party; therefore, it is important to remember that many facets of the first-century Judaism fail to appear in our available sources, " and that Judaism was much more variegated than such sources would lead us to expect."

religion as a consequence of his conversion.[1] This claim juxtaposes the
Christian Apostle against his Jewish background, and, in effect, cuts
him off from his religious tradition. Our consideration of the rabbinic
materials—often judged to be the most direct literary deposit of the
teachings of the Pharisees and their successors—will test the authenticity of this claim in light of the relevant themes and judgment vocabulary in the materials themselves.

1. Our consideration of judgment in the rabbinic writings falls into
two parts : (a) the significance of judgment for the individual, and
(b) the meaning of judgment for Israel.[2]

(a) It is impossible to discuss the significance of judgment for the
individual in an intelligent way without some grasp of the place of the
Torah in rabbinic thought. When we look at the relationship of the
Torah to the patriarchs and holy places of Israel's heritage we notice
that the rabbis view the Torah as an ahistorical entity with no relationship to the covenant. Moses and Sinai, for example, are less significant
as a person and a place against which Israel's faith is defined and her
actions judged, than they are means of authenticating the validity
of the Torah. For example, in the Midrash on Deuteronomy 1:29 the
rabbis note that Moses summons Joshua and addresses him before all
Israel, "Sei stark und fest" (Deut. 31:7). The rabbis interpret this to
mean : " 'Stark,' [d.h.] in der Tora; und 'fest,' [d.h.] in guten Wer-

---

[1] Rudolf Bultmann, *Existence and Faith*, trans. Schubert M. Ogden (Living Age Books, no. 29; New York : Meridian Books, Inc., 1960), pp. 147-157, says that in Romans 7 Paul is contrasting his Christian existence with his former life as a legalistic Jew. Mattern, *Verständnis*, p. 215, summarizes the central thrust of her work : " Es geht Paulus nicht um Addition alter Vorstellungen und Aussagen, sondern um ein grundlegend Neues : die justificatio impii, die in verantwortlichen Gehorsam stellt." Devor, "Concept of Judgment," pp. 364-365, says unequivocally : "Paul the Pharisee knew himself to be under a holy God who had made known his holy will in the revelation of the Book, his holy law. This book should have been for Paul the source of all blessings.... But that which should have been his deepest joy gradually became his deepest despair." Devor adds, p. 366, that in Christ God overcomes this human impotence : "this man, now, unbelievably hears the verdict in Christ; now no condemnation.... This is the soaring reality which unshackled Paul." For Paul "faith is the antithesis of merit." Devor, pp. 367-368, concludes : "The contrast between faith-living and his old Pharisaic days is everywhere evident .... With this background, then, Paul broke into the Christian life."

[2] This consideration ranges beyond the use of the term משפט which appears infrequently in the Babylonian Talmud.

ken."[1] Very typical is the tendency to claim authority for a saying by tracing it back to Moses, e.g., a saying by R. Joshua from Rabban Joḥanan b. Zakkai (A.D. 10-80) "who heard it from his teacher, and his teacher [heard it] from his teacher as a *halachah* [given] to Moses from Sinai."[2] The Torah, then, appears as an absolute; the tradition and personages gain their significance as witnesses to the Torah, not *vice versa*.

The glorification of the Torah as an entity within itself further reveals its isolation from its historical foundations. In the rabbinic materials the Torah is timeless. It existed before and assisted God in the creation;[3] it is by the Torah that the world is sustained,[4] and though heaven and earth pass away the Torah will not pass away.[5] The Torah can stand with God as one of the parents (the mother) of Israel,[6] and yet be called God's daughter.[7] The Torah talks with God,[8] intercedes for the righteous,[9] and carries certain prophylactic powers against snake bite.[10] Variously the Torah is called a stronghold,[11] a

---

[1] *Tannaitsche Midrashim, Sifre zu Deuteronomium*, trans. and ed. Henrik Ljungman (Stuttgart : W. Kohlhammer, 1964), p. 74.

[2] Eduyyoth, p. 50, in *The Babylonian Talmud*, trans. under the editorship of Isaac Epstein (London : The Soncino Press, 1952), p. 50. All citations from the Talmud are from this edition unless otherwise noted. Hereafter this work will be cited as BT. Cf. Kiddushin, pp. 209, 188; Yebamoth, p. 527; Megillah, pp. 118, 148; Yoma, p. 11; Pesahim, p. 180; Erubin, p. 125. For an excellent introduction to the formation of the Talmud see William F. Stinespring, "Talmud," in *Dictionary of the Bible*, ed. James Hastings, revised edition by Frederick C. Grant and H.H. Rowley (New York : Charles Scribner's Sons, 1963), pp. 954-956.

[3] *Midrash Rabbah Exodus*, trans. and ed. S.M. Lehrman (London : Soncino Press, 1939), p. 539. All references to the Midrash will be to the Soncino edition unless otherwise stated. Hereafter cited as MR. Exodus, Numbers, etc.

[4] *The Mishnah*, trans and ed. Herbert Danby (Oxford : At the Clarendon Press, 1933), p. 446.

[5] *Ibid.*, p. 9.

[6] MR Exodus, p. 353.

[7] *Ibid.*, p. 352.

[8] Solomon Schechter, *Aspects of Rabbinic Theology* (New York : Shocken Books, 1961), p. 323.

[9] Moore, *Judaism*, I, 268.

[10] *The Targums of Onkelos and Jonathan ben Uzziel on the Pentateuch*, trans. and ed. J. W. Etheridge (2 vols.; London : Longman and Co., 1862), I, 166.

[11] MR Leviticus, p. 400.

crown,[1] light,[2] medicine,[3] wine,[4] water, oil, and milk.[5] The Torah can also serve as a surrogate for the temple.[6]

C.G. Montefiore notes that the Torah has "some sort of independent and cosmic existence, even as its creation took place long before the creation of man." [7] In spite of this observation, Montefiore muses quizzically, "It is odd how a book so full of events in time could be regarded as existing before the history of man began." [8] In light of our investigation such a development should not be surprising even though it may seem "odd" to modern man. By this time the Torah no longer receives its primary significance through its historical ties. Although it is in history, it transcends both history and the community through which it was given birth. Or, to express it differently, no longer does the Torah derive its significance from God's gracious acts in his chosen community and its history. Consequently, the way is clear for the Torah to become no longer the basis of behavior as "determined by the relationship to God, but that very relationship itself." [9]

Faith, consequently, is understood as fidelity to the Torah. There is little, if any, juxtaposition of faith and works [10] in the rabbinic writings because in a very real sense faith is the performance of works. Montefiore, to be sure, cites eight pages of references to faith, many of which depict faith as an inward attitude directed toward an object.[11] Only one such reference, however, is from a rabbi in Akiba's time or before,[12] and even in this single reference faith means trust in God's benevolence. Schoeps goes too far, therefore, when he says that faith

---

[1] MR Exodus, p. 427; cf. MR Numbers, p. 112.

[2] MR Exodus 34:1, p. 427; MR Numbers 14:10, p. 613.

[3] Sifre Deut., 'Eḳeb, para 45, f. 82b, as cited in Montefiore and Loewe, *Rabbinic Anthology*, p. 125.

[4] Pes. K. 102 *a fin.* as cited in Montefiore and Loewe, *Rabbinic Anthology*, p. 312.

[5] Cant. R. I, para 2, 3, on I, 2 as cited in Montefiore and Loewe *Rabbinic Anthology*, p. 163.

[6] Schechter, *Rabbinic Theology*, p. 136.

[7] Montefiore and Loewe, *Rabbinic Anthology*, p. xxxiii.

[8] *Ibid.*

[9] Noth, *Laws*, p. 91.

[10] Schoeps, *Paul*, p. 202.

[11] Montefiore and Loewe, *Rabbinic Anthology*, pp. 334-341.

[12] *Ibid.*, p. 338 : "He who created the day, created the sustenance thereof. R. Elazar of Modi'im said : If a man has food for the day, but says, 'What shall I eat tomorrow ?' Such a one is deficient in faith. R. Eliezer the Great said : He who has yet bread in his basket, and says, 'What shall I eat tomorrow ?' belongs to those who are small in faith."

means only fidelity in the first-century rabbinic writings,[1] but there is little question but that fidelity is the overriding emphasis of the rabbinic materials.[2]

This tendency to understand faith as fidelity to the Torah is especially prominent in the rabbinic materials that treat the Abraham narrative. In the Genesis narrative (15:6) Abraham appears as a man of faith. The rabbis interpret this to mean that Abraham had kept the Torah even before it had been written. The Mishnah reads: "We find that Abraham our Father had performed the whole Law before it was given, for it is written, *Because that Abraham obeyed my voice and kept my charge, my commandments, my statutes, and my laws.*" [3] It might be argued that since Rabbi Nehorai's statement comes as late as A.D. 165-200 it has no bearing on our discussion. It seems apparent, however, that he is repeating a tradition which was already in existence when Jubilees was written (between 109-105 B.C.). In Jubilees 24:8 ff. Yahweh counsels Isaac against going to Egypt for famine relief and reaffirms his intention to bless Isaac for Abraham's faith. Abraham's faith is understood to mean fidelity to the Law even before it was given: "And in thy seed shall all the nations of the earth be blessed, because thy father obeyed My voice, and kept My charge and My commandments, and My laws and My ordinances." [4]

The pre-Christian Rabbi Shemayah (first century B.C. teacher of Hillel) ascribes meritorious value to the faith of Abraham. It is this faith which makes Israel deserving of having the sea divided for them.[5] Abraham's faith in this case also appears to mean fidelity to God's command.[6]

Although the Talmud mentions lighter and heavier commands,[7] the

---

[1] *Paul*, p. 204.

[2] Arnold Meyer, *Das Rätsel des Jacobusbriefes* (Giessen: Alfred Töpelmann, 1930), p. 137, is in basic agreement.

[3] Kiddushin, p. 329; see also BT, Yoma, p. 134, " Rab [c.a. A.D. 200] said: Our father Abraham kept the whole Torah."

[4] Charles, *Apocrypha, II*, 50.

[5] Tractate Beshallah in *Mekilta de-Rabbi Ishmael*, trans. and ed. Jacob Z. Lauterbach (3 vols.; Philadelphia: The Jewish Publication Society of America, 1933), I, 220.

[6] Moore, *Judaism*, II, 237, believes that confidence also is implicit in the use of the term here.

[7] Sifre Deut. 12:23, para 76 (90b), as cited in Montefiore and Loewe, *Rabbinic Anthology*, p. 196. See Herman L. Strack and Paul Billerbeck, *Kommentar zum Neuen Testament aus Talmud und Midrash* (5. vols.; München: C.H. Becksche Verlagsbuchhandlung Oskar Beck, 1922), I, 901 ff.

true Israelite, it is assumed, will faithfully keep all of the commandments, and will be held accountable for all of them at the Last Judgment. Ben Azzai (a contemporary of Akiba) said, "Run to fulfill the lightest duty even as the weightiest" (Aboth 4:2). His statement accurately characterizes rabbinic thought. Likewise Rabbi (Judah the Patriarch, A.D. 165) made more explicit what had long been implicit in rabbinic thought when he said, "be heedful of a light precept as a weighty one, for thou knowest not the recompense of reward of each precept." [1]

On the basis of this limited investigation one is led to conclude with Rudolf Bultmann that "in the rabbinic literature faith is understood onesidedly as obedience to the law." [2] Once again, then, we see the Torah emerging as the organizing center of Judaism. Consequently, the emphasis is shifted away from the continuing divine initiative to human activity. Man's action is no longer a response to Yahweh whose action precedes the Torah, but a response to the Torah itself. Judaism

---

[1] The Mishnah, Aboth 2:1, p. 447. Hugo Odeberg, *Pharisaism and Christianity*, trans. J.M. Moe (St. Louis : Concordia Publishing House, 1962), p. 20, is in error when he suggests that the ruling norm of all rabbinic ethics is the law of love : "[A] supreme moral norm characterizes the entire history of rabbinical ethics." Odeberg rests his case on the story of the pagan who came to Hillel saying, "Make me a proselyte, on condition that you teach me the whole Torah while I stand on one foot" (Shabbath, p. 140). Odeberg reports Hillel's reply as, "Thou shalt love thy neighbor as thyself; and what is hateful to you, you shall not do to others. This is the whole Law; everything else is application" (p. 17). It is interesting to note that in the text there is not one word about loving the neighbor : בא לפני הלל גייריה אמר ליה דעלך סני לחברך לא תעביד זו היא כל התורה כולה ואיד פירושה הוא זיל גמור. (*Der Babylonische Talmud*, ed. Lazarus Goldschmidt [8 vols.; Berlin und Wien : Benjamin Harz Verlag, 1925], I, 388).

The Soncino edition renders the text : "When he went to Hillel, he said to him, "[W]hat is hateful to you, do not to your neighbor : that is the whole Torah, while the rest is commentary thereof; go and learn it" (Shabbath, p. 140). Odeberg obviously has in mind the statement of Akiba : "[T]he greatest principle is thou shalt love thy neighbor as thyself" (Bereshit, p. 236); however, this statement is an exception to the general rule seen in Sifre Deut., 'Ekeb, para. 48 as cited in Montefiore and Loewe, *Rabbinic Anthology*, p. 155, etc. One may deplore, as does Odeberg, the tendency to present Pharisaism as the antithesis of Christianity; however, he goes beyond the evidence when he suggests a very early date for a supreme ruling norm of neighbor love for all Pharisaic conduct.

[2] "Faith," in *Bible Key Words*, trans. and ed. Dorothea M. Barton, P.R. Ackroyd, and A.E. Harvey (from G. Kittel's *Theologische Wörterbuch zum Neuen Testament* [New York : Harper & Brothers, 1960]), IV, 46.

thus becomes more of an orthopraxis than an orthodoxy,[1] and the judgment is held by this praxis.

The strong emphasis on fidelity to the Torah is coupled with a correspondingly strong doctrine of recompense.[2] Akiba's statement, "All is according to the amount of work" (The Mishnah, Aboth 3:16) accurately summarizes the general philosophy of rabbinic judaism.[3] According to the rabbis, man's good deeds will intercede for him and his bad deeds will accuse him at the last judgment.[4] All of man's deeds are preserved in a book in readiness for the great assize.[5]

Confidence that fidelity would be rewarded in the judgment is a common theme of rabbinic writings.[6] The counterpart of this emphasis is the warning: "[L]ose not belief in retribution." [7] This severe future judgment was tempered by a slight emphasis on mercy.[8] Not until the middle of the second century A.D., however, is there evidence of any awareness of conflict between the doctrine of mercy and the judgment demand. By this time we see numerous attempts to rationally explain this apparent contradiction.[9] Even in the one case cited where mercy is shown in the judgment (Rosh Hashanah, p. 64), the divine favor rests only on (1) the Jews, and (2) those who have merit to their account. Consequently, it seems accurate to say that man's status at the judgment depends principally on his fidelity to the Torah.

It is more difficult to understand how the emphasis on reward and retribution can be reconciled with the corresponding emphasis on disinterested service to God. For example, Antigonus of Soko (third century B.C.) said: "Be not like slaves that minister to the master for the sake of receiving a bounty (פרס), but be like slaves that minister to the master not for the sake of receiving a bounty; and let the fear of Heaven be upon you." [10] In commenting on this passage Herford says:

---

[1] Kurt Schubert, *Die Religion des nachbiblischen Judentums* (Freiburg-Wien : Herder, 1955), p. 26.

[2] Abraham Cohen, *Everyman's Talmud* (London : J.M. Dent and Sons, 1931), p. 188.

[3] R. Travers Herford, *Pirke Aboth* (New York : Jewish Institute of Religion, 1945), pp 88-89.

[4] The Mishnah, Aboth 4:11, p. 454.

[5] *Ibid.*, p. 447.

[6] *Ibid.*, p. 452.

[7] *Ibid.*, p. 446.

[8] BT, Rosh Hashanah, p. 64.

[9] *Ibid.*, p. 66; cf. BT, Sanhedrin, p. 245; BT, Shabbath, p. 774.

[10] The Mishnah, Aboth 1:3, p. 446; Aboth 2:8, p. 448; cf. BT, Shabbath, p. 781.

The term "reward" which is frequently used in this connection, both in Jewish and Christian writings, does not in either case refer to any thing which can be an object of selfish desire. It refers to the divine approval, God's "well done, good and faithful servant." For that "reward" a man may serve God, and such service is rendered for love and not for gain, nor for the expectation of the fulfilment of any bargain.[1]

Hugo Odeberg agrees with Herford. He acknowledges that the promise of reward and the threat of punishment were used in later rabbinic thought to motivate man to do good deeds, but he believes that in the first century A.D. there "would be more reason to say that Christianity to a certain extent adopts the morality of reward than to say this about Pharisaism." [2]

It is difficult to accept the arguments of Herford and Odeberg. Surely Herford goes too far when he suggests that early Pharisaism had no interest in earned reward. R. Eleazar (A.D. 80-120) clearly disagrees: "Be alert to study the Law and know how to make answer to an unbeliever; and know before whom thou toilest and who is thy taskmaster who shall pay thee the reward of thy labour." [3]

Morton Smith's careful study of Tannaitic parallels to the Gospels gives strong support to the position taken here.[4] While undoubtedly there are references to reward in Paul's letters as well as the Gospels,[5] it is simply incorrect to say that the promise of reward or pay had little or no currency in first century Judaism. Smith lists 117 Tannaitic references to שכר (pay) in the rabbinic materials.[6] Many of Smith's references date at least as early as the first century and may rest on pre-Christian traditions. There are, by the same token, five references in Paul's letters to $\mu\iota\sigma\theta\acute{o}s$ (Rom. 4:4; I Cor. 3:8; 3:14; 9:17, 18), although there are other contexts in which the concept of reward is present (cf. II Cor. 5:10). Smith's citation of Sifre on Deuteronomy 33:6 is especially apposite to our argument:

"Let Reuben live," in (virtue of his part in) the affair of Joseph,
"And let him not die," in (virtue of) the affair of Bilhah. R. Hananya b.

---

[1] *Pirke Aboth*, p. 23.

[2] Odeberg, *Pharisaism and Christianity*, p. 33.

[3] The Mishnah, Aboth 2:14, p. 449; cf. 4:11; 5:23, etc.

[4] Morton Smith, *Tannaitic Parallels to the Gospels* (Journal of Biblical Literature Monograph Series, vol. VI; Philadelphia: Society of Biblical Literature, 1951).

[5] For a complete list of references in the Gospels see Smith, *Tannaitic Parallels*, pp. 161-162.

[6] *Ibid.*, pp. 163-184.

Gamaliel says, "Merit is never exchanged for guilt, for merit except that of Reuben and that of David" .... And the Sages say, "Merit is never exchanged for guilt, nor guilt for merit, but pay is given for the (performance of) commandments and men are punished for the transgressions (they have committed). And why does Scripture say, 'Let Reuben live and let him not die'? Because Reuben repented."[1]

Likewise, Odeberg overstates the case when he says Pharisaism was less legalistic than Matthew. It is well to remember that the Mishnah and the Talmud include widely divergent opinions.[2] More significantly, to this writer's knowledge, there is no evidence to suggest that the rabbis felt there was any contradiction between the promise of reward for good deeds (Aboth 2:14) and the disavowal of any thought of working for a reward (Aboth 2:8). The fact that apparently contradictory ideas stand so close to each other should argue against any tendency of ours to look for a carefully developed system of belief about reward. The very fact that the early rabbis make no attempt to reconcile these two concepts (which appear on adjacent pages in the Mishnah) might suggest that they presented no difficulty to the rabbis.[3] The fact remains, however, that man was created to perform the Law (Aboth 2:8b) and the performance of the Law is equated with salvation itself.[4]

It should come as no surprise to us, therefore, that the judgment for the rabbis assumed a strongly individualistic emphasis. When man's fidelity to the Torah became decisive, it became "necessary that the individual himself should begin to be responsible for keeping its requirements."[5] This outlook stands in bold contrast to the early Old Testament texts where an individual transgression involves the whole community in the consequences of and in the responsibility for expiating the crime (e.g., Deut. 13:6; 17:7).

The individual retribution of the rabbinic materials is both a future prospect and, to a limited degree, a present reality. Illness or even death might follow some sin.[6] Natural disasters, wars, etc. were also linked to individual or corporate sin.[7] Suffering in this world was often

---

[1] Smith, *Tannaitic Parallels*, p. 177.

[2] Herman L. Strack, *Introduction to the Talmud and Midrash* (New York : Harper Torchbooks, 1965), p. 20.

[3] Moore, *Judaism*, II, 89-111.

[4] Noth, *Laws*, p. 91.

[5] *Ibid.*, pp. 97-98.

[6] BT, Shabbath, pp. 153-154.

[7] Cohen, *Everyman's Talmud*, pp. 119-120.

considered punishment for sin, but it was also believed to contain redemptive powers.¹ It is significant that the rabbis realized, however, that a direct tie could not always be made between individual suffering and sin; consequently in a later period considerable space is given over to explaining why the guilty are left unpunished in this world while the righteous continue to suffer.²

(b) Parallel to this emphasis on individual judgment is the concern with the corporate judgment. Whereas the individual cannot be sure of the outcome of the judgment, Israel can confidently expect deliverance, victory, and vindication.³ The wicked of Israel may have to undergo a period of purging by fire before entering God's blessed kingdom.⁴ This vindication of Israel stands in sharp contrast to the fate of the nations. In the view of R. Eliezer (A.D. 80-120) non-Jews would have no share in the world to come : "All the nations have no share in the world to come, even as it is said, 'The wicked shall go into Sheol, and all the nations that forget God' " (Ps. ix, 17).⁵ Rabbi Joshua (A.D. 80-120) took exception to R. Eliezer's statement when he said, "[T]here are righteous men among the nations who have a share in the world to come." ⁶ It seems probable, however, that Rabbi Joshua has hope for only *some* of the Gentiles, while Akiba, like R. Eliezer, expresses the common view that *all* of Israel "will have a share in the world to come." ⁷ Secondly, it should be added that salvation for Israel depended on their status as Israelites *per se* while salvation for the Gentiles was contingent on their conversion to Judaism.⁸ Thirdly, the continuing struggle of the Jews to maintain their identity against unremitting hellenizing forces and political pressures would have made it extremely difficult for the Jews to include representatives of these erosive forces in the new kingdom.⁹ William

---

¹ Mekilta, II, 278, R. Eliezer ben Jacob, A.D. 80-120; The Mishnah, Aboth 5:23, p. 458, "Ben He-He [a disciple of Hillel] said : according to the suffering so is the reward."

² Cohen, *Everyman's Talmud*, pp. 121 ff.

³ Mekilta, I, 238-239.

⁴ BT, Rosh Hashanah, p. 64.

⁵ Tosefta, Sanhedrin XIII, 2 as cited in Montefiore and Loewe, *Rabbinic Anthology*, p. 604.

⁶ BT, Sanhedrin, p. 601.

⁷ *Ibid.*

⁸ Schweitzer, *Mysticism*, pp. 178-179; Moore, *Judaism*, I, 232-233.

⁹ Cohen, *Everyman's Talmud*, p. xvii, says, "If the Jewish nation was to be preserved, it must be ringed round by a burning faith as by a frontier of fire."

David Davies says that the trend toward segregation began soon after the exile, and consequently "the post-exilic history of Judaism became the history of a 'fenced' community." [1] Although there were protests against this particularism (e.g., the authors of the books of Ruth and Jonah), Jewish nationalism prevailed. By the first century B.C. there is little evidence of universalism, and the attitude toward the Gentiles had hardened further still by the first century A.D.[2] R. Eliezer goes so far as to say that even those who die outside of Palestine have no share in the world to come.[3] R. Simai (A.D. 140-165) avoided this rigid and provincial exclusivism by suggesting that tunnels would be bored underground and the dead would roll to the land of Israel.[4]

Obviously there was some uneasiness over this narrow particularism for by the time of Judah ha-Nasi (A.D. 165) there is an attempt to rationalize statements in support of it. According to Judah, the Torah, the way of salvation, had been offered to the Gentiles but they rejected it. Consequently, the nations will be rejected by God at the future judgment.[5] In other words, if the Gentiles are to be treated unjustly by a narrow, particularistic judgment, they are merely getting what they deserve. Thus we see that the corporate image of Israel was primarily nationalistic. No longer is there a strong resemblance between this corporate entity and the covenantal people of ancient Israel.

The question inevitably intrudes : What is the relationship of the individual to the nationalistic community in the rabbinic materials? To answer this question a distinction needs to be made between the character of this relationship in the first century A.D. and its character in ancient Israel. Noth correctly says that in the Pentateuch "the 'thou' which occurs in the laws meant the whole of the Israelite tribe or the individual in the context of the whole." [6] According to this view the the entire community was implicated by the sin of any one member. In our period under consideration, however, it is possible to view the individual as a unity within but not fully explained by the corporate

---

[1] *Paul*, pp. 61-62.

[2] Davies, *Paul*, p. 62.

[3] Mekilta, Baḥodesh, II, 236.

[4] T.J.Ket XII, para 3, f. 35b, as cited in Montefiore and Loewe, *Rabbinic Anthology*, p. 600.

[5] Mekilta, Baḥodesh, II, 236.

[6] Noth, *Laws*, p. 97.

community. Noth traces this development to the "abolition of an antecedent social ordinance founded by God." [1] As the individual takes responsibility for himself before the judgment the actions of the whole society on behalf of the individual fall into abeyance.[2] The judgment of Israel parallels but is not dynamically related to the judgment of the individual.

2. Righteousness (צדקה) in the rabbinic materials refers almost entirely to human action. In the one hundred references under the heading "righteous" in the index to The Babylonian Talmud all refer to righteous *men*.[3] The one allusion to righteous judgment refers to man's fairness in exacting dues.[4] Aboth 5:18 interprets צדקת אל of Deuteronomy 33:21 neither as the "righteous decrees of the Lord" nor as the "righteousness of God", but the righteousness which Moses did : "Moses was righteous and caused the many to be righteous, [therefore] the righteousness of the many was [considered] dependent on him, as it is said, he executed the righteousness of the Lord and his ordinances with Israel." One late reference by Rab (A.D. 200-220) obliquely alludes to God's righteousness in the creation of the world : "By ten things was the world created : By wisdom, and by understanding, and by reason, and by strength, and by rebuke, and by might, and by righteousness and by judgment, by loving kindness and by compassion" (Ḥagigah, p. 65). The index however, lists thirty-three references to the righteousness of man.[5] Montefiore lists no references to the righteousness of God in the index to his anthology but cites forty references to the righteous man and/or Israel.[6] The rabbinic materials take for granted that in the judgment God will do right, otherwise the righteous deeds of man would avail nothing;[7] nevertheless, the emphasis remains on man and the need to present

---

[1] Noth, *Laws*, p. 97.

[2] *Ibid.*, p. 98.

[3] *Index Volume to the Soncino Talmud*, compiled by Judah J. Slotki (London : The Soncino Press, 1952), pp. 342-343.

[4] Aboth 3:16, pp. 39-40.

[5] *Index Volume to the Soncino Talmud*, compiled by Slotki, pp. 342-343.

[6] Montefiore and Loewe, *Rabbinic Anthology*, pp. 833-834.

[7] Peter Stuhlmacher, *Gottes Gerechtigkeit bei Paulus* (Göttingen : Vandenhoeck & Ruprecht, 1965), p. 177, quotes Marmorstein : "The justice of God appears in His character and name of Judge, 'Lord of Judgment', as source of law and order, as the revealer of the moral, social, and political duties, and master of reward and punishment." Cain's malicious deed, for example, is attributed to his belief that " There is neither

himself righteous before the judgment by doing the Torah.[1] This emphasis is almost opposite to that of the apocalyptic materials which focus sharply on the righteousness of God and his power to bring about his victory.

As one might expect we see no intimate tie between God's righteousness and his power to uphold his covenant. In fact, the rabbinic understanding of the covenant is an interesting phenomenon in and of itself. The index of the Babylonian Talmud lists only nine references to the word "covenant" (ברית) in the entire thirty-five volumes.[2] More significant than the paucity of references, however, are the nuances the word carries when it rarely occurs. It can mean rules of procedure or behavior,[3] an ordinance,[4] a synonym of circumcision,[5] or an oath.[6] Oblique references to the covenant are made in other contexts which carry a similar meaning.[7] In the Targum of Palestine the covenant can mean a commandment,[8] or a promise that God will not

---

judgment nor Judge, nor another world; nor will good reward be given to the righteous, nor vengeance be taken of the wicked" (Targum of Palestine, p. 171). Cf. Mekilta, Tractate Baḥodesh, II, 227-228.

[1] The Targum of Palestine reflects this viewpoint when it speaks of God's creation of "the garden of Eden for the righteous," but "Gehinnam for the wicked" (I, 168). Noah is called a " man righteous and perfect in his generation " (I, 47). In this same vein, R. Joshua b. Levi (A.D. 120-140) says, "Thou hast judged well, Thou hast condemned well, and well provided Gehenna for the wicked and Paradise for the righteous" (BT, Erubin, p. 129). Cf. Berakoth, p. 109; p. 385; Shabbath, p. 500; Yoma, p. 179; Ḥagigah, p. 48; p. 64; Yebamoth, p. 711; Sanhedrin, p. 489; p. 618; Aboth 2:7, p. 17; Mekilta, Tractate Shirata, II, 5; Tractate Amalek, II, 148, etc.

[2] *Index Volume to the Soncino Talmud*, compiled by Slotki, p. 92.

[3] Yebamoth, pp. 19-20, "Circumcision stands in a different category, for concerning it thirteen covenants were made"; Soṭah, pp. 184-185, "[T]here were forty-eight covenants in connection with each commandment."

[4] Yebamoth, pp. 486-487, says the rabbis often sought to reconcile conflicts between the Pentateuch and rabbinic traditions. For example, the *mashuk* (one whose circumcision was botched and who appears to be uncircumcised) was permitted by the Pentateuch to eat *terumah* but forbidden by rabbinic ordinance to do so. The rabbis argued that "He hath broken My covenant" referred to the eating of *terumah* by the *mashuk*.

[5] Cf. MR Exodus, p. 353, and Yebamoth, p. 480, by R. Akiba, and Sanhedrin, pp. 402-403.

[6] Pesaḥim, p. 180, "When I went and discussed the matter before R. Eleazar, he said to me, By the covenant! These are the very words which were stated to Moses at Sinai."

[7] Aboth, p. 59, " With ten trials was Abraham, our father proved, and he stood firm in them all." One of the ten trials was the covenant "between the pieces."

[8] Targums, I, 242.

judge Abram's sons.[1] Only one possible reference have we discovered where the word may carry the rich historical and theological meaning that it has in the Old Testament. Rabbi Eleazar of Modin (A.D. 80-120) says in the Mishnah : "If a man profanes the Hallowed Things and despises the set feasts and puts his fellow to shame publicly and makes void the covenant of Abraham our father ... he has no share in the world to come." [2] Danby thinks, however, that covenant here refers to circumcision and the warning is issued against anyone who would "render himself, by artificial device, uncircumcised." [3] If Danby is correct, and there is good reason to believe he is,[4] then we find no place in the rabbinic materials where covenant designates a vital divine-human relationship. It is obvious in these references that a grasp of "covenant" as a theological term was no longer considered vital for understanding the Torah. No longer do God's covenant with his people and the commandments stand in such a close relationship as we see them in the apocalyptic materials and the prophets. Martin Noth rightly says that the "loose and hazy way of using earlier definite concepts is a symptom that they no longer meant much for this late period." [5] The use of the word "covenant" for all kinds of rules, oaths, etc.[6] coupled with the severance of the concept of covenant as a gracious relationship from the Law gives us some idea of the degree to which the Torah was cut loose from its historical background. Thus in contrast to the apocalyptic materials, the Qumran sect, and the pre-exilic prophets, in the rabbinic materials God no longer preserves his righteousness by destroying the covenant breaker; he impartially rewards and punishes those who keep or transgress the Law.

3. We notice also that the wrath of God receives scant attention in the rabbinic materials and is not a function of God's righteousness as it is in the apocalyptic, Qumran and pre-exilic writings. The reluctance to speak of Divine wrath, Montefiore claims, is an attempt to modify the crueler descriptions of God.[7] In Abodah Zarah there is evidence to support Montefiore : "Our Rabbis taught : *God is angry every day*,

---

[1] *Ibid.*, p. 204.
[2] The Mishnah, p. 451.
[3] Danby (trans. and ed.), *The Mishnah*, p. 451, n. 13.
[4] Aboth, p. 34, n. 6.
[5] Noth, *Laws*, p. 95.
[6] Targums, I, 242.
[7] Montefiore and Loewe, *Rabbinic Anthology*, p. 52.

but how long does His anger last? A moment. And how long is a moment? One 53,848th of an hour."[1] While the date of the following passage is uncertain, it is of interest for the studious care with which it avoids the use of the expression "the wrath of God": "When they who engaged in whisperings in judgment multiplied, *fierceness of anger increased against Israel* and the Shechinah departed" (Soṭah, p. 252; emphasis added).

According to the general index of the Babylonian Talmud only four references directly mention God's anger.[2] One of these references minimizes the severity of God's anger: "Know now how many acts of charity I performed for you in that I did not become angry all that time, in the days of Baalam the Wicked" (Sanhedrin, p. 718). A second reference is an editorial insertion from the Mishnah which is missing in the Hebrew text (Sanhedrin, p. 768). The third reference from Abodah Zarah was noted above, and the fourth reference minimizes the severity of the anger. Joshua b. Ḳarḥah (A.D. 140-165) comments on Exodus 4:14—"And the anger of the Lord was kindled against Moses": "A [lasting] effect is recorded of every fierce anger in the Torah, but no [lasting] effect is recorded in this instance" (Zebaḥim, p. 490).

Although there are only these four references to the wrath of God in the Talmud, there are seventy-seven references to Gehenna,[3] which is an instrument of punishment although it is not connected to the divine name. This same propensity for the use of personifications of wrath in place of the expression "the wrath of God" appears also in the Targum of Palestine. In Deuteronomy nine after Moses descends from the mountain, sees the idolatry of Israel and breaks the tablets in a rage, God's wrath toward the idolaters is represented by the appearance of five angels of destruction called "Wrath, Burning, Relentlessness, Destruction, and Indignation."[4] In the interpretation which is inserted into the text no reference is made to the wrath of God.

It seems apparent in light of the above investigation that with the shift of emphasis away from the righteousness of God to the righteous man went an accompanying loss of emphasis on the wrath of God as an appropriate response toward those who violate the covenant. Judg-

---

[1] BT, Abodah Zarah, p. 15.
[2] *Index Volume to the Soncino Talmud*, compiled by Slotki, p. 21.
[3] *Ibid.*, p. 157.
[4] Targums, I, 589.

ment, therefore, in the rabbinic materials is more legalistic than in the pre-exilic prophets, the apocalyptic writings, or the Qumran scrolls.

A brief word is in order concerning the role of the community in the judgment. The בית דין between A.D. 70 and the third century A.D. was the highest religious and civil authority in the land.[1] Was it expected that this judicial arm of the Jewish people would be an instrument of God in the future judgment? There is little evidence for such a position in spite of Manson's belief that the angels play no part in the rabbinical picture of the judgment because their place is taken by Israel.[2] *The Jewish Encyclopedia* lists only one reference to a heavenly בית דין (Soṭaḥ [22b]), and in that reference there is no mention of Israel's participation in the judgment proceedings.[3] Strack and Billerbeck cite Pesiḳta (187a),[4] which speaks of the Israelites judging the world, but by Strack's own admission the collection may be as late as A.D. 800.[5] At least it is safe to say that the community does not play the same prominent role in the judgment depicted in the rabbinic materials that it does in the apocalyptic writings and the Qumran texts.

The rabbinic judgment passages, much like those in the apocalyptic materials, contain either descriptions of the judgment with no hortatory additions or they simply make a direct connection between sin and punishment with no elaboration. For example, in the Mishnah, R. Eleazar the Modiʻite (A.D. 80-120) says:

> He who profanes holy things and despises the festivals, and shames his associate in public, and makes void the covenant of Abraham our father, and gives interpretations of Torah which are not according to Halachah, even though he possesses Torah and good deeds he has no portion in the world to come.[6]

We see that these statements are not so much judgment pronouncements or even descriptions of the judgment which conform to a definite pattern as they are affirmations of the trustworthiness of God's verdict.

---

[1] *The Jewish Encyclopedia*, ed. Isidore Singer, et al. (12 vols.; New York, London: Funk and Wagnalls Company, 1902), III, 114-115.

[2] Thomas Walter Manson, *On Paul and John* (Studies in Biblical Theology, no. 38; London: S.C.M. Press, 1963), p. 19.

[3] *The Jewish Encyclopedia*, III, 115.

[4] Strack-Billerbeck, *Kommentar*, I, 672.

[5] Strack, *Introduction to the Talmud and Midrash*, p. 211.

[6] Aboth 3:12, p. 451.

While it is readily acknowledged that all kinds of cross-fertilization took place between rabbinic Judaism and Jewish apocalyptic,[1] it would be erroneous to ignore the differences between the two of them.[2] While we have noted distinct differences between these two currents within Judaism, our conclusions must point to general tendencies in these streams of thought more than to sharp cleavages between them. It should be noted, however, that eschatology is the area in which one would expect the differences to be most noticeable.

In summary, our discussion above suggests that judgment is conceived in more corporate terms in the prophetic, apocalyptic, and Qumran materials than in most rabbinic writings. The framework of their message is eschatological whereas the organizing center of the rabbinic materials is the Torah.[3] Their writings show an awareness of *Heilsgeschichte* which the rabbinic materials do not show. Instead, the

---

[1] Rössler, *Gesetz und Geschichte im Judentum*, oversimplifies the differences between apocalyptic and rabbinic Judaism, although his work is suggestive otherwise. Russell, *Method*, p. 23, emphasizes what is becoming increasingly clear, that all types of Judaism inside and outside of Palestine were open to many of the same kinds of influences.

[2] William David Davies, *Christian Origins and Judaism* (Philadelphia : The Westminster Press, 1962), pp. 19-30, rejects this kind of rigid separation but acknowledges that differences do exist between the two. Ernst Käsemann. " The Beginnings of Christian Theology " in *New Testament Questions of Today*, trans. W.J. Montague (London : S.C.M. Press, Ltd., 1969), 82-107, says Jewish apocalyptic contributed significantly to the development of early Christian theology.

[3] Nahum N. Glatzer, "Hillel the Elder in the Light of the Dead Sea Scrolls," in *The Scrolls and the New Testament*, ed. Krister Stendahl (New York : Harper and Brothers Publishers, 1957), p. 242, offers a strong argument for the belief that the Pharisaic community actively opposed apocalyptic trends. He says, "In the Hillel texts there is no reference to the messianic idea. There is no mention of retributive justice on earth and an affirmation of the life in the world-to-come, a portion of which is to be gained by the study of Torah. The silence on messianism in a period in which it was a burning issue cannot be adequately explained by the paucity of our sources. It can be assumed that, in concentrating on learning, on *hesed*, on the reconstruction of the Pharisaic community, Hillel counteracted the challenge of eschatological thought. As quite indirect evidence, the fate of Jonathan, son of Uzziel, Hillel's distinguished disciple, may be cited. Jonathan, whom the sources made also heir to the prophetic tradition of Haggai, Zechariah, and Malachi, is said to have undertaken an Aramaic translation (Targum) of the prophetic books. A voice reprimanded him for having 'revealed God's secrets to mankind.' He defended his work as being done 'that dissension may not increase in Israel.' When, continuing his labors, he came to the Book of Daniel, with its allusions to the messianic end, the Voice issued again and said : 'No more.' In this legendary report in which much is questionable, an antimessianic tendency in the Hillel circle seems at least indicated."

rabbis conceived of the traditions as a fence around the Torah.[1] In their discussion of judgment, they see a closer tie between the righteousness of God, his wrath and his covenant than do the rabbinic traditions. We noted an especially strong emphasis on the covenant in the Qumran texts. The apocalyptic and Qumran writings appear to assign a larger role to the community in the eschatological judgment than do the rabbis.

We shall now turn to our consideration of judgment in the Pauline letters in light of these findings.

---

[1] The Mishnah, Aboth 3:14, p. 452.

CHAPTER THREE

JUDGMENT TERMINOLOGY, FORM, AND THEMES IN PAUL'S LETTERS

This chapter is divided into three parts: (A) a study of Paul's judgment terminology, (B) an examination of his judgment form, and (C) a discussion of the place of judgment in the structure of his thought.

A. Judgment Terminology in Paul's Letters

In the first section of this chapter we shall briefly look at some of Paul's most important judgment language and seek to understand how he draws from and reinterprets his Jewish tradition. Our study of righteousness, wrath, the Day, and death must necessarily be limited since any one of these pregnant terms could well be the subject of a monograph.

1. Although our treatment of righteousness is limited, it is necessary,[1] since in Paul's letters as well as in the Old Testament and apocalyptic literature righteousness appears almost entirely in a forensic context.[2]

Righteousness (δικαιοσύνη) is one of the most important words in Paul's vocabulary,[3] yet one of the most difficult to understand. Many call God's righteousness the ruling theme of Romans,[4] yet they

---

[1] Mattern, *Verständnis*, pp. 59-75, omits any consideration of righteousness from her word study.

[2] E.R. Achtemeier, "Righteousness in the OT," in *The Interpreter's Dictionary of the Bible*, ed. George Arthur Buttrick (4 vols.; New York, Nashville: The Abingdon Press, 1962), IV, 81.

[3] Werner Georg Kümmel, "Die Bedeutung der Enderwartung für die Lehre des Paulus," in *Heilsgeschehen und Geschichte*, herausgegeben von Erich Grässer, Otto Merk und Adolf Fritz (Marburger theologische Studien, vol. III; Marburg: N.G. Elwert Verlag, 1965), p. 46, says, "Nun kann es keine Frage sein, dass der Rechtfertigungsgedanke für Paulus die eigentliche Denkform für das eschatologische Geschehen ist."

[4] Charles Kingsley Barrett, *A Commentary on the Epistle to the Romans* (New York, Evanston, and London: Harper & Row, Publishers, 1957), p. 29, says of 1:17, "Here for the first time we touch on the dominating theme of the epistle." Anders Nygren, *Commentary on Romans*, trans. Carl C. Rasmussen (Philadelphia: Muhlenberg Press, 1949), pp. 65-92, heads his discussion of 1:16-17 with the topic "The Theme of the

sharply disagree over the meaning this term has for Paul. Since the discussion between Rudolf Bultmann and Ernst Käsemann has helped define the problem of interpreting righteouness in Paul, a consideration of their opposing positions will frame the study of this word.

Bultmann takes the phrase δικαιοσύνη θεοῦ to mean the righteousness which comes from God,[1] or the righteousness which is bestowed as a gift from God.[2] Through the preaching of the Word this gift becomes a possibility, and through the decision of faith becomes a reality for the hearer of the Gospel.[3] As we can see, Bultmann begins with man and his response to righteousness, and consequently rejects any substantival approach to understanding righteousness. Conzelmann characterizes Bultmann's methodology as an "existential interpretation through which he presents the theology of Paul as anthropology." [4]

Righteousness understood in anthropological terms, Käsemann believes, dissolves into individualism, and consequently distorts Paul's central doctrine.[5] Instead, Käsemann takes δικαιοσύνη θεοῦ as a subjective genitive and interprets the phrase to mean "the righteousness which belongs to God and issues from him" rather than the righteousness "which is valid before God and is given us by him." [6] In summary, Käsemann says, the righteousness of God "for Paul is God's dominion over the world, which is being revealed eschatologically in Christ." [7] Righteousness is that right with which God carries out his claim over the world which though fallen from him still belongs to him. In other words, God's righteousness is his power to bring about his victory.[8] Therefore, Käsemann reasons, "Paul does not relate God's righteousness primarily to the individual. And it must not be under-

---

Epistle." Hans Conzelmann, " Current Problems in Pauline Research," *Interpretation*, XXII (1968), 186, says, "The actualization of the understanding of the world and the parenesis, the understanding of church and office, anthropology, eschatology—all these themes are held together and normalized by the one central theme of justification."

[1] *Theology*, I, 285.

[2] "ΔΙΚΑΙΟΣΥΝΗ ΘΕΟΥ," p. 12.

[3] *Ibid.*, p. 16.

[4] "Current Problems in Pauline Research" p. 175.

[5] "God's Righteousness in Paul," p. 109.

[6] *Ibid.*

[7] *Ibid.*, p. 107.

[8] Eduard Schweizer, "Dying and Rising with Christ," *New Testament Studies*, XIV (1967), 11, agrees with Käsemann that the righteousness of God is correctly understood as "power."

stood exclusively from the context of anthropology, as must be the case if its character as gift is the first and only concern." [1]

Käsemann concedes that anthropology is a part of Paul's theology, but only a part, and not the central part at that. The main theme is rather the establishment of the eschatological, reconciling rule of God over the whole world. Thus, according to Käsemann, justification deals primarily not with individual forgiveness but with release from the old eon and entrance into the new. Bultmann's view, in his opinion, tragically narrows Paul's doctrine of the righteousness of God by focusing too exclusively on the individual. Pauline eschatology, Käsemann says, "proclaims the sovereignty of God in the doctrine of justification : equally, it proclaims the sovereignty of God in its apocalyptic. 'Yet Christ must triumph' is its central theme, as the enthronement of the Lamb is that of the apocalypse. The inward-oriented eschatology is only *one* section of this proclamation." [2]

Bultmann challenges Käsemann on a number of interpretations. He points to Philippians 3:9 and Romans 10:3 as evidence for his claim that δικαιοσύνη θεοῦ is a gift of God. In Philippians 3:9 the righteousness ἐκ θεοῦ ἐπὶ τῇ πίστει is contrasted with the righteousness of the Law, and in Romans 10:3 the righteousness of God is juxtaposed to man's own righteousness.[3] Bultmann calls this genitive "ein Gen. auctoris." [4] To Käsemann's claim that δικαιοσύνη θεοῦ in Romans 1:17 and 10:3 ff. is personified as power, associating the power and gift concepts,[5] Bultmann objects that this is a "rhetorische Formulierung" which does not modify the meaning of δικαιοσύνη θεοῦ seen elsewhere. Even if δικαιοσύνη θεοῦ as gift is grounded in God's power, he continues, δικαιοσύνη does not designate God's act but the result of the act.[6] Although Bultmann agrees with Käsemann that God's gift has the characteristic of power, he adds that it is power only in the believers who commit themselves in the reception of the gift.[7]

Bultmann rejects Käsemann's understanding of righteousness as a

---

[1] "God's Righteousness in Paul," p. 109.
[2] *Essays on New Testament Themes*, trans. W.J. Montague (Studies in Biblical Theology, no. 41; London : S.C.M. Press, 1964), p. 82 (emphasis added).
[3] "*ΔΙΚΑΙΟΣΥΝΗ ΘΕΟΥ*," p. 13.
[4] *Ibid.*, p. 12.
[5] "God's Righteousness in Paul," p. 101.
[6] "*ΔΙΚΑΙΟΣΥΝΗ ΘΕΟΥ*," p. 14.
[7] *Ibid.*

gift with present and future dimensions. The references to righteousness in the future (Rom. 2:13, 3:20; Gal. 3:24) as well as in the present (Gal. 2:16) have no "zeitlichen Sinn." [1] Only Romans 5:19, Bultmann believes, speaks of righteousness in a genuinely future sense, and even in this passage the genitive τοῦ θεοῦ is missing.

Bultmann attacks the heart of Käsemann's argument when he argues that the expression δικαιοσύνη θεοῦ originated with Paul rather than in Jewish apocalyptic. Nowhere in the literature of late Judaism, Bultmann argues, does this expression appear as a formula as in Paul. Bultmann defines a formula as a special creation with a special meaning for a special situation. εὐαγγέλιον, for example, as a *terminus technicus* of the Christian proclamation, means something quite different in the synoptic Gospels than it does in the Septuagint. Similarly, Bultmann believes, it is erroneous to see the Qumran texts as the conceptual home of the Pauline formula, the righteousness of God. The Pauline formula qualifies as a formula because it designates the eschatological gift of God which rests on a concrete event. Bultmann concludes: "Die paulnische Rede von δικ. θεοῦ ist also nicht eine 'Radikalisierung und Universalisierung' der jüdischen Rede von Gottes Gerechtigkeit auf die auch der impius hoffen darf, sondern eine Neuschöpfung des Paulus." [2]

While at first glance this debate may appear unrelated to Paul's doctrine of judgment, in reality, it has the greatest relevance. If Käsemann's position is viable then this lends support to our claim that judgment which is closely related to righteousness in Paul's letters must be understood in other than strictly individualistic terms. While one may wish to reserve any final judgment on the strength of one position as opposed to another, three considerations lead us to prefer Käsemann's argument to Bultmann's:

a. Bultmann's "formula" test which he uses to support his claim that δικ. θεοῦ is a Pauline creation will not stand examination. By the same test one could argue that such expressions as "the wrath of God" and "the judgment of God" are Pauline formulae.

b. Contextually, δικαιοσύνη θεοῦ in Romans 1:17 must be understood in relationship to the verb ἀποκαλύπτεται, which designates an active, not static, work of God.[3] That this righteousness is power rather

---

[1] "ΔΙΚΑΙΟΣΥΝΗ ΘΕΟΥ," p. 15.

[2] *Ibid.*, p. 16.

[3] I am indebted to Professor James L. Price for this insight.

than mere gift is indicated by the parallel construction in Romans 1:16. There Paul is not ashamed of the Gospel for it is the δύναμις θεοῦ "unto salvation to all those believing." That this power has a universal rather than a strictly individualistic application is indicated by the expression παντὶ τῷ πιστεύοντι.

c. Historically, Käsemann's understanding of righteousness in Paul stands well within Old Testament and Jewish apocalyptic traditions, and, as such, deserves careful consideration.

(1) In the Old Testament, as we have noted above,[1] righteousness is synonymous with that salvation or deliverance which reveals the power of God to bring about his victory. In Psalms 98:3 this connection is clear:

> The Lord has made known his victory (MT : ישועתו; LXX : σωτήριον αὐτοῦ) he has revealed his vindication (MT : גלה צדקתו; LXX : ἀπεκάλυψεν τὴν δικαιοσύνην αὐτοῦ) in the sight of the nations.

A similar tie between righteousness and salvation appears in Isaiah 46:13 :

> I will bring near my deliverance (MT צדקתי; LXX : δικαιοσύνην μου) it is not far off,
> And my salvation (MT : תשועתי; LXX : σωτηρίαν) will not tarry (cf. Isa. 51:5 ff.).

In this same regard Isaiah 56:1 is especially suggestive :

> Thus says the Lord :
> "Keep justice (MT : משפט; LXX : κρίσιν)
> and do right (MT : צדקה; LXX : δικαιοσύνην)
> for soon my salvation (MT : ישועתי; LXX: σωτήριόν μου)
> will come and my deliverance (MT : וצדקתי; LXX : ἔλεός μου)
> be revealed" (LXX : ἀποκαλυφθῆναι).

While the RSV translators have not given us a literal translation of the Hebrew text, few would deny that they have captured its true meaning.

E.R. Achtemeier sees the same basic understanding of righteousness in the Old Testament that Käsemann sees in Paul. Mrs. Achtemeier believes that צדקה is portrayed most often in the Old Testament as a forensic term and Yahweh does right as the judge of the earth (Pss. 9:4, 8; 50:6, 96:13, 99:4; Isa. 5:16, 58:2; Jer. 11:20).[2] As a righteous

---

[1] *Supra*, pp. 16-18.
[2] "Righteousness in the OT," p. 82.

judge God restores the right of those who have it taken from them. Thus, Israel can appeal to Yahweh's righteousness, "for deliverance from trouble (Pss. 31:1; 88; 143:11), from enemies (Pss. 5:8; 143:1), from the wicked (Pss. 36; 71:2); for vindication of her cause before her foes (Ps. 35:24)." [1] This same understanding prevails when the RSV translators render צדק in Psalms 48:10 as "victory," and in I Samuel 12:7 צדקה is rendered quite correctly "saving deeds."

> Now therefore stand still, that I may plead with you before the Lord concerning all the saving deeds of the Lord (כל צדקות יהוה).

Achtemeier concludes, "Yahweh's righteous judgments are *saving* judgments (Ps. 36:6).... As judge of the earth, Yahweh decides for his people, delivering and saving them. This is his righteousness. And this is Israel's 'triumph' (Judg. 5:11; Isa. 45:25), God's 'victory' (Ps. 48:10)." [2]

(2) Even more striking are the terminological similarities between Paul and the Qumran texts. One of the rules of the community is that "the priests shall recount the righteousness of God" (I QS 1:21; צדקות אל). The community must be hedged about "to maintain faithfulness and mighty judgment according to the righteousness of God" (I QS 10:25; לצדקת אל). Likewise, the covenanter exults, "My justification (משפטי) in the righteousness of God (בצדקת אל) will stand everlastingly" (I QS 11:12). Although there are numerous references to "Thy righteousness" in the apocalyptic materials as well as in the Qumran texts and in the Old Testament, the phrase "the righteousness of God" (צדקת אל) apparently is shared with the Qumran community only by Paul.[3]

Not only do we see Paul and the covenanters using the same terms, but also in the Qumran texts as in Paul righteousness is a dominant theme. The passages which deny man any righteousness of his own (I QH 9:14, 13:17, 16:11) only draw the contrast more sharply between God's righteousness and man's unrighteousness. The psalmist ex-

---

[1] *Ibid.*, pp. 82-83.

[2] *Ibid.*, p. 83. Cf., *supra*, pp. 17-18.

[3] Peter Stuhlmacher, *Gerechtigkeit Gottes bei Paulus* (Göttingen : Vandenhoeck & Ruprecht, 1965), p. 144, believes the Masoretes mispointed צדקות as a singular צדקת. He points to the abstract meaning of the word in Deuteronomy as evidence that it was intended as a plural. At any rate, this is the only reference to צדקת יהוה in the Old Testament (Deut. 33:21).

claims, "Thy judgments I will declare righteous" (I QH 9:9; cf. 9:14; 12:31; 13:17; 16: 11), and asks how the perverse "reply to the judgment of righteousness" (1:26). He acknowledges that God's judgment is just : "Thy righteous punishment accompanies my sins" (9:33), and in 1:26 the psalmist bursts into a hymn praising God's righteousness : "Thine, Thine, O God of knowledge are all the works of righteousness" (cf. 4:30 f., 4:37, 7:19, 8:2, 11:7, 11:30f., 16:9, 17:17, 17: 20).

Although the verbal and theological similarities between Paul's concept of righteousness and that of Qumran are striking, significant differences remain. In the Qumran texts the vindication of God's righteousness remains in the future whereas in Paul it is taking place in the present.[1] Käsemann, therefore, goes too far when he says that "the Thanksgiving Psalms of Qumran offer evidence that already in apocalyptic Judaism the *present* manifestation of God's righteousness could be extolled with as much emphasis as in Paul." [2] It is true that the psalmist can speak of God who is *now* righteous,[3] and can summon the covenanters to works of righteousness; however, in contrast to Paul the vindication of God's righteousness remains in the imminent future. In the Psalms of Thanksgiving 14:15 f. we see how the psalmist's belief in the future vindication of God's righteousness undergirds the present affirmation :

> Thou art righteous and all Thine elect are truth, and all perversity [and ungod] liness, Thou *wilt* destroy (תשמיד) for ever and Thy righteousness shall be revealed (ונגלתה) to the eyes of all Thy works.[4]

One section in the Manual of Discipline (11:14 f.) which apparently speaks of justification as both past and future forces some qualification of our position :

> In His compassion He has brought me near,
> And in His dependable mercy He *will bring* my justification

---

[1] Helmut Koester, "The Role of Myth in the New Testament," *Andover Newton Quarterly*, VIII (1968), 189 touches a genuine Pauline emphasis when he says, "Resurrection, thus, vindicates the righteous man as well as God's own righteousness." Jesus' resurrection for Paul means God's righteous act is no longer merely a matter of hope but a present reality.

[2] "God's Righteousness in Paul," p. 107.

[3] E.g., 17:20, "For Thine, Thine is righteousness"; cf. 11:7.

[4] Emphasis added. Dupont-Sommer, *Essene Writings*, p. 243, is plainly in error when the Qal imperfect יִצְדָּק in 13:17 is translated "is justified," i.e., "It is by Thy goodness alone that man is justified." Rather, the translation should be, "It is by thy goodness alone that a man will be right."

> In His steadfast righteousness He *has justified me* (שפטני)
> And in His great goodness He *will pardon* [or, atone for] all my iniquities
> And in His righteousness He *will cleanse* me from man's impurity
> And from the sin of the children of men.[1]

The Qal perfect of שפטני may suggest a justification which already has taken place. Man's final justification is in some sense anticipated by his reception into the Qumran community, but the time when the community will be finally vindicated and God's righteousness victorious remains in the future. The covenanters are called "sons of righteousness," but they still struggle against the sons of perversity. God will resolve this struggle only in the future. Members of the sect are now called "sons of light," but the War Scroll clearly shows that the final future battle which will establish the sons of light and vindicate God's righteousness remains in the future. The Teacher of Righteousness has come indeed, but there is no reference to his resurrection which would signal God's vindication of his ministry in the present. The community endures suffering, but release from this suffering must await God's final Day. It is noteworthy, moreover, that even though the scribe speaks of justification in the perfect tense, he does so in a context which calls for pardon, mercy, and cleansing in the future. While one may allow that there is some degree of overlap between the ages in the Qumran outlook, there is no gainsaying the fact that for Paul the time is later. The Last Day is already present. The Messiah has come. The resurrection has already signalled the beginning of the New Age. The heavenly forgiveness has begun. The Gentiles already are included. Krister Stendahl distinguishes between the two outlooks by calling "the degree of anticipation greater" in Paul than in Qumran.[2] Cross calls the hour "later." [3] It would appear that the general tendency in the Qumran texts is to view the final justification of God's righteousness as still outstanding. Nowhere in the Qumran texts do we find anything like the affirmation of Paul that "the righteousness of God is being

---

[1] *The Dead Sea Manual of Discipline*, trans. William Hugh Brownlee (Bulletin of the American Schools of Oriental Research, Supplementary Studies, Nos. 10-12; New Haven, Conn.: American Schools of Oriental Research, 1951), p. 44 (emphasis added).

[2] "The Scrolls and the New Testament : An Introduction and a Perspective," in *The Scrolls and the New Testament*, ed. Krister Stendahl (New York: Harper and Brothers, Publishers, 1957), p. 17.

[3] *Ancient Library of Qumran*, p. 240.

revealed" (Rom. 1:17). So although the covenanters do believe God's final vindication is near, it is not yet present.[1]

The Qumran community also does not see God's vindicating act in the same universal terms as does Paul. The Apostle, unlike the Qumran community, envisions a day when through God's mission to the Gentiles, the wayward Jews will also be included in God's redemptive action (Rom. 9-11). The Gospel, according to Paul, embraces both "Jew and Greek."

Braun notes another difference between Paul and Qumran. Righteousness in Paul is oriented not primarily toward the Law but the cross.[2] James L. Price correctly notes that even though Paul, like the Qumran community, cites Habakkuk 2:4 this passage for Qumran "concerns all the doers of the Law in the house of Judah whom God will deliver in the Judgment" whereas for Paul God's righteousness "had been manifested *apart from Law*, and those who are experiencing salvation 'in the place of judgment' are not the pious, but sinners from among Jews and Gentiles."[3]

(3) Other materials from the Apocrypha and Pseudepigrapha parallel the justification-of-God theme in Paul. Romans does refer to the relationship of righteousness to man; however, this righteousness is a righteousness which comes from *God* (i.e., as God's vindicating action)[4] and this obedience is an obedience which is a fitting response to *God's* saving work.[5] In Romans 1:17-3:20 the central issue apparently is theodicy, not individual salvation.[6] This issue recurs again in the Apocrypha and Pseudepigrapha. The Psalms of Solomon in particular trumpet this theme. Even though God's judgment is painful the psalmist says:

> I will justify Thee, O God, in uprightness of heart
> For in Thy judgements is thy righteousness (displayed),
> O God
>
> (Pss. of Sol. 2:16-17).

---

[1] This position is also at variance with that taken by Herbert Braun, *Qumran*, II, 171-172. Cf., however, Siegfried Schulz, "Zur Rechtfertigung aus Gnaden in Qumran und bei Paulus," *Zeitschrift für Theologie und Kirche*, LVI (1959), 182-183, who says that Qumran sees righteousness as a *goal* of the earnestly observed Torah demand.

[2] *Qumran*, II, 170.

[3] James L. Price, *Interpreting the New Testament* (New York: Holt, Rinehart and Winston, 1961), p. 403.

[4] Rom. 4:3, "Abraham believed God, and it was reckoned to him [i.e., by God] as righteousness." Cf. 4:5; 4:6; 4:9; 4:11; 4:22; 5:17, etc.

[5] Rm. 6:13; 6:16; 6:18; 6:19; etc.

[6] I owe this idea to James L. Price, my professor in a seminar on Romans.

Meditating on the siege of Jerusalem the writer says—

> I thought upon the judgements of God since the creation of heaven and earth; I held God righteous in His judgements which have been from of old, God laid bare their sins in the full light of day; all the earth came to know the righteous judgements of God (Pss. of Sol. 8:7-8).

Similarly, I Enoch speaks of the punishment for those who deny the "righteous judgment" of God (60:6). It is noteworthy that the expression " righteous judgment " is a common one in some apocalyptic materials (I Enoch 27:3, 60:6, 91:12, 91:14, 93:5; II Baruch 67:4, etc.), but appears infrequently, if at all, in the rabbinic materials.[1]

As in the Qumran texts, so here also, significant differences exist between the concept of righteousness in Paul and the Apocrypha and Pseudepigrapha. In the latter the vindication of God's righteousness meant condemnation for the Gentiles and salvation, or at least no more than chastisement, for the Jews.[2] To Paul on the other hand, Jews and Gentiles were both alike subject to God's vindicating action, both his wrath and his redemption, for God does not play favorites. The " Jew first and also the Gentile"—a fairly common expression in Paul's letters [3]—both alike experience Paul's Gospel either for good or for ill. God's righteous judgment falls on all men whoever they are (Rom. 2:1).

(4) The rabbinic materials refer to the righteousness of the Messiah,[4] but they allude to God's righteousness infrequently if at all. As we noted above (Chapter II, section 3), the rabbinic materials are less concerned with the righteousness of God than how man can present himself as righteous before God.[5] By contrast, the righteousness of God is a theological *"Grundthema"* of the whole body of apocalyptic materials.[6]

While the above discussion has been limited to the righteousness of God, there is little doubt in the Qumran and apocalyptic writings about the claim this righteousness lays on man. God's righteous deeds

---

[1] The one reference this writer has located (BT, 'Abodah Zarah, p. 91) must be dated with Resh Laḳish about A.D. 250.

[2] We noted, however, in the Qumran texts that more antipathy is expressed toward apostate Jews than against the Gentiles.

[3] Rom. 1:16; 2:9; 3:9; cf., Rom. 1:13; 9:24; I Cor. 10:32; 12:13.

[4] Gottlob Schrenk, "Righteousness ($\Delta\iota\kappa\alpha\iota\sigma\sigma\nu\nu\eta$) in the New Testament," in *Bible Key Words*, trans. J.R. Coates (from G. Kittel's *Theologisches Wörterbuch zum Neuen Testament* [New York : Harper & Brothers, Publishers, 1951]), I, 31.

[5] Strack-Billerbeck, *Kommentar*, III, 163.

[6] Stuhlmacher, *Gerechtigkeit Gottes bei Paulus*, p. 175.

call man to a life of fidelity and hope. In our view, D. Moody Smith, Jr. is entirely correct in his closely reasoned and well documented study of Romans 1:17. Paul's phrase ἐκ πίστεως should be taken with the verb ζήσεται rather than the subject δίκαιος. Paul's major concern with parenesis well supports Smith's claim that "Paul regards righteousness or justification not only as God's gracious act, but also as a state of human existence characterized by faith. 'The righteous shall live by faith.' "[1] While dealing with different materials, Smith's conclusion supports our claim that it is erroneous to read justification by faith as the central theme of Romans, or indeed of Paul's theology.

In summary, then, Paul's understanding of righteousness, while showing significant differences, strikingly resembles the understanding and vocabulary of the Qumran texts and of the Apocrypha and Pseudepigrapha. Emphasis on the righteousness of God instead of the rightness of man, the understanding of righteousness as God's power to bring about his victory, the concern with the question of theodicy as it relates to righteousness, and the intimate tie between judgment and the righteousness of God are all motifs which Paul shares with Jewish apocalyptic.

If it can be maintained on the strength of this evidence that the background of Paul's doctrine of the righteousness of God is in a Jewish apocalypticism similar to what we see at Qumran, then Käsemann's position, though exaggerated at points, appears basically sound.[2] While it is true that the phrase δικαιοσύνη θεοῦ gains a new dimension when Paul interprets it in light of the Christian Gospel, it is no mere Pauline creation.[3] On the basis of our investigation, it would appear that Paul uses concepts, terms, and themes still in touch with Jewish tradition. If this conclusion is sound, then some of its implications for Paul's doctrine of judgment are readily apparent. No longer need judgment in Paul be understood in purely individualistic terms; rather, it applies to the whole inhabited world. No longer does Paul's central question appear to be "How can a man get right with God and thus escape the impending judgment?" but rather "How is God's right-

---

[1] "Ο ΔΕ ΔΙΚΑΙΟΣ ΕΚ ΠΙΣΤΕΩΣ ΖΗΣΕΤΑΙ" in *Studies in the History and Text of the New Testament : In Honor of Kenneth Willis Clark*, ed. Boyd L. Daniels and M. Jack Suggs (Studies and Documents, vol. XXIX; Salt Lake City : University of Utah Press, 1967), pp. 13-25.

[2] *Supra*, pp. 69-70. See his statement that Qumran shows as much a sense of God's present righteous action as does Paul.

[3] Bultmann, "ΔΙΚΑΙΟΣΥΝΗ ΘΕΟΥ," p. 16.

eousness vindicated so that *all* men are manifestly without excuse, unable in *any* way to impugn God's judgments of men?" [1] Through his Gospel, Paul answers, God is vindicating his righteousness. For repentant sinners God vindicates his righteousness through his saving action, but for those who impugn his justice and reject his Son, God's Gospel is wrath and fury.

Covenant for Paul has some of the same rich and varied coloration that we see in the Qumran materials (Chapter II, section 3). Only in Romans 9:4, where Paul refers to "the covenants" do we find anything like the rabbinic tendency to make ordinance and covenant synonymous. It is obvious in II Corinthians 3:4-18, Galatians 4:24 ff., and Romans 11:27 that the covenant for Paul forms the same basis of a theology of history that we see in Qumran and the Old Testament, and is consequently closely related to God's righteousness, or his covenant loyalty to his people.[2]

2. Paul's use of ὀργή reveals some of the same traces of his theology which we saw evidenced in his use of righteousness. Three of these emphases are worthy of special attention.

a. Contrary to the view of some, ὀργή in Paul is closely related to and serves as a function of the righteousness of God.[3] As such, righteous-

---

[1] Others taking positions similar to this one are : Stuhlmacher, *Gerechtigkeit Gottes bei Paulus*; Adolf Schlatter, *Gottes Gerechtigkeit* (2d ed.; Stuttgart : Calwer Verlag, 1952); Price, *Interpreting*, pp. 403 ff.; Howard Kee, Franklin W. Young, Karlfried Froehlich, *Understanding the New Testament* (2d ed.; Englewood Cliffs, N.J.: Prentice Hall, Inc., 1965), pp. 193-194.

[2] Johannes Behm, "The NT Term διαθήκη," in *Theological Dictionary of the New Testament*, ed. Gerhard Kittel, trans. and ed. Geoffrey W. Bromiley (Grands Rapids, Mich.: Wm. B. Eerdmans Publishing Company, 1964), II, 129-131.

[3] Hans Lietzmann, *Einführung in die Textgeschichte der Paulusbriefe, An die Römer* (4th ed.; Handbuch zum Neuen Testament, vol. VIII; Tübingen: J.C.B. Mohr [Paul Siebeck], 1933), p. 31, says that 1:18-3:20 describes the period prior to the Gospel. The revelation of the wrath, therefore, designates the past epoch when prior to the advent of the Gospel all humanity had fallen under the wrath of God. Otto Michel, *Der Brief an die Römer* (Kritisch-exegetischer Kommentar über das Neue Testament; Göttingen : Vandenhoeck & Ruprecht, 1955), p. 53, n. 1, sees the gospel and the wrath of God as separate entities. Nygren, *Commentary*, pp. 95 ff., juxtaposes God's righteousness and his wrath. Calvin R. Schoonhoven, *The Wrath of Heaven* (Grands Rapids, Mich.: Wm. B. Eerdmans Publishing Company, 1966), p. 36, calls wrath a "property of God," which is not to be "identified with the righteousness of God." Archibald Macbride Hunter, *The Epistle to the Romans* (London : S.C.M. Press, 1955), p. 44, says, "[T]he gospel proclaims not God's wrath, but his righteousness." Mattern, *Verständnis*, p. 71, says

ness has a double character. Salvation and condemnation, deliverance and punishment are all functions of God's righteousness.[1] This suggests that Romans 1:17 and 1:18 are closely related and not juxtaposed, as is often assumed.[2] The close relationship is supported by γὰρ and the repetition of the verb Ἀποκαλύπτεται in 1:18. That 1:18 cannot refer to the era before Christ as the time of wrath seems evident from Paul's reference in 3:25 to God's patient endurance. The revelation of God's wrath, then, is not a mere prerequisite to the proclamation of the Gospel to show man's need of salvation, but is part of the Gospel itself.[3] As Karl Barth rightly says, it is good news that God acknowledges man's sin and is doing something about it.[4] The tendency to individualize righteousness has supported the juxtaposition of wrath and righteousness in spite of Paul's treatment here and elsewhere. The revelation of salvation and wrath at once is more easily understood in a universal than in an individual context.

b. God's wrath has universal application. God's righteousness is wrath to all those who reject God's Gospel, whoever they are, Jew or Gentile. Miss Mattern inaccurately calls Romans 1:18-32 an address to Gentiles only.[5] That Gentiles and Jews, Christian and non-Christian, are in view throughout the section seems evident from the numerous inclusive references in the section. In 1:18 the wrath of God is revealed on all ἀδικίαν ἀνθρώπων (pl.). The Διὸ in 2:1 connects 1:18-32 with what follows, and again in 2:1 Paul surveys his audience : " Therefore you have no excuse, O man, when you judge another" (ὦ ἄνθρωπε πᾶς ὁ κρίνων). This same emphasis is carried forward in 2:9 where tribulation and distress are promised to πᾶσαν ψυχην ἀνθρώπου who do evil, and in 3:9 where Paul charges that πάντως are under the power of sin.

" der ὀργή Rö 1,18 steht die δικαιοσύνη Rö 1,17 gegenüber." Stuhlmacher, *Gerechtigkeit Gottes bei Paulus*, p. 80, sees the righteousness of God in 1:17 and the wrath of God in 1:18 in antithetical parallelism.

[1] Achtemeier, "Righteousness in the OT," p. 83. See *supra*, pp. 72-73.

[2] Smith, "Ο ΔΕ ΕΚ ΠΙΣΤΕΩΣ," pp. 13-25, delivers a severe blow, we believe, to this traditional interpretation.

[3] Franz J. Leenhardt, *The Epistle to the Romans*, trans Harold Knight (London : Lutterworth Press, 1961), p. 60. Charles Harold Dodd, *The Epistle of Paul to the Romans* (London : Hodder and Stoughton, 1932), pp. 20-24, speaks of the wrath as preliminary to the Gospel.

[4] *A Shorter Commentary on Romans*, trans. D.H. van Daaler (Richmond, Va.: John Knox Press, 1959), pp. 25-31.

[5] *Verständnis*, p. 59; Michel, *Der Brief an die Römer*, p. 5, feels that 1:18-32 is addressed to the Gentiles and 2:1-29 to the Jews.

Wrath then must be seen in its more inclusive context and not as a preliminary act of God designed to lead individual men to the Gospel.

c. Wrath in Paul is charged with the same eschatological current that runs through all of his theology. The experience of wrath for Paul is a present possibility, for the wrath of God "is being revealed" (Rom. 1:18; Ἀποκαλύπτεται). The Law is at work in the present producing wrath (Rom. 4:15; ὀργὴν κατεργάζεται). In performing its police function the state executes God's wrath on the wrongdoer in the present (Rom. 13:4). God's wrath at last, Paul claims, has actually come upon the persecutors of the church (I Thess. 2:16). In 1:18-31 God's wrath manifests itself in handing the offenders over to the consequences of their sin.

At the same time Paul speaks of wrath as a future prospect. The hardhearted and impenitent are warned in Romans 2:5 f. that they are storing up wrath for themselves for "he will render (ἀποδώσει) to each one according to his works." The threat of this future possibility carries forward to 2:8 where Paul promises "wrath and fury" to those who are factious and do not obey the truth. As recipients of God's promises Paul joins other Christians in saying, "we shall be saved (σωθησόμεθα) through him from the wrath" (Rom. 5:9; cf. I Thess. 1:10).

A comparison of these emphases with those we have noted in Chapter Two is instructive. It is only necessary to take brief note of the Old Testament view of wrath as it relates to Paul. We observed above that the pre-exilic prophets speak primarily of God's wrath against Israel while the post-exilic prophets speak mainly of God's wrath on the Gentiles and the apostate Jews but not on faithful Israel.[1] In contrast to Paul we shall see how this same emphasis appears in the literature of late Judaism.

The similarities between the apocalyptic and Pauline concept of wrath are striking. In both wrath is a function of God's righteousness (Jub. 36:10; Rom. 1:17 f.). In both the wrathful judgment is corporate (I Enoch 5:6 f., 84:4, 92:9, 103:7 ff., etc.; Rom. 1:18-3:20). In both an outpouring of wrath comes on the Last Day (I Enoch 91:7; Rom. 2:5 f.). In both God shows his forbearance by holding back his wrath (II Baruch 59:6, 48:14, 17; Rom. 2:3-5). In both God's wrath falls on men who act as if they are Lord (Jub. 5:6; Rom. 1:18-32).

---

[1] *Supra*, pp. 18-19.

In spite of these similarities the differences are considerable. As it is true of judgment,[1] so also it is true that wrath in apocalyptic literature is poured out primarily on the heathen (I Enoch 92:9), and apostate Jews (I Enoch 91:7).[2] In I Enoch 5:9 the elect are promised that they will not "die of (the divine) anger or wrath." Redemption is promised to the righteous but terror and dismay are in prospect for the wicked at the end of the world (I QM 3:28). "Eternal perdition" awaits those who live in "the spirit of error" (I QS 4:12). In II Baruch 59:6 even the delay of God's wrath means he shows special favoritism to Israel. Paul on the other hand sees God's wrath in a more universalistic sense. Being a Jew exempts no one from the claims of the Gospel; being a Gentile allows no one to plead ignorance (Rom. 1:18-3:20), nor does being a Christian in some ontological sense offer any protection from the wrath. It is rather those sinners who respond in believing obedience to God's Gospel who know God's vindicating action as grace instead of wrath (Rom. 5:9; I Thess. 1:10, 5:9). It perhaps is more correct to say the Christians are exculpated from the wrath than that they are excluded from it.[3]

Paul also differs from the apocalyptic writers in his understanding of eschatological wrath as a present possibility. It is clear in the apocalyptic writings that even though God's wrath is manifested in history,[4] this historical manifestation merely anticipates the future Day of Wrath. There was also a growing tendency to speak less and less of wrath as a present historical possibility and to speak more and more of wrath on the Last Day.[5] To Paul, conversely, the Last Day is already

---

[1] *Supra*, pp. 29-32.

[2] I Enoch 84:4 seems to suggest that God's wrath is universal : "Upon the flesh of men abideth Thy wrath until the great day of judgment." However, the following lines show that "flesh of men" means sinful men : "And now, my Lord, destroy from the earth the flesh which has aroused Thy wrath. But the flesh of righteousness and uprightness establish as a plant of the eternal seed" (84:6).

[3] Hermann Kleinknecht, Johannes Fichtner, Gustav Stählin, *et al.*, "Wrath," in *Bible Key Words*, trans. and ed. Dorothea M. Barton and Peter Runham Ackroyd (from G. Kittel's *Theologisches Wörterbuch zum Neuen Testament* [New York, Evanston : Harper and Row, Publishers, 1964]), IV, 122-123.

[4] The post-exilic prophets and apocalyptic materials are unanimous in seeing the exile as an expression of God's wrath (Pss. of Sol. 2:7-10). Jubilees 24:28, 30; 36:10 sees the threat of the Philistines as a sign of God's wrath whose full fury will be known in the future. The Damascus Document speaks of Israel's history as a monotonous story of apostasy and the outpouring of God's wrath, but this memory magnifies the conviction of the community that it preserves the righteous remnant.

[5] *Supra*, pp. 26-27.

proleptically present and its final manifestation stands in the imminent future.

In contrast to Paul and the apocalyptic materials, the rabbinic materials show a general reluctance to ascribe wrath directly to God.[1]

It seems likely, therefore, that Paul's wrath concept has its roots in some type of Jewish apocalyptic thought. Again, we notice, as in the comparison above,[2] that the points at which Paul differs significantly from apocalyptic views are in his universalization of the wrath concept and in his contemporarization of wrath while retaining its future dimension. These alterations are obviously closely associated with Paul's understanding of the Gospel he preaches.

3. ἡμέρα, like other forensic terminology in Paul, has a double meaning. The church can look forward to the Day as the Day of Salvation (II Cor. 6:2; ἡμέρα σωτηρίας). It is Paul's hope that the spirit of the incestuous man will be saved on the Day of the Lord (I Cor. 5:5). Paul expects to boast of the Corinthians on the Day of the Lord Jesus (II Cor. 1:15). The good work begun in the church at Philippi will be brought to completion on the Day of Jesus Christ himself who will be glorified with his saints on that Day (II Thess. 1:10).

While for the saints the Day brings victory and fulfillment, the end-time also portends terror and loss. The unpredictability of the Day's advent calls for continued vigilance in faith and works for it comes like "a thief in the night" (I Thess. 5:2,4). On that Day the secrets of man's heart will be judged (Rom. 2:16); the Day brings wrath for the hard-hearted and impenitent (Rom. 2:5). On that Day the Christian's work will meet the test of fire (I Cor. 3:13-15). As was true in his use of righteousness and wrath terminology, so also here Paul sees the Day as already present but in some sense still outstanding. The Day of the Lord means both that the Lord has come, and the Lord will come. Paul speaks to the Corinthians of the *parousia* and the future judgment as τῇ ἡμέρᾳ τοῦ κυρίου Ἰησοῦ Χριστοῦ (I Cor. 1:8; cf. II Cor. 1:14; Phil. 1:10, 2:16). He harbors hope that the spirit of the incestuous man will be saved ἐν τῇ ἡμέρᾳ τοῦ κυρίου (I Cor. 5:5; cf. I Thess. 5:2). Paul expects to be proud of the Corinthians ἐν τῇ ἡμέρᾳ τοῦ κυρίου Ἰησοῦ (II Cor. 1:14). Ethical behavior gains new seriousness in light of the imminent Day. Paul's summary in

---

[1] *Supra*, pp. 63-65.
[2] *Supra*, p. 78-79.

Romans 13:12 f. brings into focus the long parenetic section in chapters twelve and thirteen : "...the night is far gone, the day is at hand. Let us then cast off the works of darkness and put on the armor of light; let us conduct ourselves becomingly as in the day" (13:12 f.).

It is apparent, however, that for Paul the eschatological Day in some sense is already present. The Christians at Thessalonica are reminded that they are sons of the Day (I Thess. 5:5; υἱοὶ ἡμέρας). Paul identifies with the Thessalonian church when he says, " [W]e are of the Day" (I Thess. 5:8 ἡμεῖς δὲ ἡμέρας ὄντες). In II Corinthians 6:2 Paul makes one of his characteristically powerful affirmations : ἰδοὺ νῦν καιρὸς εὐπρόσδεκτος (II Cor. 6:2). So here as elsewhere we see the eschatological tension between the Day which now is but which is yet to come.

The term "Day," like righteousness and wrath, has corporate connotations. Paul will be proud of the church at Corinth on the Day of the Lord Jesus (II Cor. 1:14). God will sustain the Corinthian church (ὑμᾶς, pl. "you all") until the "day of our Lord Jesus Christ" (I Cor. 1:8). Paul makes the same promise to the church at Philippi : "I am sure that he who began a good work in you (ὑμῖν, pl.) will bring it to completion at the day of Jesus Christ" (1:6; cf. 1:10). Although Paul is interested in the salvation of the incestuous man "on the day of the Lord" (I Cor. 5:5), his ultimate goal is the purification of the church : "Clean out the old leaven that you may be fresh dough" (I Cor. 5:7). With slightly different terminology Paul makes the same point in II Corinthians 5:10: "For we must all stand before the judgment seat of Christ" (cf. Rom. 14:10).

We have noted in our discussion above the tendency of the postexilic prophets to think of the Day (יום) more and more as a future time and event when God would reward the Jews and punish the pagan nations.[1] As best we can tell, this outlook is present in both apocalyptic and rabbinic materials; however, the concept of "the Day" plays a more decisive role in apocalyptic than in rabbinic literature.[2] In contrast to I Enoch, for example, which carries numerous references to the Day (1:1, 10:12, 16:1, 22:4, 48:8, 55:3, 94:9, 97:1, 98:10, etc.), the index to the Babylonian Talmud lists only one reference to the eschatological Day,[3] and the index to the Montefiore and Loewe

---

[1] *Supra*, p. 27.

[2] *Supra*, pp. 38-39.

[3] *The Babylonian Talmud, Index Volume*, compiled by Judah J. Slotki (London : The Soncino Press, 1952), p. 102.

anthology lists only one such reference.[1] The Targums carry references to the Day which have been inserted into the text, but they apply to individuals, not to Israel as a whole.[2]

Paul, as we have learned from past comparisons, while sharing much of the apocalyptic viewpoint differs here also at the same three points noted above : (1) he sees the eschatological Day as already present, (2) he applies the terminology universally, and (3) he ties the Day to the life, death, resurrection and *parousia* of Jesus.

4. An understanding of Paul's use of θάνατος as it relates to judgment is as difficult as it is important. It is important because of the close tie between judgment and death. It is difficult because Paul speaks about death on so many different levels. He speaks of death as a result of sickness, injury (Phil. 2:27, 30), martyrdom (II Cor. 1:9, 11:23; Phil. 1:20), or deprivation (I Cor. 9:15). He speaks of death as a natural expiration at the end of one's normal length of days (I Cor. 15:32). He speaks of death as a daily self-denial of the flesh (I Cor. 15:31; Rom. 8:13). He speaks of death as a cosmic power with a dispensation (II Cor. 3:7) which has ruled mankind since Adam (Rom. 5:14). He speaks of death as eschatological punishment for sin (Rom. 1:32, 5:12, 7:13, 8:13, etc.). He speaks of deliverance from slavery to death now (Rom. 6) by proleptically experiencing the future death in baptism. He speaks of Jesus' death which overcomes the rule of death and reconciles dying man (I Cor. 11:26). Since it is impossible within the space of this study to explore all of the dimensions of death in Paul's understanding we shall limit ourselves to those with eschatological connotations.

Just as righteousness, wrath and the Day are all present eschatological realities for Paul, so also is death. Death, Paul believes, comes in the present to those who do not properly discern the body when they celebrate the Eucharist (I Cor. 12:3). Apparently expulsion from the church, Paul thought, brought an attack by Satan and then death (I Cor. 5:5). Death is more than a present physical fact; it is a cosmic

---

[1] *A Rabbinic Anthology*, p. 589.

[2] Targums, I, 295, Joseph refuses to have sexual intercourse with Tamar lest he be condemned on "the day of the great judgment of the world to come." On p. 167 (Gen. 3) Adam's sentence is pronounced : "By the labour of thy hands thou shalt eat food, until thou turn again to the dust from which thou wast created : for dust thou art, and unto dust thou shalt return; for from the dust it is to be that thou art to arise, to render judgment and reckoning for all that thou hast done, in the day of the great judgment."

power against which Christ now struggles (I Cor. 15:25 f.) and it is at the same time the Christian's enemy.

Death, according to Paul, is God's eschatological verdict for those who reject Christ.[1] Those filled with all "manner of wickedness" (Rom. 1:29), "who know God but do not honor him as God" (Rom. 1:21), "deserve to die" (Rom. 1:32). Slaves of sin are "led to death" (Rom. 6:21). The old life ends in death (Rom. 6:21). Sin will pay its wages in the currency of death (Rom. 6:23). Sin works to produce death (Rom. 7:13), and preoccupation with the flesh brings death (Rom. 8:6), etc. Through his baptism the Christian proleptically tastes this eschatological death in the present and thus forestalls the tyranny of this death over the present or future. Not only does the Christian participate in Christ's death (and proleptically the eschatological death), but also he shares proleptically in Christ's victory over death in the present (Rom. 6:5). The final victory remains in the future, and death remains in the present and future, but it has lost its sting and power to tyrannize (I Cor. 15:54 f.). It is this victory through hope that frees the Christian to fight against sin and death in the present; it is this foretaste of victory that enables the Christians to live "as dead men made alive" and to employ their members as "weapons of the righteousness of God" in the present.[2]

Death, however, even for Paul remained a painful future reality. The ultimate victory over death when Christ shall put all powers and dominions under his feet remains in the future (I Cor. 15:24-25). The destruction of this enemy will only be finally accomplished at the *parousia* (I Cor. 15:26). Thus, death remains as a cosmic threat to God's purpose being realized in the church, his instrument of a judgment of condemnation and a judgment of victory. As long as this issue remains unresolved the church, including all her members, remains under the threat of death and awaits redemption.[3] This future threat puzzled the Corinthian church. Evidently believing in some kind of realized eschatology, they thought they had already passed from death to life. Paul reasserts the necessity of a future resurrection which some

---

[1] Bultmann, "*ΔΙΚΑΙΟΣΥΝΗ ΘΕΟΥ*," p. 15.

[2] Nygren, *Romans*, p. 263.

[3] See the note on the personification of death and sin by Thomas Wilfred Manson, *On Paul and John* (Studies in Biblical Theology, no. 38; Naperville, Ill.: Alec R. Allenson, Inc., 1963), pp. 27-28.

question (I Cor. 15:12 f.), and deals with the confusion that death has brought to the community (I Cor. 15:6, 20).[1]

In the above discussion on death as a present reality we saw death as a negative eschatological judgment. Paul believes, therefore, that a man dies because he deserves to die.[2] This does not prevent Paul from seeing death in some characteristically positive sense. The death of Christ has the power to reconcile (Rom. 5:10). It is in Christ's death that God shows forth his righteousness (Rom. 3:24 f.), and in his death that a debt is paid (Rom. 6:10).[3] Likewise, as we have noted above, it is in the Christian's death with Christ that he comes to share in his life. Where death has a purely negative connotation Paul frequently attaches a statement pointing to the new life, new spirit, or victory that comes through Christ's death or Christian baptism (cf. Rom. 5:12-15, 5:21, 6:3, 6:5, 6:16, 6:23, 7:5, 8:2, etc.). All too often the Christian's death with Christ is interpreted in an individualistic context. Paul's allusions, however, to the "fellowship of his sufferings" in Philippians 3:10, and of being "baptized into his body" in I Corinthians 12: 13 reinforce our argument that this death is understood corporately by Paul.

As we have noted in our study of other judgment terminology, so also here we see the corporate dimension of death. Romans 5:12-21 speaks of the unity of mankind in Adam's sin and death.[4] In this

---

[1] John Coolidge Hurd, Jr., *The Origin of I Corinthians* (New York : Seabury Press, 1965), pp. 229-233. Cf. *infra*, pp. 138-139.

[2] Bultmann, *Theology*, I, 17.

[3] Karl G. Kuhn, "Rom. 6:7," *Zeitschrift für die neutestamentliche Wissenschaft*, XXX (1931), 306. Kuhn turns our attention to the Old Testament for the understanding of Rom. 6:7: "For the one who dies is justified from sin." He notes that according to Numbers death pays all debts : "When a man ... commits any of the sins that men commit by breaking faith with the Lord, and that person is found guilty ... he shall make full restitution for his wrong ... giving it to him to whom he did wrong. But if the man has no kinsman to whom restitution may be made for the wrong, the restitution for the wrong shall go to the priest, for the Lord in addition to the ram of atonement with which atonement is made for him" (Numbers 5:8 f.). If he dies before he can make the sin offering, then his heirs do not have to make the sin offering for him because his death itself provides the expiation (p. 306). This tradition could easily stand behind Paul's claim that death with Christ in baptism frees one from the debt to sin, or slavery to the old age (cf. references to slavery in 6:6).

[4] Heinrich Emil Brunner, *The Letter to the Romans*, trans. H.A. Kennedy (Philadelphia: The Westminster Press, 1959), p. 44. Cf. Robin Scroggs, *The Last Adam* (Philadelphia : The Fortress Press, 1966), pp. 76-82; Paul Schubert, "Paul and the New Testament

section Paul is not concerned with the origin of sin but its universality.[1] He knows sin as a corporate reality,[2] and death as corporate judgment. This emphasis on corporeity carries forward into chapter six, where the first person plural appears regularly in the discussion of death and new life (vss. 1-9, 15), and the second person plural appears in verses 10, 14, and 16-22.[3]

Since Miss Mattern argues that the final judgment is synonymous with destruction she takes the absence of any reference to a second death for Christians to be proof that Christians do not face the final judgment of condemnation.[4] She compares Paul's doctrine of judgment to that of the Fourth Gospel in which by man's response to the claim of the Gospel he places himself among the believing who will not be judged or among unbelieving who remain under the wrath of God.[5] In this connection Miss Mattern argues that Paul juxtaposes righteousness and judgment terminology in order to show the righteous the condemnation from which they will be delivered.[6]

While her position is closely reasoned, it seems to us that her argument suffers from some basic weaknesses. (1) With her tendency to minimize the importance of the final judgment for the Christian, Miss Mattern seriously weakens the eschatological tension which appears to us to run through all of Paul's judgment thought. This weakness is particularly evident in her comparison of Paul to the Fourth Evangelist. While there are some future references in the Fourth Gospel, few would deny that the sharp eschatological tension so evident in Paul is not a major concern of the Fourth Evangelist. The overriding emphasis of

---

Ethic in the Thought of John Knox," in *Christian History and Interpretation: Studies Presented to John Knox*, ed. W.R. Farmer, C.F.D. Moule, and R.R. Niebuhr (Cambridge: At the University Press, 1967), p. 86, says Paul speaks of our solidarity with Adam in Romans 5. Karl Barth, *Christ and Adam*, trans. T.A. Small (New York: Harper & Brothers, Publishers, 1956, '57). Rudolf Bultmann, "Adam and Christ According to Romans 5," in *Current Issues in New Testament Interpretation: Essays in Honor of Otto A. Piper*, eds. William Klassen and Graydon F. Snyder (New York: Harper & Brothers, Publishers, 1962), pp. 143-165, attempts to refute Barth's position. Bultmann argues that Adam is changed into an idea of man and Christ becomes the ideal man at the head of the new humanity. The figures are changed into ideal types by Paul, in Bultmann's opinion.

[1] Price, *Interpreting*, p. 408.
[2] *Ibid.*
[3] Tannehill, *Dying and Rising with Christ*, pp. 7-39.
[4] *Verständnis*, p. 67.
[5] *Ibid.*, p. 75.
[6] *Ibid.*, p. 74.

the Gospel of John is on the present. (2) We have noted above how closely Paul ties wrath to righteousness and we have argued that wrath and judgment are not juxtaposed to righteousness but are expressions of righteousness.[1] If our position is allowed to stand then Miss Mattern's position is placed in question. (3) It seems erroneous to argue that since there is no condemnation for those who are in Christ, there is no final judgment for the Christian. She acknowledges that the works of the Christian are judged in some individual, intermediate judgment; however, the final judgment means only condemnation for the non-Christians. If the evidence in this word study will support a sound position, then we believe that the Christian does face the Last Judgment, but he faces it in confidence because there God's righteousness will be completely vindicated. This eschatological event means victory for the Christian as well as defeat for those who have impugned God's justice.[2]

When one examines Paul's concept of death in the light of his background it is readily apparent that he shares the view expressed in most of these sources. In the Old Testament, it is a commonplace that death comes from sin (e.g., Gen. 3:3, 19). Likewise in the apocalyptic materials sin and death are commonly placed in a cause and effect relationship. In Ezra's last prayer before ascending to heaven, he acknowledges the tie of death to sin and praises God for his mercy (IV Ezra 8:53). In II Enoch 30:16, God thinks about Adam's fate: "After sin what is there but death?"[3] I Enoch sets the death penalty in an eschatological context; for this writer the punishment is no mere natural death, but is associated with the apocalyptic woes. After listing a long series of woes (98:9-16), the writer says of the sinners, "They shall have no peace but die a sudden death" (98:16).

The rabbinic materials, likewise, know a connection between sin and death. The statement of Rabbi Hanina b. Dosa (A.D. 80) illustrates the position of the rabbis in this connection: " 'And Moses fled from before it' another reason of his flight is because he had sinned by his words. Had he not sinned, he would not have fled, for not the serpent brings death, but sin."[4]

---

[1] *Supra*, pp. 79-81.

[2] *Supra*, pp. 81-83.

[3] II Enoch is not among the books we have considered throughout this study however, this citation is worthy of mention.

[4] MR Exodus, p. 71. This view prevails as late as Rabbi Ammi (c.a., A.D. 380), who said "There is no death without sin" (Shabbath, p. 255). Cf. Strack-Billerbeck, *Kommentar*, I, 815-816; III, 155-157, 228.

Although Paul shares the viewpoint of the Old Testament, apocalyptic, and rabbinic materials, he naturally differs in the particular way he places his materials in Christocentric focus. In the apocalyptic and rabbinic materials deliverance from the eschatological visitation of death and destruction remains future, whereas for Paul these powers are under attack and are being overcome in the present time.

In summary, our word-study has traced three themes through some of Paul's judgment terminology. We have seen that Paul shares a number of eschatological emphases and judgment terminology with Jewish apocalyptic. Like the apocalyptic writers, Paul sees the double function of righteousness, wrath and the Day. Like the apocalyptic writers, he sees righteousness, wrath, the Day and death in corporate terms. Like the apocalyptic writers, the imminent judgment impinges sharply on the present.

Paul differs from Jewish apocalyptic at those points where his Gospel dictates a change in emphasis. Men receive condemnation in the judgment not because they are Gentile or apostate Jews, but because they reject "Christ crucified." In the universal judgment God is no respecter of persons. No man can appeal to his ancestry, and no man is excused by his ignorance. Unlike the apocalyptic literature, Paul sees the judgement as proleptically present; no longer is it a future prospect only.

While our study has concerned itself with specific words, its implications extend beyond the words themselves. Paul not only uses apocalyptic terminology for the communication of his Gospel. He also appropriates its eschatological framework. It is this appropriation that distinguishes Paul from the rabbinic writers. While the rabbinic materials are interlarded in some measure with eschatological references, the Torah is plainly the integrating factor in the rabbinic materials. In the apocalyptic materials concern with the Torah is prominent, but the integrating factor is eschatology. It is in this use of the eschatological framework for the proclamation of his Gospel that Paul most closely resembles the apocalyptic writers.

If this conclusion may be drawn from our study, then it is basically erroneous to attempt to view judgment in Paul too narrowly and in individualistic terms, as has been the perennial tendency. While the individual is included in both apocalyptic and Pauline thought, their proclamation begins not with the individual but the broad sweep of God's activity.

In the following two sections of this chapter we shall look more closely at the framework of the judgment speech in Paul, and the structure of his proclamation itself.

B. The Judgment Form in Paul's Letters

In Chapter Two (section 2) we outlined the position of Claus Westermann on the prophetic judgment form. We saw that the pre-exilic form had four basic parts with some variations to increase the flexibility of the form. The four divisions were—

1. Summons to hear : "Now therefore, hear the word of the Lord."
2. Accusation : "You say, 'do not prophesy ' " etc.
3. Introduction to the announcement of the sentence by the formula "therefore" (a message formula).
4. Announcement : " Your wife shall be a harlot " etc.[1]

In our investigation in Chapter Two we saw also that apparently no similar form was used either by the apocalyptic or rabbinic writers.[2] Since the prophetic form dropped into disuse one might assume that no such form exists in Paul. According to Krister Stendahl's thesis, however, Paul understood his Damascus Road experience not as a conversion but as a call like that of the prophets.[3] Similarly, Ernst Käsemann believes that Paul pronounces a prophetic judgment in I Corinthians 5:3-5.[4] In the light of these views, the question is worth asking if there is some type of judgment form in Paul's letters and if so how does it resemble or differ from the prophetic form ?

Our investigation uncovered two types of judgment materials in Paul's letters. First, there is the judgment pronouncement which Käsemann places in the tradition of early Christian prophecy. Because of the special significance this type of material has for our considera-

---

[1] *Supra*, p. 21.

[2] *Supra*, pp. 41, 65.

[3] "The Apostle Paul," p. 204. Stendahl sees Paul's "conversion as a call to become the Apostle to the Gentiles. This [Stendahl says] was the task for which he—in the manner of the prophets of old—had been earmarked by God from his mother's womb."

[4] " Sentences of Holy Law in the New Testament," in *New Testament Questions of Today*, trans. W.J. Montague (New Testament Library; London : S.C.M. Press, Ltd., 1969), 66-81. Munck, *Paul*, pp. 11-35, speaks of Paul's Damascus Road experience not as a conversion but as a call to a particular mission, like the Old Testament prophetic call. Paul's apostolic ministry, therefore, is not a "soul game" but a part of God's Salvation History.

tion of I Corinthians 16:22, we postpone our discussion of the judgment pronouncement until we examine that passage.[1] Second, there is judgment parenesis which aims to warn, comfort, admonish, and encourage the church through hortatory devices. It is the latter type which we shall discuss here.

As one might expect, the tie of punishment to sin forms the nucleus of Paul's judgment parenesis (e.g., I Cor. 3:16-17; 6:9-11; 10:1-10; 11:17-34; I Thess. 4:3-8; II Thess. 2:1-12; Gal. 6:7-10, etc.). Sometimes Paul draws from familiar Jewish tradition to warn the church (I Cor. 10:1-13). Occasionally he uses non-Jewish sources (e.g., the catalog of vices in I Cor 6:9-11 and Gal. 5:18-21a). In places Paul takes up the specific offenses of his readers (I Cor. 11:21, 28) or the wrongs of those who oppose his Gospel (I Thess. 2:13-16). In the sense that they deal with the relationship of sin and punishment, Paul's parenetic judgment materials are informed by a commonplace of Old Testament, rabbinic, and apocalyptic traditions alike.

Paul, however, differs from the apocalyptic and rabbinic writers in two ways: (1) He adds an hortatory or parenetic element to his description of the punishment of sin. In framing this addition Paul makes explicit what, at best, is only implicit in apocalyptic and rabbinic materials.[2] The following passage from I Corinthians 11:17-34 well illustrates this tendency in Paul:

1. Introduction:	In the following instructions I do not commend you, because when you come together it is not for the better but for the worse (v.17).
2. Offense:	For in eating, each one goes ahead with his own meal, and one is hungry and another is drunk (v.21).
	Whoever ... eats or drinks the cup of the Lord in an unworthy manner will be guilty of profaning the body of the Lord (v. 28).
	For anyone who eats and drinks without discerning the body
3. Punishment:	eats and drinks judgment upon himself. That is why many of you are weak and ill, and some have died (vss. 29 f.).

---

[1] *Infra*, pp. 142-158.

[2] The apocalypticists do announce the triumph of God's righteousness, and this message undoubtedly was a source of hope for the community. The preservation of the apocalyptic materials proves that they were valued by the community; nevertheless, parenesis is not integrated into the judgment proclamation (cf., *supra*, p. 41). Likewise, it is clear in the rabbinic materials that while the judgment proclamation assured the Jews of the trustworthiness of God, the hortatory element cannot be isolated as a regular feature of the judgment material (cf., *supra*, p. 65).

| 4. Hortatory Conclusion: | So then, my brethren, when you come together to eat, wait for one another ... lest you come together to be condemned (vss. 33f.). |

Even where Paul speaks of judgment over non-Christians,[1] he does so to warn, instruct, or nurture the church. In II Thessalonians 2:1-15 this pattern is clear:

1. Introduction:	that day will not come unless the rebellion comes first (v. 3).
2. Offense:	[The son of perdition] opposes and exalts himself against every so-called god or object of worship, so that he takes his seat in the temple of God, proclaiming himself to be God (v. 4).
3. Punishment:	then the lawless one will be revealed, and the Lord Jesus will slay him with the breath of his mouth and destroy him by his appearing and his coming (v. 8).
2. Offense:	[The disciples of the "lawless one" are culpable also] because they have refused to love the truth and be saved.
3. Punishment:	Therefore God sends upon them a strong delusion so that all may be condemned who did not believe the truth but had pleasure in unrighteousness (vss. 9-12).
4. Hortatory Conclusion:	So then, brethren, stand firm and hold to the traditions which you were taught by us, either by word of mouth or by letter (v. 15).

(2) Paul also differs from his Jewish forebearers when he views God's judgment as already beginning in an ultimate sense. Through the cross of Christ the whole inhabited world is now being called to give an account (Rom. 1:18 ff.). Judgment is now beginning on the enemy of the Gospel (I Thess. 2:13-16). Erring Christians also are culpable before God's righteous action (I Cor. 11:29 f.). The completion of the judgment, however, remains in the future. Only then will God be completly victorious over his adversaries (II Thess. 2:8; 2:12; Gal. 6:8. etc.).

Since Paul's hortatory emphasis in these materials is pastoral in tone, it is erroneous to see the prophetic, oracular form behind his eschatological parenesis dealing with the judgment. Whether he cuts his pronouncement form from the prophetic bolt of cloth is a question we must consider below. There is no evidence, however, in the judgment parenesis to support the view that Paul here imitates the prophetic

---

[1] Braun, *Gerichtsgedanke*, p. 44, observes that Paul speaks of judgment over the Christians about sixty times versus about twenty times over the non-Christians. It should be noted, however, that even sections which speak of judgment over the non-Christians are usually addressed to the church.

mode of address. The apostle's frequent switch from the indicative to the subjunctive mood when he moves from his introduction to the delineation of the offense and punishment (e.g., I Cor. 3:16-17), his tendency to use the indirect ("if *anyone*") rather than the direct mode of address (" because *you* ") characteristic of prophecy, and his use of the hortatory element as his conclusion ("stand firm", "take heed," etc.) rather than the flat judgment announcement ("God will destroy you"), argue against the position that Paul used the basic form of prophetic speech as his model. Paul's regular use of the hortatory element, however, shows in a significant way the strong corporate slant of his judgment allusions. It is erroneous, also, to assume that Paul's address to a congregation requires a corporate emphasis. We know from the Fourth Gospel as well as later Gnostic writings that materials intended for a circle of believers could carry a strong individualistic emphasis. This observation, therefore, argues for a consideration of Paul's judgment pronouncements in an ecclesiastical and corporate rather than an individualistic context.

C. Judgment Themes in Paul's Letters

We turn now to consider the relationship of judgment to some important themes in Paul's letters. Uncertainty over the extent to which Paul uses traditional materials, or the degree to which a redactor interpolates materials into his text [1] added to the fact that different occasions may have evoked varying but appropriate responses from Paul, makes it difficult, if not impossible to speak of the Christology of Paul.[2] There is general agreement, however, that the emphasis on the cross forms the nucleus of Paul's theology.[3] For example, Paul counterba-

---

[1] Ernst Käsemann, "Zum Verständnis von Röm. 3:24-26," in *Exegetische Versuche und Besinnungen* (2 vols.; Göttingen : Vandenhoeck & Ruprecht, 1960), I, 96-100; Bultmann, *Theology*, I, 46; Charles H. Talbert, "A Non-Pauline Fragment at Romans 3:24-26 ?" *Journal of Biblical Literature*, LXXXV (1966), 287-296; Joachim Jeremias, *The Eucharistic Words of Jesus*, trans. (3rd German ed.) and ed. Arnold Ehrhardt (New York : The Macmillan Co., 1955), pp. 103-104, 187-188.

[2] Kee-Young-Froehlich, *Understanding the New Testament*, p.191.

[3] Rudolf Bultmann, *Theology of the New Testament*, trans. Kendrick Grobel (2 vols.; New York : Charles Scribner's Sons, 1951), I, 293, can say that the cross is so central for Paul that "Jesus' death-and-resurrection, then, is for Paul the decisive thing about the person of Jesus and his life experience, indeed, in the last analysis it is the sole thing of importance to him."

lances the Corinthian enthusiasm with the statement, "I decided to know nothing among you but Jesus Christ and him crucified" (I Cor. 2:2; cf. 1:23; Gal. 3:1). Although some might object that this emphasis cannot be taken as normative since it appears in a polemical context, there is no reason to doubt that this represents the core of Paul's Gospel. This emphasis surfaces in varying contexts and numerous letters. Paul understands baptism, for example, as participation in the death of Jesus (Rom. 6); he notes that in the Eucharist the church proclaims the Lord's death "until he comes" (I Cor. 11:26). In I Corinthians 1:18 Paul refers to the "word of the cross" as the "power of God." The proclamation of "Christ crucified," Paul acknowledges, is a "stumbling block" to the Jews and "folly to the Greeks" who, both alike, reject the Gospel. Paul calls the haters of the Gospel " the enemies of the cross" (Phil. 3:18), and condemns those who accept circumcision to avoid persecution for " the cross of Christ " (Gal. 6:12). Paul glories not in circumcision but in "the cross of our Lord Jesus Christ" (Gal. 6:14). Although the cross and resurrection belong together the priority of the cross is clear.[1]

For our purposes it is unnecessary to decide how and in what sense Paul's proclamation of the cross was fashioned out of traditional materials. Not the source of the materials but their position in Paul's letters is our concern. Paul's message is distinguished from that of Jewish apocalyptic not by its eschatological tension, because we saw in Chapter Two [2] that tension between the "then" and the "not yet" is present in the apocalyptic materials as well. The distinctive element in Paul's outlook is a tension between the "then" and "not yet" with Christ as both magnetic poles. Or, to put it another way, the foci of Paul's eschatological ellipse are the cross and the *parousia*, but the axis between them extends beyond them to include the Israel of the past and the Israel of the eschatological future. Peter Stuhlmacher, therefore, is quite right when he says with special emphasis that, "*Die paulinische Eschatologie ist eine proleptische und darin christologische Eschatologie.*" [3] Oscar Cullmann makes a similar point when he talks about all Salvation History being latently present in the

---

[1] Bultmann, *Theology*, I, 293. Käsemann, *Perspectives on Paul*, translated by Margaret Kohl (Philadelphia : Fortress Press, 1971), pp. 32-59.

[2] *Supra*, p. 49.

[3] "Erwägungen zum Problem von Gegenwart und Zukunft in der Paulinischen Eschatologie," *Zeitschrift für Theologie und Kirche*, LXIV (1967), 449. Italics are his.

Christ event.[1] It is this Christocentric focus that makes Paul's eschatology three dimensional. The tension in Paul's theology is between the "then-now-not yet," or between a "now-not yet" whose "now" is rooted in the "then" and brought to fruition in the "not yet." Eduard Schweizer characterizes the cross in Paul's theology as the sign post that stands at the turning of the ages "which separates the new creation from the old."[2] It is this present dimension which Christ gives Paul's eschatology which differentiates it from that of Jewish apocalyptic. We shall now consider this present dimension.

1. It seems almost superfluous to speak of the contemporaneity of God's act for Paul. Both the righteousness and wrath of God are revealed in the present (Rom. 1:17 f.). The outpouring of God's Spirit, a powerful manifestation of the Messianic Age, is now taking place. The believers already are tasting "the first fruits ($ἀπαρχή$) of the Spirit" (Rom. 8:23).[3] This Spirit, likewise, "helps us in our weakness" (Rom. 8:26) in the here and now.[4] Those who are now "in Christ" are already members of the eschatological congregation;[5] they are now members of the new creation : "The old has passed away, behold, the new has come" (II Cor. 5:17). Members of Christ's body are "heirs" in the present time (Rom. 8:17). Already Paul knows the new life in Christ

---

[1] *Salvation as History*, trans. Sidney G. Sowers and the staff of S.C.M. Press (New Testament Library; London : S.C.M. Press, Ltd., 1965), p. 166.

[2] "Spirit of God," in *Bible Key Words*, trans. A.E. Harvey (from G. Kittel's *Theologisches Wörterbuch zum Neuen Testament* [New York : Harper & Brothers, Publishers, 1960]), III, 68. Maurice Goguel, "Le caractère, à la fois actuel et future, du salut dans la théologie paulinienne," in *The Background of the New Testament and Its Eschatology : In Honour of Charles Harold Dodd*, ed. W.D. Davies and D. Daube (Cambridge : At the University Press, 1956), pp. 322-341, sees eschatological tension in Paul's understanding of faith. He is, however, according to our view, in error when he concludes that there are two unreconciled types of eschatology in Paul—one collective, which is rooted in Jewish apocalyptic, and one individualistic (p. 336). J. Louis Martyn, "Epistemology at the Turn of the Ages : II Corinthians 5:16," in *Christian History and Interpretation : Studies Presented to John Knox*, ed. W.R. Farmer, C.F.D. Moule, and R.R. Niebuhr (Cambridge : At the University Press, 1967), p. 273, and Werner Georg Kümmel, "Jesus und Paulus," in *Heilsgeschehen und Geschichte*, herausgegeben von Erich Grässer, Otto Merk und Adolf Fritz (Marburger theologische Studien, vol. III; Marburg : N.G. Elwert Verlag, 1965), p. 95, both support the position taken here.

[3] Johannes Weiss, *Der erste Korintherbrief* (10th ed.; Göttingen : Vandenhoeck & Ruprecht, 1925), p. 356, says that if Christ's resurrection is the first fruits there is no doubt but that the harvest ("*Ernte*") will and must follow.

[4] Schweizer, "Spirit of God," p. 71.

[5] Bultmann, *Theology*, I, 311.

at least in a partial way (Gal. 2:20). God's mighty acts are now being manifested in the work and witness of the apostles. In II Corinthians 6:2 Paul exults, "Behold, now is the acceptable time; behold now is the day of salvation." The close association of $\nu\hat{v}\nu$ with God's eschatological deeds emphasizes this contemporaneity (Rom. 3:26, 5:9, 5:11, 6:19, 6:21, 8:1, 8:18, 8:22, 11:5, 11:30, 11:31, 13:11, etc.).

2. Like apocalyptic writers Paul sees God's eschatological deeds in relationship to Israel's history and vice versa. Paul understands the Christ-event not as an outrageous novelty but as a part of God's plan announced to Abraham to bless all nations through his "seed" (Gal. 3:16; i.e., Christ). Paul was sensitive to the charge that his Gospel was a crude aberration, unfaithful to the God of Abraham, Isaac, and Jacob, and, therefore, to be repudiated. Paul replies that God's mission to the Gentiles has traveled through Israel and that even God's mission to the pagan nations has Israel as its goal. It is not God who has forsaken Israel but Israel which has forsaken God.

Schoeps gives an entire chapter to Paul's conception of *Heilsgeschichte* and concludes cynically that it is "far-fetched speculation," "arbitrary typological treatment of the history of Israel," " much fantasy" and "highly subjective opinions." [1] Schoeps fails to appreciate, however, Paul's belief that in the Christ the Jewish "ideal of a holy people" is fulfilled and through him and "through the gift of the Spirit an ever-widening, inclusive fellowship was being formed as the means of further realizing this ideal." [2] Schoeps also overlooks the common belief, obviously shared by Paul, that in the Messianic Age the Scriptures would be truly and fully understood.[3] Thus Paul was following a common exegetical principle when he sought to understand the Scriptures through the person and work of the Messiah. In the following paragraphs we shall mention briefly some of the ways Paul interprets Israel's history in light of the Christ-event.

Stuhlmacher very perceptively notices Paul's propensity to use the preposition $\pi\rho o$ as a prefix when he alludes to Israel's history.[4] God, for

---

[1] *Paul*, p. 244.

[2] Price, *Interpreting*, p. 396.

[3] E.g., John 4:25 : "I know that Messiah is coming (he who is called Christ); when he comes he will show us all things." Otto Michel, *Paulus und seine Bibel* (Beiträge zur Förderung christlicher Theologie; Gütersloh : Druck und Verlag von C. Bertelsmann, 1929), p. 134, shows how in apocalyptic thought the revelation of the true meaning of the scriptures was seen as a spiritual blessing reserved for the Endtime.

[4] "Erwägungen zum Problem von Gegenwart und Zukunft," p. 434.

example promised the Gospel (προεπηγγείλατο) ahead of time through his prophets (Rom. 1:2). All of the Old Testament was written in the former days (προεγράφη) for our instruction (Rom. 15:4). In Galatians 3:8 Paul says the writers of the Scriptures "saw ahead of time" προιδοῦσα) "that God would justify the Gentiles by faith," and the Scriptures "preached the Gospel beforehand (προευηγγελίσατο) to Abraham." In Romans 8:29 Paul assumes that Israel's election is identical with the election of the church. Those whom God foreknew (προέγνω) he decided upon beforehand (προώρισεν) as his elect.[1] From this observation, Stuhlmacher concludes—

> Paulus trifft bereits im Alten Testament auf den Gott, der ihn vor Damaskus zum Boten des Christus berufen hat. Anders formuliert : Gott ist als Vater Jesu Christi für Paulus schon im Alten Testament anwesend, und die alttestamentliche Vergangenheit wird darum ganz folgerichtig vom Apostel als Verheissung, besser; als eine die Gegenwart tragende Ankunft des in Christus erwählenden Gottes erfahren. Das aber bedeutet : *Nicht nur Gegenwart und Zukunft, sondern auch die geschichtliche Vergangenheit werden dem Apostel zu Aussageweisen des Kommens Gottes.*[2]

When we look at Paul's treatment of Old Testament figures we see a similar pattern. In Romans 4 Paul answers the charge that this Gospel would make God go back on his word. If God's promises are made to Abraham's descendants, Paul's accuser asks, how can he now exclude the majority of the Jews from the eschatological community which represents the fulfillment of God's promise ?[3] In reply Paul questions the assumption that God's promises were made to Abraham on the basis of his good works (Rom. 4:2-8). Appealing to Genesis 15:6 Paul says that Abraham was reckoned righteous by faith in God's promises while still a Gentile before becoming the progenitor of the covenanted people. Therefore, his righteousness did not depend on circumcision (Rom. 4:9-12), or on observance of the Law (Rom. 4:13-17a). "Reckoning," Paul argues from Psalms 32, does not mean counting good works but the non-reckoning of sin. Thus Paul argues it is those who have faith in Christ who are childern of the promise instead of those who can claim fidelity to the Law, or are circumcised, or who are blood descendants of Abraham (Gal. 3:6 f.).[4] Consequently, the history which began with

---

[1] "Erwägungen zum Problem von Gegenwart und Zukunft," pp. 434-435.

[2] *Ibid.*, p. 435.

[3] For a good summary of the accusation and Paul's response see Price, *Interpreting*, pp. 387-388; 395-396.

[4] In Gal. 3:16 Paul notes that the promise is made to Abraham's "seed" which he interprets as referring to Christ, not Israel. Cf. David Daube, "The Interpretation of

Abraham, Paul believes, reaches its true goal in Christ.[1] Thus Paul can speak of the non-reckoning "not for his sake alone, but for ours also" (Rom. 4:23b-24). It is evident that in Galatians 3 and Romans 4 Paul is not merely citing illustrative material from the past; Paul considers Abraham "not merely as a 'paradigm' of a believer, but as progenitor of Israel, the elect people."[2]

In Paul's discussion of Sarah and Hagar (Gal. 4:21-31), Sarah and Isaac appear as the recipients of the promise which comes to fruition in Christ and the church.[3] Paul also views Adam and Moses through the prism of Christ. Adam is seen not only as the head of the community of sin and death and thus the first recipient of the promise of God's punishment, but also as the inadequate antithesis to Christ the head of the new humanity and guarantor of God's promise of redemption (Rom. 5:12-31). Again Paul understands the deed of an Old Testament figure through Christ.[4] Even if one makes a distinction between Salvation History and typology, as does Cullmann, one must still acknowledge that in Romans 5:12-21 the typology "is imbedded in a total salvation-historical understanding."[5] As in Paul's references to Adam so also in his allusions to Moses, Christ is the controlling image (II Cor. 3:7-15). The splendor of the Law is eclipsed by the splendor of Christ.

Some might use the references to Adam and Moses to support their claim that Paul, to be correctly understood, must be seen in juxtaposition to his background. It must be noted, however, that Paul in-

---

a Generic Singular in Galatians 3:16," *Jewish Quarterly Review*, XXXV (1944), 227-230; Price, *Interpreting*, p. 396.

[1] Christian Dietzfelbinger, *Heilsgeschichte bei Paulus?* (Theologische Existenz Heute; München : Chr. Kaiser Verlag, 1965), p. 10.

[2] Cullmann, *Salvation in History*, pp. 263-264.

[3] Dietzfelbinger, *Heilsgeschichte bei Paulus?*, p. 12.

[4] Klaus Galley, *Altes und neues Heilsgeschehen bei Paulus* (Arbeiten zur Theologie, series I, vol. XXII; Stuttgart : Calwer Verlag, 1965), p. 36, says, "Paulus kann so verfahren, weil der Gegensatz nicht das Erste ist, sondern schon vorher eingefasst ist von dem einen, zielgerichteten Willen Gottes, der über dem Gegensatz steht. Sein Plan gibt dem Gegensatz einen Sinn und ein Ziel; weil Gott der Herr ist, sind Adam und Christus vergleichbar. Adam, der sündigte und dem Tod verfiel, ist Gottes Geschöpf und untersteht seinem Willen. Gott kann die Sünde der Adamiten seinem Heil in Christus dienen lassen, weil auch diese Sünde nicht ohne ihn geschehen ist. Ja, Adam und seine Wirkung gehört in Gottes Plan, dessen Ziel Christus und sein Heil für die Menschen ist. So hat Gott Adam und Christus zueinander geordnet, dass Christus in Adam seinen Beruf habe und Adam durch Christus gerettet werde." See Barth, *A Shorter Commentary on Romans*, pp. 25-31.

[5] Cullmann, *Salvation in History*, p. 129.

cludes himself in the Jewish tradition and can speak of his Jewishness in a very positive way : "I myself am an Israelite," Paul says, "a descendant of Abraham, a member of the tribe of Benjamin" (Rom. 11:2; cf. II Cor. 11:22; Phil. 3:5).[1]

Paul also shares certain key terms with the Old Testament which refer to God's gracious acts toward his covenant people. Romans 9:4f., for example, is crammed with words which refer to the election of Israel through which God would achieve his purpose.[2] υἱοθεσία points to the election of Israel (Ex. 4:22; Deut. 14:1); δόξα refers to the presence of God with Israel in the wilderness (Ex. 16:10, 24:16, 40:34f.). διαθῆκαι [3] may refer to the ordinances of God or to God's different covenant resolutions with Israel. λατρεία designates the temple service and sacrifices. The fulfillment of the promises (ἐπαγγελίαι) given to the prophets and fathers would come in the Messianic Age. πατέρες is to be understood in the broad sense as the men of Israel's early history. Finally, ὁ Χριστὸς refers to the Jewish Messiah himself.[4] Here, as we have noticed earlier, Paul interprets Israel's history in the light of God's present redemptive act.[5]

In Romans 9-11 Paul's *heilsgeschichtliche* orientation is evident. Here, Paul's accuser asks how God can be called righteous if he excludes the majority of Israel from his new covenant community. Has God's purpose failed?[6] Christian Müller quite properly notes that the central motif of Romans 9-11 is not the justification of man but the vindication of God's claim over man for believing obedience.[7] Müller argues, against Bultmann, that Paul's teaching on justification does not begin with the question of how the sinner can be righteous but rather how the right of God over his creation is realized.[8] While Paul answers the ob-

---

[1] *Ibid.*

[2] Barret, *The Epistle to the Romans*, p. 178.

[3] See my "Διαθῆκαι in Romans 9, 4," *Biblica*, LI (1970), 377-390.

[4] Howard Rhys, *The Epistle to the Romans* (New York : The Macmillan Company, 1961), pp. 119-120; William Sanday and Arthur C. Headlam, *The Epistle to the Romans* (11th ed.; The International Critical Commentary; New York : Charles Scribner's Sons, 1906), pp. 230-231 ; Barrett, *The Epistle to the Romans*, pp. 177-178.

[5] Dietzfelbinger, *Heilsgeschichte bei Paulus?*, p. 18, says that although Paul does make negative references to Israel here Paul "lässt die ursprüngliche positive Perspektive durchscheinen."

[6] Price, *Interpreting*, pp. 411-412.

[7] *Gottes Gerechtigkeit und Gottes Volk*, p. 27, says Paul's teaching of righteousness is freed from the "Prokrustesbett des Individualismus."

[8] *Ibid.*, p. 108.

jection of the Jew, at the same time he defines the relationship of the church to Israel. The new covenant community exists in relationship to Israel. The Gentiles, Paul reminds the church, are wild olive branches which have been grafted into the olive tree (Rom. 11:17-24). Müller properly says, "Wer Israels Geschichte nicht versteht, versteht weder die Geschichte der 'Welt' noch seine eigene." [1] Müller thus disagrees with Rudolf Bultmann's view that decisive history for Paul is not world history ("*Weltgeschichte*") but what each man experiences for himself.[2] However just the criticism against Cullmann that he schematizes the Bible too rigidly on the *heilsgeschichtliche* model,[3] one can hardly question his statement that what Paul offers in Romans "is a salvation-historical interpretation of events in the mission field. Through Israel's unbelief, the full number of Gentiles come in. Thus the path leads through Israel." [4]

Paul's call to preach to the Gentiles, therefore, is a call not just to preach to individuals but a summons to participate in God's plan of salvation which began with Israel's election and includes Israel in its final goal. God's saving acts in the present, Paul argues, do not contradict or nullify his gracious deeds of the past; on the contrary, God's work in Christ and his church fulfills his saving purpose begun in Israel. The exclusion of the majority of Israel cannot be attributed to God's failure but to Israel's stubborn heart.[5]

From the observations above it is easy to see that Paul, like the apocalyptic writers, ties God's future acts to his deeds and promises of the past.[6] The eschatological tension between God's promises and their fulfillment runs through all of Paul's thought. It is evident from

---

[1] *Gottes Gerechtigkeit und Gottes Volk*, p. 106.

[2] *History and Eschatology* (Gifford Lectures, 1955; Edinburgh : The University Press, 1957), p. 42, says eschatological bliss is thought of in reference to the individual. Paul, according to Bultmann, exchanges the history of the world for the history of the human being. See his *Glauben und Verstehen* (Tübingen : J.C.B. Mohr [Paul Siebeck], 1933), pp. 101-102. For a further discussion of the relationship of the individual to world history in Paul see Günter Klein, "Individualgeschichte und Weltgeschichte bei Paulus," *Evangelische Theologie*, XXIV (1964), 126-165.

[3] Stuhlmacher, "Erwägungen zum Problem von Gegenwart und Zukunft," pp. 440-441, n. 40.

[4] *Salvation in History*, p. 251.

[5] *Ibid.*, p. 264.

[6] Davies, *Paul*, pp. 316-317, rightly points to the tension which is expressed in the rabbinic materials between the two phases of the '*ôlâm ha-bâ*', and cites Strack-Biller-

our investigation above that the eschatological νῦν for Paul is no ahistorical entity as it was for the Gnostics. It is a "now" whose significance is enhanced by its tie to the past and by the impingement of the future upon it. It is to that future emphasis that we now turn.

3. The day when God will complete his work of salvation stands on the near horizon of Paul's thought. The appointed time is short (I Cor. 7:29); indeed, "the Lord is at hand" (Phil. 4:4, 5). The imminent "day of the Lord" will break forth suddenly and the Lord will come unexpectedly like a thief in the night (I Thess. 5:2). The eschatological moment, Paul warns, is closer now than we at first believed; "the night is far gone, the day is at hand" (Rom. 12:11 f.).

This impending Day so strongly conditions the present in Paul's thought that it is necessary to talk not just about the Day itself but the ways in which God's present eschatological deed is held in tension with the future consummation. Almost random selections from Paul's letters will reveal the now-not-yet tension. The Christians *are* "heirs" (Rom. 8:17), but they *"will* inherit" the Kingdom of God (I Cor. 6:9; emphasis added). The word of the cross is the power of God to those who are now being saved (I Cor. 1:18), but salvation itself usually appears as a future expectation (I Cor. 3:15, 5:5, 7:16, 9:22, 10:33, etc.)[1] The

---

beck for support: "Yet the striking phenomenon that the Rabbinic teachers have used the expression *há-'ólâm ha-bâ'* to designate both the heavenly world of the souls and also the future Age of Consummation would have made it clear to us, as it were, that the heavenly Aeon of the Souls and the future Aeon of Consummation were regarded as one and the same great *'ólâm ha-bâ'*. This great *'ólam ha-bâ'* at present had its place in heaven (I Enoch 71:14 ff.)... into it the souls of the righteous entered at the hour of death for a preliminary blessedness. That is their first phase in which it serves as the world of the souls until it enters through the resurrection of the dead into its second phase to become the earthly sphere of the Aeon of full blessedness." One cannot but notice that Strack-Billerbeck cites I Enoch as support for their position. One could add a number of references from IV Ezra (4:11-27; 6:20; 7:12-47, 50, 112 f.; 8:1, 52) as well as allusions from II Baruch (83:4 f.), all of which predate the rabbinic sources. See Martin Dibelius, *Die Geisterwelt im Glauben des Paulus* (Göttingen: Vandenhoeck & Ruprecht, 1909), p. 64, who emphasizes the fact that Paul's idea of the two ages has its roots in Jewish apocalyptic. While Paul does not explicitly mention the age to come except possibly in Ephesians 1:20 (ἐν τῷ μέλλοντι), references to ὁ κόσμος and ὁ αἰών οὗτος are common in Paul's letters (e.g., I Cor. 1:20; 2:6; 2:8; 3:18, etc.). Fundamental to Paul's thought, however, is the belief that the Christian lives in the overlap between the two ages (cf. Manson, *On Paul and John*, p. 26).

[1] It is noteworthy that with the possible exception of Rom. 8:24 (τῇ γὰρ ἐλπίδι ἐσώθημεν [aor. ind. pass.], the verb σώζω has a future orientation in Paul. Even 8:24, however, is set in a future context. Cf. Rom. 5:9, 10; 9:27; 10:9, 13; 11:26; II Cor. 2:15; I Thess. 2:16; 2:10.

creation now groans for redemption but only then will it "be set free from its bondage to decay" (Rom. 8:21). We now enjoy the "first fruits of the Spirit" but we must wait for "the redemption of our bodies" (Rom. 8:23). The present ἀρραβών of the Spirit (II Cor. 1:22, 5:5) will be fulfilled in the future. The resurrection of Jesus is a sign of the presence of the Age to Come,[1] but the final installment will come only at the end when all will be raised. Paul acknowledges that his present insight into God's mystery is dim but then he will see face to face (I Cor. 13:12). He acknowledges that his present knowledge of God is incomplete, but then he will know as he is known (I Cor. 13:12). In Philippians 3:8-12 Paul can speak of God's eschatological victory as both present and yet still outstanding:

> I count everything as loss because of the surpassing worth of knowing Christ Jesus my Lord. For his sake I have suffered the loss of all things, and count them as refuse, in order that I may gain Christ... that I may know him and the power of his resurrection... Not that I have already obtained this or am already perfect; but I press on to make it my own, because Christ Jesus has made me his own.

While salvation is known in a limited way now, Paul still struggles against Satan. The Devil frustrates his travel plans (I Thess. 2:18), and destroys men (I Cor. 5:5; II Cor. 12:7). Paul still battles the flesh (Rom. 8:4), yet he struggles in the assurance that God's victory in Jesus Christ is near (I Cor. 15:57).

This same eschatological tension runs through Paul's concept of the sacraments. In baptism one dies with Christ in the present, but he is raised with Christ only in the future. In Romans 6:5 Paul says: "For if we have been united with him in a death like his, we shall certainly be (ἐσόμεθα) united with him in a resurrection like his." Paul adds in Romans 6:8: "[I]f we have died with Christ, we believe that we shall also live (συζήσομεν) with him."

When speaking of baptism Paul can speak of dying with Christ (Rom. 6:8; ἀπεθάνομεν σὺν Χριστῷ), of being buried (συνετάφημεν) with Christ (Rom. 6:4), of being grafted together (σύμφυτοι) with Christ (Rom. 6:5), or of being crucified together (συνεσταυρώθη) with Christ (Rom. 6:6) all in the present.[2] This emphasis, however, is held in tension with being with Christ in the *parousia*.[3] On the Last Day Jesus "will

---

[1] Davies, *Paul*, p. 298.
[2] Note the frequent use of συμ.
[3] Schweizer, "Dying and Rising with Christ," pp. 1-14.

bring with him those who have fallen asleep" (I Thess. 4:14). In Romans 8:32 Paul speaks of God's giving "us all things with him" (i.e., Jesus) in the future.

The same tension is evident in Paul's association of baptism and the Kingdom of God. Paul does not deny that a real change takes place at baptism but he refrains from saying the Kingdom of God is fully realized. Although the Kingdom of God is proleptically experienced now (I Cor. 4:20; I Thess. 2:12; Rom. 14:17), the full inheritance will come only in the future (I Cor. 6:9, 10; 15:24, 15:50; Gal. 5:21; II Thess. 1:5).[1]

The Eucharist, like baptism, is held in tension between the cross and the *parousia*. As often as the church eats the bread and drinks the cup of the messianic banquet it proclaims "the Lord's death until he comes" (I Cor. 11:26).[2]

Paul's ethics also stand in the magnetic field between the anode of death and the cathode of the *parousia*.[3] When Paul answers the charge of antinomianism in Romans 6, he refutes the accuser finally by setting the behavior of the Christians in an eschatological context. The $νῦν$ of 6:22 signals the eschatological hour which gives the actions of the Christian a new seriousness. The fruits of holiness which the Christian has in his life now result in eternal life. In Romans 6:12-14 the imperative which the future lays on the present strengthens the Christian for his continuing struggle against sin and its dominion.

The $οὖν$ in Romans 12:1 links the imperative of chapters 12-13 with the preceding indicative. The long parenetic section in chapters 12-13 ends with a summary of the Law—"you shall love your neighbor as yourself" (13:9)— and an eschatological warning: "[T]he night is far gone, the day is at hand. Let us then cast off the works of darkness and put on the armor of light. Let us conduct ourselves becomingly as in the day" (Rom. 13:12 f.). It is very evident that Paul understands the ethical demand in an eschatological context.

In Romans 14:10 f. Paul holds both the strong and the weak responsible for the unity of the church with the reminder that "we shall all stand before the judgment seat of God." In I Corinthians 7:25-31

---

[1] Schweizer, "Dying and Rising with Christ," p. 7.

[2] Cullmann, *Salvation in History*, pp. 259-260.

[3] Schubert, "Paul and the New Testament Ethic," p. 379, speaks of the tension in Paul's ethic between the "now" and "not yet" with the "then" extending into the "now."

Paul's view of marriage is heavily influenced by his belief that the Day of the Lord is at hand.

Stuhlmacher believes that this tension characterizes Paul's understanding of his apostolic office as well.[1] Paul's call is rooted in the Old Testament tradition (Gal. 1:12-17), but it functions in tension between the "now" and "not yet." Paul's vision of the risen Lord is a prolepsis of the *parousia*. The work which Christ began in his earthly ministry and will complete at the consummation, Paul does now on earth as the Lord's apostle.[2]

Keith F. Nickle argues convincingly that the collection for the Jerusalem church is to be seen in this same eschatological perspective.[3] Paul based his Gentile mission on an emphasis which, though secondary, is present in the Old Testament nonetheless. Because of Israel's stubbornness God would reverse the order of salvation.[4] Instead of reaching the Gentiles through Israel, God would save Israel through the pagan peoples. Consequently, the trip to Jerusalem, Nickle argues, was more than a benevolent gesture; it was an "eschatological pilgrimage."[5] If Nickle's position is sound, then here again we see tension between the beginning and the end of God's eschatological deed.

Some who believe that the delay of the *parousia* causes Paul to relax the sharp eschatological tension in his later letters might take issue with our position that this tension pervades most of Paul's language and letters, whether early or late. Charles Harold Dodd, for example, says:

> It is noteworthy that as his interest in the speedy advent of Christ declines, as it demonstrably does after the time when he wrote I Corinthians the "futurist eschatology" of his earlier phase is replaced by this "Christ mysticism." The hope of glory yet to come remains as a background of thought, but the foreground is more and more occupied by the contemplation of all the riches of divine grace enjoyed here and now by those who are in Christ Jesus.[6]

---

[1] "Erwägungen zum Problem von Gegenwart und Zukunft," pp. 429-430. See Walter Schmithals, *Das kirchliche Apostelamt* (Forschungen zur Religion und Literatur des Alten und Neuen Testaments, vol. LXI; Göttingen : Vandenhoeck & Ruprecht, 1961), pp. 34-36.

[2] "Erwägungen zum Problem von Gegenwart und Zukunft," pp. 429-430.

[3] *The Collection* (Studies in Biblical Theology, no. 48; London : S.C.M. Press, Ltd., 1966), pp. 129-143.

[4] Rom. 9:33 (Isa. 28:16); 10:21 (Isa. 65:2); 11:8 (Isa. 29:10), as cited by Nickle, *The Collection*, p. 133, n. 248.

[5] *The Collection*, p. 142.

[6] *The Apostolic Preaching* (New York : Harper & Brothers, Publishers, 1962), p. 63;

William David Davies shares Dodd's view. Although he acknowledges that the expectation of the *parousia* persists in Romans and Philippians, he argues that in these later letters Paul is more concerned with translating the meaning of the coming age into present experience than with the impending Day.[1] August Strobel believes that Paul emphasizes the righteousness of God to deal with the question of theodicy which is raised by the delay of the *parousia*. Strobel questions the opinion that the apostle lived under the impression that the end was near.[2]

In response to the position of Dodd, Davies and Strobel it should be noted that references to the *parousia* appear throughout Paul's letters, and there is little evidence that the expectation of an imminent, though unpredictable Day fades into the background in Paul's later letters.[3]

Charles Harold Dodd, *New Testament Studies* (Manchester : At the University Press, 1953), p. 111, says, "In Romans we have the one passage, xiii. 11-14, 'Our salvation is now nearer than it was when we became Christians. The night is advanced : the day has drawn near.' The whole passage echoes I Thess. v. 1-11; but a comparison of the two passages reveals an unmistakable change of tone. In the earlier epistle the tone is one of intense, almost excited, urgency. *At any moment* the Lord may be here. In the latter the tone is (shall we say ?) that of an earnest preacher, but not that of the herald of an imminent catastrophe."

Dodd, *The Epistle of Paul to the Romans*, p. 210, says of verse 13 that "the eschatology has become little more than an imaginative expression for the urgency which belongs to all moral effort when it is thought of in relation to the eternal issues of life."

[1] *Paul*, p. 319.

[2] *Untersuchungen zum eschatologischen Verzögerungsproblem* (Supplements to Novum Testamentum, vol. II; Leiden, Köln : E.J. Brill, 1961), p. 201. Charles, *Eschatology*, pp. 437-438, divides Paul's eschatology into four successive stages.

[3] Cf. I Thess. 4:13 ff.; 5:1 ff.; Phil. 2:12 ff.; 3:20 f.; Gal. 5:5; 6:7 ff.; I Cor. 15:20 ff.; II Cor. 5:1-10; Rom. 13:11 ff.; 14:10, etc. as cited by Stuhlmacher, "Erwägungen zum Problem von Gegenwart und Zukunft," pp. 448-449, n. 53. Arthur Lewis Moore, *The Parousia in the New Testament* (Supplements to Novum Testamentum, vol. XIII; Leiden : E.J. Brill, 1966), p. 61, says, "beneath the surface of Paul's letters, which changes according to the needs and circumstances being addressed, there is a constant and consistent eschatological framework in which the past, dominated by the Cross and Resurrection, the present, dominated by the Spirit, and the future, dominated by the Parousia, all have their necessary place." John William MacGorman, "An Analysis of the Factors which Relate to the Possibility of Tracing Development in Pauline Eschatology" (unpublished Ph. D. dissertation, Duke University, 1965), pp. 278 ff., argues convincingly that Paul does not relax his emphasis on the eschatological crisis in his later epistles. Neill Q. Hamilton, *Holy Spirit and Eschatology in Paul* (Scottish Journal of Theology, Occasional Papers, no. 6; Edinburgh : Oliver and Boyd Ltd., 1957), p. 68, claims, against Dodd, that the same linear tension is present in Rom. 13:11-14 that Dodd sees in I Thess. 5:1-11.

In section 1 of this chapter we saw that Paul's eschatological language is pervasive.[1] In this section we have seen that the eschatological tension does not weaken in Paul's later letters (e.g., Romans). One is compelled to agree, therefore with Schoeps that "we should misunderstand Paul's *letters as a whole*, and the governing consciousness from which they spring, if we failed to recognize that Paul only lives, writes, and preaches in the unshakeable conviction that his generation represents the last generation of mankind.[2]

The discussion of the structure of Paul's theology has at least two implications for our study.

(1) Since the cross is central to Paul's soteriology and eschatology we can expect it to stand at the heart of his judgment thought as well. In the cross God fulfills his promises to Israel; therefore, to reject the cross of Christ is to incur God's righteous judgment. The cross is "a stumbling block" (I Cor. 1:23) to those who reject it and " the power of God " (I Cor. 1:18) to those who respond in repentance and faith. No appeal to heritage, or ignorance can evade its claim. No attempt to discredit the justice of God's judgment can neutralize God's right to believing obedience. Just as judgment through the cross is to move Israel and the nations to repentance and faith, so also is it intended to move the church to watchful and faithful obedience. The judgment of the cross, therefore, is not addressed primarily to individuals one by one but to the whole inhabited world. We have seen that Paul shares the corporate emphasis and his eschatological framework with Jewish apocalyptic thought, but that the central place of the cross clearly distinguishes Paul's thought from that of Jewish apocalypticism.

(2) The eschatological tension which runs through Paul's theology we would expect to serve as a model for his judgment thought as well.

Since we saw that Paul's eschatology is corporate in outlook and that all of his letters reveal some eschatological tension, and since we dis-

---

[1] *Supra*, pp. 68-91. Note that in the later letters Paul can speak of "eager longing" ἀποκαραδοκία; Phil. 1:20; Rom. 8:19), of "groaning" στενάζω; Rom. 8:23) which show the fervent hope and eager expectation of God's final Day. In Phil. 4:5 Paul can say ὁ κύριος ἐγγύς. In Rom. 13:11 f. Paul can speak of the καιρός as the dawn of God's eschatological Day.

[2] *Paul*, p. 102. William Manson, "Mission and Eschatology," *International Review of Missions*, XLII (1953), 391, sees this tension in the church's mission as well. He says, " The Christian Church and the world mission therefore fulfill themselves under conditions of tension."

covered that Paul's judgment sections aim to edify the church and urge it to watchful obedience, it is appropriate now to turn to a consideration of judgment and the church in some of Paul's letters.

CHAPTER FOUR

THE CHURCH AND JUDGMENT

This chapter is divided into two parts : (1) an exegetical study of the passages which treat the judging church in Paul's letters, and (2) a consideration of Paul's teaching concerning the church under judgment. I am aware of a certain circularity of approach that considers first the background and then the texts of the letters themselves which were used first of all to guide the investigation of the background. This approach, however, is less likely to lead to the misinterpretation and distortion of key themes than is atomistic exegesis.

Before turning to the texts themselves we must briefly consider the purpose of I Corinthians. Because of the inordinately large number of references to judgment in I Corinthians, and because of the special way one's predisposition about the situation prompting this letter influences one's interpretation of these passages, this treatment is required.

What was the situation at Corinth which led Paul to write this letter to the church? Of course, the answer to this question may be at best an intelligent guess, but some amount of conjecture, if restrained, is permissible and even necessary if one is to understand this correspondence. If it can be presumed that Paul's preaching in Corinth carried the same apocalyptic shading that we see in his letters, and if his audience, Greek or Jewish, had been influenced by Hellenistic thought forms, then one might wonder if the problem between Paul and the Corinthian church may have been rooted in a basic conceptual misunderstanding.

Edward Schweizer suggests that men influenced by Greek thought would have had difficulty understanding the Hebrew concept of progressive and purposeful history. If the Corinthians were dualists, he says, they would have thought in terms of opposing spheres, and would have found the message of one age succeeding another strange indeed. Therefore, Schweizer adds—

> ... they certainly could not conceive of the Spirit as a mere *sign* of that which is to come. If it were part of the heavenly world, it must be the reality itself.... If Jesus were the bringer of the Spirit, he must have been a bearer of celestial matter, with which he endowed believers and so united them with the celestial

world. Thus for the first time, a radical solution became possible. The meaning of Jesus' mission lay in his bringing the celestial power-substance, πνεῦμα, into the world. Union with him meant union with his substance, that is to say, *salvation itself*.[1]

In his study of αἰών Hermann Sasse corroborates Schweizer's observations. To the Greeks, Sasse observes, αἰών meant "unending time" or "the eternal today," "uninterrupted time," or "time as prolongation." [2] Therefore, Paul's announcement of a new αἰών which upon its arrival stands in opposition to but fulfills the old age would have sounded incredible to a Greek. Even more incomprehensible would have been Paul's proclamation of an age which has been inaugurated but whose full realization remains future.

Likewise, the term ἡμέρα had connotations for the Hebraic mind which were strange to the Greek. For those who had never seen the use of "the Day" as a moment of personal confrontation or for whom "the Day" had only temporal connotations, it must have seemed strange to see these terms used as symbols of promise or threat. The problems in the church at Corinth may have been rooted in the inability of Paul's Hellenistic audience to come to terms with his temporal dualism. If this be so, it would be easy to understand how the Corinthians would come to adopt a kind of realized eschatology which Schweizer, Funk, Käsemann and others believe evoked Paul's letters.

Schweizer observes: "From the premise that Christ, like Adam, controls all humanity that belongs to him, it is a short step to the Corinthians' conclusion that all who belong to him *are* already ἐπουράνιοι." [3]

Robert W. Funk basically agrees with Schweizer when he says, "The basis of factions in Corinth lies in the fact that some of the Corinthians have forgotten that the eschaton still lies before them and so understand their freedom as absolute." [4]

Ernst Käsemann was one of the first scholars to assert that a form of realized eschatology evoked I Corinthians. He says that the "enthusiasts" felt they were above temptation and—

---

[1] "Spirit of God," III, 55-56.

[2] Hermann Sasse, "αἰών" in *Theological Dictionary of the New Testament*, ed. Gerhard Kittel, trans. and ed. Geoffrey W. Bromiley (Grands Rapids, Mich.: William B. Eerdmans Publishing Company, 1964), I, 198.

[3] "Spirit of God," III, 62.

[4] *Language, Hermeneutic, and the Word of God* (New York: Harper and Row, 1966), p. 278.

... thus above responsibility to any earthly ordinance because they were convinced that baptism had endowed them with a heavenly nature and the freedom of a truly spiritual man. They celebrate the Eucharist as those who have been translated out of the old aeon—it is for them the banquet of the saints in bliss—and deny (we must surely interpret I Cor. 15 thus) the necessity of a bodily resurrection in the future, because they wrongly believe that they have already experienced the resurrection in the sacrament.[1]

Hans Conzelmann likewise believes that spirit-enthusiasts were responsible for the trouble in the church at Corinth. The Corinthians believed they had already entered the Kingdom in a complete sense. "They could conclude : if Christ is risen so are also his people... they had separated the resurrection of Christ from his death and spiritually left his death behind." [2]

Johannes Weiss thinks that the arrival and preaching of Apollos started the reaction in the church at Corinth. Using the Alexandrian method of Scripture proof, and compelling his hearers with his expert reasoning, Apollos led a group of Corinthians to trust in their knowledge. In this new wisdom the final blessedness of the vision of God, according to Apollos, is already achieved. Then these "superior Christians," instructed by Apollos, demonstrate their new freedom by eating meat offered to idols.[3]

Although Apollos would be a likely figure to stand behind the Corinthian aberration if one follows the account in Acts 18:24-19:6, his presence is not necessary to explain the problem. Apollos, then, need not have created the problem, but may have only aggravated an incipient tendency in the church toward realized eschatology. Funk aptly describes the situation in Corinth : "Inasmuch as they were united with a transhistorical Sophia, they understood themselves to be united to transhistorical existence and thus privileged to leap over the mundane realities of historical existence."[4]

One can easily see how the Corinthians might think that their freedom from the transitory and their supposed direct apprehension of the

---

[1] *Essays*, p. 171.

[2] "On the Analysis of the Confessional Formula in I Corinthians 15:3-5," *Interpretation*, XX (1966), 24-25. Conzelmann opposes Schmithals' argument that a group at Corinth has a Gnostic Christology. Walter Schmithals, *Die Gnosis in Korinth* (2d ed.; Forschungen zur Religion und Literatur des Alten und Neuen Testaments, vol. XLVIII; Göttingen : Vandenhoeck & Ruprecht, 1965).

[3] *Earliest Christianity*, trans. Frederick C. Grant (2 vols.; New York : Harper Torchbooks, 1959), I, 334-335.

[4] *Language*, p. 290.

transhistorical Sophia would relieve them from depending on historically conditioned authority. In the face of such an attitude Paul is forced to defend his apostolic vocation and prerogatives (ch. 9); he feels that he is on trial before the congregation (4:2 ff.). The Corinthians, moreover, could even consider themselves "above Scripture" (4:6). To their superior wisdom they could subordinate not only the Scriptures and the apostles but also Christ and the cross. Consequently, what was central to the Christian faith had suddenly become peripheral. In this transhistorical state the Corinthians could claim that "all things are lawful" (6:12), and show contempt for Paul's scrupulous behavior. Sarcastically Paul asks these "free" Corinthians in 9:1, "Am I not free?" Being "free" they could presume to live above temptation (ch. 7). Already they could feel entitled to rule and assume that they enjoyed the riches of the Kingdom. Already they dared to claim full participation in the messianic banquet (4:8 ff.; 11:17 ff.). Confident that they were completely in the New Age, they could refuse to share with Paul the messianic woes which precede the full birth of the eschaton. Presuming to be in the Kingdom already, they could live as if the judgment were in the past and as if there were nothing in the future to bring their works to the test (3:10-17). Their direct union with the transcendent God could prompt unrestrained, highly individualistic expressions of worship and total disregard for the "unenlightened" members of the community (8:1-13). They could be indifferent to the very existence of the church itself (3:16-17). Factionalism which is endemic to such proud assertions and individualistic expressions, Paul knew, could easily destroy the church which he had founded. It is perhaps this kind of spiritual enthusiasm and its attendant ills which evoked Paul's early correspondence to the Corinthians.

A. The Church as an Instrument of Judgment

Two interlocking themes run through Paul's discussion of the church and judgment. First, it will soon be apparent [1] that the church in the Pauline letters is both an instrument and an object of divine judgment. Second, this judgment has both present and future dimensions which are held by Paul to exist in tension. It is only for the sake of an orderly

---

[1] *Infra*, p. 115.

discussion that we shall subsume the eschatological aspects of the judgment under the ecclesiological. This ordering of the evidence, however, reflects in no way the order of Paul's interests and emphasis. Both emphases are so intimately intertwined in Paul's statements concerning judgment that it is impossible to disentangle them without doing violence to them.[1]

Before discussing the role of the church in judgment it is necessary to raise the question: Whence does Paul derive the church's authority for judgment? It is evident in many of Paul's letters that the judgment now breaking forth is God's judgment (Rom. 1:17 f.; I Thess. 2:16; 4:6; II Thess. 1:5-12; I Cor. 3:17). This judgment, however, is closely tied to the Christ event. Paul's statement that "the wrath of God is revealed" (Rom. 1:18), we have seen,[2] is inseparable from his earlier statement, "For I am not ashamed of the Gospel" (Rom. 1:16). Furthermore, those on whom the wrath of God falls for attempting to destroy the church at Thessalonica (I Thess. 2:16) are accused of killing the Lord Jesus (I Thess. 2:15). Also, to the statement that anyone who destroys God's temple (i.e., the church) faces God's destruction (I Cor. 3:16) is coupled the declaration that Christ is the foundation of the church (I Cor. 3:11). God's judgment and the Christ event are so intimately associated in Paul's mind that he can speak alternately and without distinction of standing before the judgment seat of God or of Christ (Rom. 14:10; II Cor. 5:10). In his mind, God's judgment is realized in the Christ event.

It is from Christ whose cross judges the whole world that the apostle and the church derive their authority for judgment. Either explicitly or implicitly, it is in his name that the judgment is pronounced. In I Corinthians 5:4 the gathered church is commanded to perform the

---

[1] G.W.H. Lampe, "Church Discipline and the Interpretation of the Epistles to the Corinthians," in *Christian History and Interpretation : Studies Presented to John Knox* ed. W.R. Farmer, C.F.D. Moule, and R.R. Niebuhr (Cambridge : At the University Press, 1967), pp. 337-361, considers the church's judging function apart from any reference to the eschatological framework of this disciplining act. This is a major weakness of Lampe's treatment. C.F.D. Moule, "The Judgment Theme in the Sacraments," in *The Background of the New Testament and its Eschatology : In Honour of Charles Harold Dodd*, ed. W.D. Davies and D. Daube (Cambridge : At the University Press, 1956), pp. 464-481, alludes to but does not fully develop the future element in Paul's doctrine of judgment. Moreover, he fails to view judgment in the sacraments as a part of Paul's broader understanding of the role that the church plays in the judgment procedure.

[2] *Supra*, pp. 79-83.

judgment on the offender (I Cor. 5:3), and his spirit is present as the church gathers for its judicial act. The judgment, however, is only in the name of the apostle exercising his Lord's authority (I Cor. 5:4).

Elsewhere the apostle renders direct judgment but, again, the authority for his judgment is clearly a derived one. Of course, Paul does not always explicitly state that the authority for his judgment rests with the Lord Jesus, nor need he do so. Inherent in his apostolic office reside the power and authority of the sender. He is authorized to represent the one who commissioned him.[1] It is in this authority that Paul is empowered to judge (I Cor. 5:3 f.) as well as to do signs, wonders, and mighty works (II Cor. 12:12). In places, but not universally, the authority for judgment is mentioned along with the judgment pronouncement. In I Corinthians 5:3 f. Paul states that he has pronounced judgment in the name of the Lord Jesus on the offender. Likewise in I Corinthians 16:22 Paul pronounces judgment directly—"If anyone does not love the Lord, let him be $\dot{\alpha}\nu\dot{\alpha}\theta\epsilon\mu\alpha$ "— and then invokes the name of the Lord—"Our Lord come ($M\alpha\rho\alpha\nu\alpha$ $\theta\alpha$)." Paul, as an apostle, possesses the authority to issue commands, but this authority is anchored in his special relation to the Lord Jesus. In II Thessalonians 3:6 Paul commands the "brethren in the name of the Lord Jesus Christ, that you keep away from any brother who is living in idleness." [2] But, in Galatians 1:9 Paul can pronounce judgment in defense of the Gospel without actually invoking the name of the Lord : "If any one is preaching to you a gospel contrary to that which you have received let him be accursed." Thus it is evident that whether or not Paul explicitly recites the name of the Lord Jesus when he pronounces a judgment, by virtue of his conception of his apostolic office, Paul's judgment is in the name of the Lord Jesus nevertheless.

At a number of points in I Corinthians Paul deals with the Corinthian

---

[1] Karl Heinrich Rengstorf, "$\dot{\alpha}\pi\dot{o}\sigma\tau o\lambda o\varsigma$," in *Theological Dictionary of the New Testament*, ed. Gerhard Kittel, trans. and ed. Geoffrey W. Bromiley (Grand Rapids, Mich.: William B. Eerdmans Publishing Company, 1964), I, 407-451. For an excellent survey of the most important literature on apostleship and the problems of background, function, etc., see Wilhelm Schneemelcher, "Apostle and Apostolic," in Edgar Hennecke, *New Testament Apocrypha*, ed. Wilhelm Schneemelcher, trans. R. McL. Wilson (2 vols.; Philadelphia : The Westminster Press, 1965), II, 25-34. Worthy of special mention is the pivotal work of Hans Frhr. von Campenhausen, *Kirchliches Amt und geistliche Vollmacht in den ersten drei Jahrhunderten* (Beiträge zur historischen Theologie, vol. XIV; Tübingen : J.C.B. Mohr [Paul Siebeck], 1953).

[2] See II Thess. 3:14.

propensity to contest his apostolic authority. In response evidently to the accusation that his authority is compromised because he has not known the earthly Jesus, Paul asks rhetorically in 9:1, "Have I not seen our Lord?" He calls on the Day of Judgment to attest to the authority of his office: "The Lord is my judge" (4:4). He cautions the Corinthians against making judgments which have to be reversed: "Therefore do not pronounce judgment before the time, before the Lord comes, who will bring to light the things now hidden in darkness and will disclose the purposes of the heart" (4:5). In the face of Corinthian disrespect for his authority Paul calls on the words of the Lord Jesus more often in this letter than any other (7:10; 9:14; 11:23 ff.). Before those who would judge him (ἀνακρίνουσίν; 9:3) Paul makes his defense. The community, in Paul's mind, has overstepped all bounds of propriety. It has presumed to bring the apostle to trial even before it acknowledged itself to be on trial. It refuses to view his work as it refused to view its own, in light of the final judgment. Throughout this entire discussion Paul examines the church and his own commission from the perspective of the judgment of the cross and of the *parousia* instead of the wisdom teaching of the Corinthians. Thus Paul obviously sees Jesus Christ as the basis of his apostolic authority to judge. Likewise, Paul argues, the church will recognize and accept his authority as an apostle in direct proportion to the degree they recognize and accept the authority of the Lord. It is from the authority of this lordship over the church that both derive their authority.

In our consideration of the judging church we shall see how Paul's discussion is structured on an eschatological model. The church is an instrument of judgment in the present (e.g., I Cor. 5; 6:1-11), and can expect to participate in the future judgment (I Cor. 6:2-3).[1] We now turn to a consideration of some relevant passages.

1. In I Corinthians 5 we see Paul's deep dismay over the church's failure to perform its judicial duties. In verses 9-13 we get a glimpse of the situation in the Corinthian church which evoked Paul's concern.

---

[1] Paul's statement in I Cor. 4:5—"do not pronounce judgment before the time, before the Lord comes "—is not a general prohibition against judging, but rather must be seen in the immediate, polemical context. The one who appoints the apostle, i.e., the Lord, will also judge him (4:4). How ludicrous it is that a church which no longer knows itself as a church under judgment should presume to judge. Even that judgment is in the light of its own "day," i.e., wisdom, and not by the final eschatological Day. It is in this sense that Paul issues his prohibition against judging himself as an apostle.

Here Paul refers to a previous letter (II Cor. 6:14-7:1 ?) in which he advised the Corinthians not to associate with any Christian who is "guilty of immorality or greed, or is an idolater, reviler, drunkard, or robber" (I Cor. 5:11-12). Out of their belief in "realized eschatology," the Corinthians may have objected that a truly spiritual church cannot be defiled by the grossly immoral.[1] Confronted with this defiant church (5:2), Paul pronounces judgment on the backsliding Christian in the name of the Lord Jesus and commands the gathered church to implement the judgment in the "power of the Lord Jesus" (5:4 f.). The judgment has a dual purpose : (a) the cleansing of the community, and (b) the redemption of the individual.[2]

a. We noted above how the Old Testament often speaks of the judgment of an individual offender for the purpose of purifying the community, and how the entire community can be implicated by the sin of one of its members.[3] In Leviticus the death penalty is frequently prescribed for offenses which violate the holiness either of God or of his people. In Leviticus 20:11, for example, we see an allusion to incest : "The man who lies with his father's wife has uncovered his father's nakedness; both of them shall be put to death, their blood is upon them."

In an illuminating article, Otto Betz observes that the formula applied frequently to a gross offender—"that man shall be cut off from the midst of his people" [4]—is used in the Priestly Code to refer to punishment directly inflicted by a human court for the purification of the community.[5] According to the Mishnah, Kerithoth ("extirpa-

---

[1] Hurd, *Origin*, pp. 50-53; 77-78. Lampe, "Church Discipline," p. 344, believes that Paul is especially severe with the incestuous man to show the church the error of its broad and easy tolerance. Thus Paul's severe judgment on the sinner is a hyperbole which for a moment hides his pastoral concern. Since Lampe believes that such a vehement judgment does not square with Paul's pastoral concern, he plays down the harsh aspects of the judgment. Although one must allow for the depth of Paul's pastoral concern, a careful reading of Paul's judgment passages will show that this concern does not blunt his emphasis on the sharpness of the judgment (e.g., I Cor. 11:30; 10:12, etc.). If Paul, as Lampe believes, pronounced an especially vengeful judgment on the incestuous man in order to impress the church with the seriousness of its careless attitude, one might ask why Paul was not more severe with the church itself.

[2] I Cor. 5:7, "cleanse out the old leaven"; 5:5, "that his spirit may be saved."
[3] *Supra*, pp. 58-59.
[4] ‎נכרת האיש ההוא מקרב עמו.
[5] "The Dichotomized Servant and the End of Judas Iscariot," *Revue de Qumran*, V (1964), 52-53.

tions"), 1:2, however, capital punishment is inflicted by God; extirpation is "at the hands of heaven." [1] Later Jewish writings say that God will extinguish serious offenders through sudden or premature death between twenty and fifty years, usually without posterity.[2] Betz argues further that in the time of Jesus, when the Romans limited the judicial authority of the Jews, the "conception of extinction by God found its expression in parenetic speeches or in a curse." [3] The Christian church, Betz suggests, used the curse then as a kind of divine sanction to protect the *kerygma* from the unbelieving world and to purge the community of unfaithful members. The curse served to warn and direct the Christians toward God who knows the hearts of men and whose strong arm can reach all mankind.

Although Betz's article is interesting and in many respects illuminating, one need not accept his thesis *in toto*. It is not necessary, for example, to explain the shift of capital punishment to God as resulting from Roman restrictions placed on the Jews. Given the tendency in Jewish apocalyptic to shift judgment more and more into a realm beyond history, shifting the administration of the death penalty to God might be expected. However, this did not alter the view that was common in apocalyptic circles that God could call upon demons or natural powers to inflict bodily illnesses, paralysis, fever, or even death.[4] Ample precedent exists, therefore, for viewing present affliction or death as God's righteous action to protect the integrity of his covenant with his people. The new element in Paul, however, is his belief that the *final* vindication has already begun.

Paul's concern for the purity of the church resembles not only the emphasis of the priestly writers, but also the preoccupation of the Qumran community with purging the community of unclean members. Since membership in the Qumran sect was considered proleptic membership in the new covenant community of the future, strict discipline was imposed to keep life in the present congregation consistent with membership in the future family. Various degrees of punishment were imposed on offenders from a small fine to total exclusion in order to maintain a state of readiness for the coming Kingdom of God.

---

[1] See Mishnah, Yebamoth, p. 225, כרת בידי שמים.

[2] Betz, "The Dichotomized Servant," pp. 52-53.

[3] *Ibid.*, p. 53.

[4] Emil Schürer, *A History of the Jewish People*, trans. J. Macpherson and S. Taylor (2 divs., 5 vols.; Edinburgh : T. & T. Clark, 1924), div. II, vol. II, p. 133. Cf. Wis. of Sol. 2:24; Heb. 2:14; Weiss, *Der erste Korintherbrief*, p. 131.

Although Paul's concern for the purity of the elect resembles that of Qumran, and although the role of the community and even the cultic setting of I Corinthians 5:3-5 are undeniable, it is too much to draw a direct parallel between the Qumran practice of judgment "by majority rule" and the process in Corinth.[1] Even if through theological arrogance (5:2, 6) or moral failure (5:1) the church neglects to ready itself for the coming Day, judgment comes nevertheless. In I Corinthians 5:12 we see that even though the church has failed to judge those within, judgment through apostolic pronouncement is already a *fait accompli* (5:3, ἤδη κέκρικα). To be sure, Paul asks the community to cooperate by ratifying the action which the Spirit (i.e., the Lord) has already taken through him. Nevertheless, however much it may offend our modern sensibilities, judgment for Paul was not essentially democratic. Käsemann is entirely correct when he says the community possesses "only the right of assent."[2] Implicit in Paul's call for Corinthian "assent" or ratification of the judgment is a summons to a new self understanding. If the church admits the need for continuing judgment, or if it views Paul's announcement as a prolepsis of the future judgment, then it must disavow its pretension to be beyond the judgment in eschatological perfection. If this pretension is surrendered then all grounds for "boasting" are removed.

Whereas we shall see later that Paul is concerned with the salvation of the individual, there is no gainsaying the fact that Paul's primary emphasis in this chapter is on the purity of the community. Paul knew that the case of incest was no mere matter of individual sin; the congregation was implicated in the transgression.[3] Therefore, Paul

---

[1] Sherman E. Johnson, "The Jerusalem Church in Acts," in *The Scrolls and the New Testament*, ed. Krister Stendahl (New York : Harper & Brothers, Publishers, 1957), p. 139. C.K. Barrett, *A Commentary on the First Epistle to the Corinthians* (Black's New Testament Commentaries; London : Adam & Charles Black, 1968), p. 124, also thinks the judgment in I Cor. is democratic, although he makes no link with the Qumran practice. This democratic judgment, he says, is informed by the church's memory of Paul as they "reflect on what they can remember of his convictions, character, and ways, and what they know of his mind in this present matter." Eduard Schweizer, *Church Order in the New Testament* (Studies in Biblical Theology, no. 32; London : S.C.M. Press, 1961), p. 23, likewise emphasizes the democratic character of the judgment through which Paul "is obviously striving to establish the church as the real bearer of responsibility." These positions, however, unduly minimize the power of the apostolic pronouncement.

[2] *New Testament Questions*, p. 71.

[3] Paul devotes eight of thirteen verses (6-13) in this chapter exclusively to the role of the church in the judgment. While he prescribes the action to be taken against the

commands the church to "cleanse out the old leaven" (5:7). In obvious response to the cynical objection of the Corinthians that it is impossible to avoid evil men in this world, Paul asks in 5:12, "Is it not those inside the church whom you are to judge?" Finally, he orders the church, "Drive out the wicked person from among you" (5:13). It hardly needs saying that Paul is calling for these rigorous measures to equip the church to stand in the final Day. The first fruits of the Kingdom are tasted in the present, but these preliminary signs summon the church to special watchfulness. Paul knew that foolish and careless preoccupation with the present manifestations might cause the church to miss the future glory or forfeit it altogether (Rom. 13:11 ff.; I Thess. 5:1 ff.). There can be little doubt that Paul places the church's judging role in eschatological perspective.

While granting the eschatological character of the church's judging role, how is one to understand the action which Paul prescribes? Many scholars, perhaps most, have read the phrase παραδοῦναι τὸν τοιοῦτον τῷ σατανᾷ εἰς ὄλεθρον to mean expulsion or excommunication from the congregation.[1] When the church expels a member from the realm, where Christ rules and hands him over to the realm where Satan reigns, then death is inevitable.[2] One must ask, however, if expulsion inevita-

---

man in verses 1-5, he also castigates the church for permitting such grossly immoral behavior. Paul does not address the individual directly. He makes the church responsible for the man. Lampe, "Church Discipline," p. 354, takes the same position we take here.

[1] E.g., Weiss, *Der erste Korintherbrief*, p. 129; Campenhausen, *Amt*, p. 147, n. 1; Käsemann, *New Testament Questions*, p. 71; and Robertson and Plummer, *A Critical and Exegetical Commentary on the First Epistle to the Corinthians*, p. 99. Hans Conzelmann, *Der erste Brief and die Korinther* (11th ed.; Kritisch-exegetischer Kommentar über das Neue Testament, vol. V; Göttingen: Vandenhoeck & Ruprecht, 1969), p. 118, rightly sees the exclusion as a "dynamistische Zeremonie."

[2] Note in Heb. 2:14 Satan has the power of death, and in John 8:44 he is called a "murderer from the beginning." See also I Tim. 1:20 where Hymenaeus is delivered to Satan so "they" may learn not to blaspheme. While these materials are post-Pauline they reflect a pre-Pauline outlook. For example, the Wisdom of Solomon (1 cent. B.C.) presents a similar view: "through the devil's envy death entered the world, and those who belong to his party experience it" (2:24). The prominence of Satan in this passage, however, in no way suggests that a radical dualism dominates Paul's cosmology. Satan is indeed an uncanny (I Cor. 7:5; II Cor. 2:11) and powerful creature (II Thes. 2:9); he afflicts even those within the church (e.g., Paul himself, I Thess. 2:18); nevertheless, he remains an instrument of God (II Cor. 12:17). Although he is "the god of this world" (II Cor 4:4) his dominion is passing away (I Cor. 10:11; 2:6) and he will soon be trampled under foot (Rom. 16:20).

bly means death for the victim? Has the church expelled the offender mentioned in II Corinthians 2:5-8 who has received punishment from the majority? If so, why has not Satan received his due from him? Why instead is the congregation urged to "forgive and comfort him" so he will not be "overwhelmed by excessive sorrow"? Is the exclusion in I Corinthians 5 more severe than that envisioned in II Corinthians 2? Is the exclusion permanent, or is it coupled with a curse similar to that in I Corinthians 16:22 or in Galatians 1:8-9? If the social ostracization prescribed in II Thessalonians 3:14 means excommunication, why does this expulsion allow for restoration short of death (3:15)? Three different solutions of this exegetical puzzle are commonly offered:

(1) The death of the offender in I Corinthians was forestalled by his repentance; therefore, the exclusion here as elsewhere in Paul has its intended result short of death.
(2) The punishment in II Corinthians 2:5-8 and II Thessalonians 3:14 is not expulsion from the community but temporary exclusion from the Eucharist; therefore, the difference is one of kind not degree.
(3) In I and II Corinthians we have two types of exclusion—one for severe cases of wrong which is coupled with a curse, and the other for less serious offenses. One is permanent; the other is temporary. One is irrevocable and leads to death; the other is revocable after the wrongdoer repents.

The first proposal which solves this exegetical riddle in one swift move has some evidence in its favor. Lampe, for example, identifies the incestuous man of I Corinthians 5:1 with the person in II Corinthians 2:5 who has caused pain not only to Paul as some might expect but "to you all." [1] He believes that the man whom Paul encourages the church to forgive and restore (II Cor. 2:5-11),[2] as well as the one in whom "godly grief" has produced repentance (II Cor. 7:10-12), may be the chastened and remorseful offender of I Corinthians 5. The temporary exclusion of the impenitent sinner from the church and

---

[1] Lampe, "Church Discipline," pp. 350-354.

[2] Paul says, "if anyone has caused you pain, he has caused it not to me, but in some measure—not to put it too severely—to you all. For such a one this punishment by the majority is enough; so you should rather turn to forgive and comfort him, or he may be overwhelmed by excessive sorrow. So I beg you to reaffirm your love for him" (II Cor. 2:5-8).

especially from the Lord's table,[1] Lampe thinks, may have led to his repentance.[2] Although Lampe's solution is neat, it suffers from serious weaknesses. Kümmel's objection to this solution is especially weighty. He says—

> Paul's command to deliver the sinner to Satan (I 5:3 f.; i.e., to exclude him from the congregation) in no wise harmonizes with the mildness of II 2:6 ff. ... It is inconceivable that the Paul who wrote I 6:12 ff.; I Thess. 4:3 ff.; Rom. 13:12 ff., etc., sometime later should have accepted so lightly that gross case of sexual lapse.[3]

If one views I Corinthians 5 in light of 11:30—"that is why some of you are weak and ill, and some have died"—it is difficult to deny that in chapter five Paul is thinking of a real destruction of the flesh and no mere renunciation of the sin of the flesh.

The second solution to our riddle is plausible enough; however, it remains primarily an argument from silence, and for that reason should be accepted only if other alternatives are lacking. One might note that Paul nowhere makes the fine distinction we see here between expulsion and exclusion. That different degrees of punishment do exist, however, none can deny. It is this awareness that leads us to the next alternative.

In light of the evidence, the third proposal is preferable. Paul had sufficient precedent for linking the curse with exclusion. In his extended note on this passage Weiss saw that already in Ezra 10:8 a connection is made between excommunication and anathema.[4] Likewise, the Qumran sect regularly used two types of exclusion, each of which had its own distinctive character and function. First, there was the temporary suspension which allowed the chastened and repentant brother to return to the community. I QS 6:25-27, for example, speaks of a year's suspension for the member who lies about his income, is disrespectful of a brother, or who physically assaults another member of the sect.[5]

---

[1] I Cor. 5:11; cf. Paul's command "not even to eat with such a one." It is more likely, however, that this command applies to all table fellowship. Strack-Billerbeck, *Kommentar*, IV, 304, shows us that in the ban from the synagogue all table fellowship except with wife and children was forbidden.

[2] Lampe, "Church Discipline," pp. 341-342.

[3] Paul Feine and Johannes Behm, *Introduction to the New Testament*, trans. A.J. Matill, Jr. (14th ed.; revision by Werner Georg Kümmel; Nashville, New York: Abingdon Press, 1966), p. 183.

[4] *Der erste Korintherbrief*, pp. 130-133.

[5] Cf. 7:4-25; 8:26-27, and 9:1-23 for a list of offenses and corresponding punishments.

Second, there was the permanent exclusion coupled with a curse; banishment or being "rooted out of the pure thing of the Many" was the functional equivalent of being placed on "death row." CD 9:1 speaks of a man who is anathematized by the community and handed over to the gentiles (instead of the Devil!) to be put to death. Grumbling against the community was sharply penalized: "they shall banish him [i.e., the one who grumbles] and he must never come back" (I QS 7:17). The backslider who uses the promise of the covenant in a selfish way is severely judged:

> May God's wrath and his angry judgment flare up against him for everlasting destruction and may all the *curses* of his covenant stick to him. May God *separate* him for evil, that he may be *cut off* from all the sons of light.[1]

Long before the Qumran materials were discovered, Adolf Deissmann read I Corinthians 5:4 f. in light of the ancient custom of execration.[2] The service culminated in the devotion of a person to the gods of the underworld.[3] In our passage Deissmann sees traces of technical expressions which are adopted from the cursing ritual:

> The phrase "deliver unto Satan that ...," recurring in I Tim. i. 20, corresponds to the formula in the London Magical Papyrus 46:334 ff.: "Daemon of the dead, ... I deliver unto thee (such a man), in order that ...," and even the unobtrusive little word, "with," "in fellowship with," is technical in just such contexts as this .... All of this proves therefore that the apostle advises the Corinthian church to perform a solemn act of execration.[4]

While Deissmann is drawing from materials which are late (4th century A.D.) and while they presume a radical dualism which Paul does not espouse, his point is essentially correct. The delivery unto Satan is tantamount to placing the accused under a curse. The believer is excluded from the body of Christ and placed in the realm of wrath where he receives the punishment which the Law prescribed for his offense (Lev. 20:11).[5] We see, therefore, in Paul two forms of exclusion: (1) the severe form coupled with an anathema (cf. I Cor. 16:22; Gal. 1:8 f.), and the milder form which is temporary (II Thess. 3:14-15; II Cor.

---

[1] I QS 2:18, emphasis added.

[2] *Light from the Ancient Near East*, trans. Lionel R.M. Strachan (4th ed.; Grand Rapids, Michigan: Baker Book House, 1965).

[3] *Light from the Ancient Near East*, pp. 302-303.

[4] Käsemann, *New Testament Questions*, p. 71, rightly identifies the realm of Satan as the realm of the wrath of God.

[5] See my discussion of I Cor. 16:22, *infra*, pp. 142-162.

2:5-11; 7:10, 12-13). While they differ in intensity, they agree in purpose—the salvation of the individual and the purification of the church.

b. While Paul's primary emphasis does not rest on the individual but the church, he is concerned about the future of the offender nevertheless. The apostle hopes that the present judgment, though severe, will forestall the fateful consequences of the last judgment. Consequently, Paul orders the church "to hand over" ($\pi\alpha\rho\alpha\delta o\hat{v}\nu\alpha\iota$) the man for the "destruction of the flesh" ($\ddot{o}\lambda\epsilon\theta\rho o\nu$ $\tau\hat{\eta}s$ $\sigma\alpha\rho\kappa\acute{o}s$) "in order that the spirit may be saved" (5:5). Käsemann believes the salvation of the man is assured because he has been baptized. The community can separate the person, he says, but baptism cannot be nullified.[1] Paul, however, does not understand the sacraments as a *pharmakon athanasias* but as a work of God's righteousness through which he preserves his own valid deed which he has wrought in the Christian.[2] This deed, according to Eduard Schweizer, is the "spirit" of the sinner or the "I" which was conferred at baptism. This "I" represents the totality of the man created through God's sacramental act. This spirit, which is not to be confused with what we call "soul," is more than the sum total of man's powers and potentialities; it is God's work, and it is this work in both the individual offender and the church which is preserved.[3]

W.D. Davies adds a new dimension to this discussion through his study of Paul's use of the word $\sigma\acute{\alpha}\rho\xi$. According to Davies, "flesh" in Paul's thought is the place where sin manifests itself.[4] Although *sarx* is morally neutral, it is the beachhead for sin's attack. Flesh is a "corrupted not corrupting element; the involuntary accomplice to the act of sin but not the criminal."[5] In Paul's acceptance of the Jewish concept of the two *yetzers*, the evil *yetzer* under the power of sin has its headquarters in man's flesh.[6] In the Qumran Scrolls the cosmic struggle between the good and evil spirits, between the sons of light

---

[1] *New Testament Questions*, p. 71.

[2] *Essays*, p. 116.

[3] "Spirit of God," pp. 85-86. Weiss, *Der erste Korintherbrief*, p. 132, errs in reading "destruction of the flesh" as platonic.

[4] "Paul and the Dead Sea Scrolls : Flesh and Spirit," in *The Scrolls and the New Testament*, ed. Krister Stendahl (New York : Harper & Brothers, Publishers, 1957), pp. 157-182.

[5] *Paul*, p. 19.

[6] *Ibid.*, pp. 20-27.

and the sons of darkness, is reproduced microcosmically in man. The evil impulse has its base of operations in the flesh.[1] It is conceivable, therefore, that for Paul the destruction of the flesh of the incestuous man means that after the base of operations is taken away from the enemy, salvation again becomes a possibility for the Christian brother. We see, therefore, that the work of Davies lends additional support to the position of Käsemann and Schweizer.

We have noted in Chapter Two that a preliminary judgment of God's elect was a commonplace in the intertestamental literature.[2] It was commonly believed that the present judgment would forestall the condemnation of the future.[3] It seems probable that Paul, likewise, thought that even such severe punishment, if owned and accepted,[4] could have a positive outcome.

We see from the discussion above that Paul views the offense in I Corinthians 5 as much more than a single case of immorality.[5] The

---

[1] "Paul and the Dead Sea Scrolls," p. 162.

[2] *Supra*, pp. 37-38.

[3] We note, for example, that the Qumran texts also speak of the restoration of the erring brother who is properly punished and duly penitent (I QS 7:18-21).

[4] There is abundant evidence for the belief that the death had to be owned as punishment for sin in order for it to have saving significance. This is already assumed in very early Old Testament tradition (especially II Sam 12:13, but also 24:10; Josh. 7:16-21; I Kgs. 8:33-39). Likewise, Sanhedrin 6:2 of the Mishnah draws on the experience of Aachan (Josh. 7) to urge confession. The condemned is instructed to confess his sin and if " he knows not how to make his confession they say to him, 'Say, May my death atone for all my sins.' " Note that the emphasis falls not on the death but the confession of sin and trouble experienced "this day" so that "in the world to come" the condemned may know an "untroubled existence." Eduard Lohse, *Märtyrer und Gottesknecht* (2d ed.; Forschungen zur Religion und Literatur des Alten und Neuen Testaments, new series, vol. XLVI; Göttingen : Vandenhoeck & Ruprecht, 1963), pp. 32-37, proved the pre-Christian origin of this teaching. Lohse also shows the undeniably close relationship between confession and atoning death among the Tannaites for whom "die Umkehr unbedingt notwendig ist, wenn der Tod Sühnkraft erhalten soll" (p. 50). For Paul also, the aim of the milder form of exclusion is repentance and restoration. In II Thess. 3:14-15 ἵνα ἐντραπῇ is clearly a synonym for repentance. See also II Cor. 2:5-11 where repentance is implied (also *infra*, p. 139). Note that the same tradition was operative in Judaism during the persecution of Trajan (116/117), in Adolf Büchler, *Studies in Sin and Atonement in the Rabbinic Literature of the First Century* (Reissued in Library of Biblical Studies; New York : KTAV Publishing House, Inc., 1967), pp. 203-207. We see, therefore, that though confession is not mentioned by Paul in this context it is probably implied.

[5] Lietzmann, *An die Korinther I-II*, p. 119, n. 43, reads μικρός in 5:6 as a *Stichwort* reflecting the Corinthian view that the case in question is that of only one individual and, therefore, need not concern the whole community. This observation well supports our own study.

indulgence of the man and the indifference of the church both stem from an arrogant or boastful attitude which jeopardizes the work of God, offends the Spirit, and betrays the church's calling as the eschatological community of the Spirit. Paul's call, therefore, for the judgment of the offender requires more than a perfunctory compliance. By pointing to the preliminary character of the church's eschatological experience and thus to the need for continuing vigilance, he demands a change in the church's understanding of the Gospel and of itself.

2. Several ties link I Corinthians 6:1-11 to chapter 5.[1] Not only is I Corinthians 6:1-8 sandwiched between references to specific types of immorality,[2] but also a typically Pauline pattern is manifested here which may be represented as "a-b-a," with "b" appearing as a kind of insertion.[3] Not only do we see a further development of Paul's earlier injunction "not to associate with immoral men" (I Cor. 5:9),[4] but also both chapters contain references to the purity of the church (I Cor. 5:7; 6:11). Most importantly, however, in 6:1-8 as in chapter 5 Paul is dealing with the judging function of the church. It is absurd, therefore, to attempt to justify this order by suggesting that in chapter 6 the husband of the violated woman (5:1) brings the offender to court.[5] In 6:7 Paul plainly states that fraud, not incest, is the offense requiring the church's attention and judgment.

Paul's treatment of the use of heathen courts falls naturally into three parts: (1) 6:1-6 deals with the Corinthian use of the courts to resolve disputes between church members; (2) 6:7-8 shows that both offended and offender are culpable, and (3) 6:9-11 ties the eschatological imperative to the indicative (a) by negatively noting that the *adikoi*

---

[1] Against the view of Heinrich August Wilhelm Meyer, *A Critical and Exegetical Handbook to the Epistles to the Corinthians*, trans. Douglas Bannerman, revised by William D. Dickson (5th ed.; New York: Funk & Wagnalls, Publishers, 1884), p. 127, who says that 6:1-11 is "a new section not connected with what has gone before."

[2] Weiss, *Earliest Christianity*, I, 145. Cf. the reference in I Cor. 5:11 to the one who is guilty of "immorality or greed, or is an idolater, reviler, drunkard, or robber," and the reference in 6:9 f. to the "immoral, idolaters, adulterers, homosexuals, thieves, greedy, drunkards, revilers, and robbers."

[3] *Ibid.*

[4] Hurd, *Origin*, p. 222; cf. Clarence Tucker Craig, "The First Epistle to the Corinthians: Introduction and Exegesis," in *The Interpreter's Bible* (12 vols.; New York, Nashville: Abingdon Press, 1953), X, 69.

[5] J.H. Bernard, *Studia Sacra* (London: Hodder and Stoughton, 1917), pp. 232-247, as cited by Hurd, *Origin*, p. 84, n. 1.

will not inherit the Kingdom of God (vss. 9-11a) and (b) by positively pointing to the implications of baptism (v. 11b).[1]

It is difficult, if not impossible, to know if Paul is referring to one offense, i.e., one lawsuit,[2] or to a general practice.[3] In any case it is not separate, unrelated instances of bad conduct which require Paul's attention, but the entire outlook and style of life of which they are a part. Here as in chapter five Paul deals with life within the church and the relationship of the church to the world (cf. 5:9-13).

When Paul speaks of judging disputes within the church as well as the participation of "the saints" in the future judgment, he is using familiar Jewish concepts.[4] He objects not to the lower ethical standards of the heathen courts,[5] but to the church's own moral and theological failure.[6] In light of continuing research on I Corinthians the dimensions of that failure are becoming more and more obvious.[7] The realized

---

[1] See a similar division in Erich Dinkler, "Zum Problem des Ethik bei Paulus, Rechtsname und Rechtsverzicht (I Kor. 6,1-11)," originally in *Zeitschrift für Theologie und Kirche*, XLIX (1952), p. 169; now in *Signum Crucis, Aufsätze zum Neuen Testament und zur christlichen Archäologie* (Tübingen : J.C.B. Mohr [Paul Siebeck], 1967), p. 206. See Lukas Vischer, *Die Auslegungsgeschichte von I. Kor. 6,1-11, Rechtsverzicht und Schlichtung* (Beiträge zur Geschichte der neutestamentlichen Exegese, vol. I ; Tübingen : J.C.B. Mohr [Paul Siebeck], 1955), pp. 7-19.

[2] Thomas Walter Manson, *Studies in the Gospels and Epistles*, ed. Matthew Black (Philadelphia : The Westminster Press, 1962), p. 241; Werner Meyer, *Der erste Korintherbrief* (2 vols.; Prophezei : Schweizerisches Bibelwerk für die Gemeinde; Zürich : Zwingli Verlag, 1947, 1945), I, 194. Hurd, *Origin*, p. 86.

[3] E.-B. Allo, *Saint Paul, Première Épître aux Corinthiens* (Études Bibliques; Paris : Librairie Lecoffre, 1934), p. 132, believes, I think rightly, that such a restriction is impossible to make in light of the general terms which Paul uses here. Robertson and Plummer, *A Critical and Exegetical Commentary on the First Epistle of St. Paul to the Corinthians*, p. 110, take a similar position.

[4] *Infra*, pp. 129-131.

[5] Against Robinson and Plummer, *First Epistle of St. Paul to the Corinthians*, p. 110. Note that Paul can speak quite positively of the Roman rule (Rom. 13:1-8).

[6] Albert Stein, "Wo trugen die korinthischen Christen ihre Rechtshändel aus ?" *Zeitschrift für die neutestamentliche Wissenschaft*, LIX (1968), 86-90, takes καθίζετε in 6:4 juridically ("Why do you lay them (καθίζετε) before those least esteemed by the church ?") and argues that this verse refers to judicial channels not open formerly to the accused Christian, i.e., the synagogue courts. If what we say is correct then Stein's point is irrelevant.

[7] See Jack H. Wilson, "The Corinthians Who Say There Is No Resurrection of the Dead," *Zeitschrift für die neutestamentliche Wissenschaft*, LIX (1968), 90-107, and Dieter Georgi, *Die Gegner des Paulus im 2. Korintherbrief* (Wissenschaftliche Monographien zum Alten und Neuen Testament, vol. XI; Neukirchen : Neukirchener Verlag, 1964), pp. 1-16, for good summaries of scholarly opinion on the identity of Paul's opponents in Corinth.

eschatology which allowed for all kinds of contradictions is the source of the trouble.¹ Those full of eschatological preoccupation exploit the material resources of their brothers (perhaps on the order of II Thess. 3:6, 13-14). Those who feel victimized object that such eschatological pretensions are used as a pretext to defraud them ($\dot{a}\pi o\sigma\tau\epsilon\rho\epsilon\hat{\iota}\sigma\theta\epsilon$; 6:7) and to deal injustice ($\dot{a}\delta\iota\kappa\epsilon\hat{\iota}\sigma\theta\epsilon$; 6:7). Given the indifference of the "brothers" to the quarrels which do not touch them directly, the injured resort to the civil courts. The strife of brother against brother combined with the failure of the church to mediate the disputes or reconcile the estranged brothers, poses a real threat to the congregation and the success of the mission. Not only, therefore, does Paul see the wrong headed nature of the quarrel and all that it presupposes, the damage the victim suffers, and the loss that will come to the offender, he also knows the potential harm to the eschatological community. Consequently, we see again that Paul views the factuous and divisive spirit of the Corinthians in its corporate, eschatological dimensions.

Paul responds to this problem on all three levels. First he addresses the church.² Drawing from traditions common to Jewish apocalyptic he speaks of the participation of the saints ($\ddot{a}\gamma\iota o\iota$) in the future judgment.³ Paul's argument runs from the greater to the lesser. How silly, he suggests, that those who will soon judge the heathen (or even angels) ⁴ should now turn to the heathen to judge them. Surely, if the church is soon to be involved in decisions of cosmic proportions, it can now judge disputes of trivial dimensions ($\dot{\epsilon}\lambda a\chi\acute{\iota}\sigma\tau\omega\nu$). Is it not ironic,

---

¹ Note, for example, immorality and celibacy (5:1 and 7:1-5) in the same church, are apparently motivitated by the same error.

² The reference to judging disputes within the church (6:1-6) and the admonition to suffer wrong rather than go to court (6:7-8) is probably not so much a graduation from less desirable to higher righteousness as it is an attempt to address all of the relevant people in the way most fitting for them.

³ Mathias Delcor makes a false distinction between the arbitrating function by the "ordinary Christian" and the administration of "spiritual matters" by the "saints"; "The Courts of the Church of Corinth and the Courts of Qumran," in *Paul and Qumran, Studies in New Testament Exegesis*, ed. Jerome Murphy-O'Connor (London : Geoffrey Chapman, 1968), pp. 69-84, especially pp. 77, 84. We know, of course, that *hagioi* is a synonym for the eschatological community, not a designation for "spiritual" leaders (e.g., Rom. 15:26, 31; 1:7; I Cor. 1:2; Phil. 1:1. etc.).

⁴ We need not tarry over the question of whether the church would judge good or bad angels, for the relative righteousness or unrighteousness of the angels does not alter Paul's basic point. Cf. Hurd, *Origin*, p. 184, n. 4, for a good summary of the different positions on this question.

moreover, that those who pretend to possess eschatological fulfilment in the present should be unable to exercise their eschatological function, i.e. judgment.[1] In 6:5 Paul asks with biting sarcasm, "Can it be that there is not a single person among you wise (σοφός) enough to give a verdict (διακρῖναι) in the case of his brother?"[2] Surely, here Paul is taunting those who profess to a wisdom associated with the end of the age (I Cor. 1:18-2:16; 3:18-23; 8:1). Why is it, Paul asks, if they possess eschatological sovereignty (I Cor. 4:8), that they do not exercise it? Paul, therefore, sees judgment here as having broad implications.[3] Even those not directly involved in the dispute have a responsibility to become involved.

In verse 7a Paul turns to the outcome of such factuous behavior. To have lawsuits at all can only mean eschatological loss, or utter defeat (ἥττημα).[4] The strife of brother against brother jeopardizes God's own proper work. It would be better, Paul suggests (7b), to suffer material loss than eschatological defeat. Perhaps Paul knows that the theological outlook of the Corinthians makes no allowances for suffering. James M. Robinson has suggested that the suffering which the Corinthians reject is not subjectivistic or individualistic, but that which is rooted in the earth's incompleteness, its negativity and absurdity. Paul thus found it necessary to reassert "the earthly literalness of suffering...with the eschatological reservation as the inevitable concomitant of that earthiness (I Cor. 4:11-13)."[5] We see, therefore, that while Paul disallows eschatological fullness in the present, he allows for eschatological defeat (cf. ἤδη with ἐστιν, present tense!), and in so doing affirms the eschatological character of the suffering. Not only are the "wise" unwilling to *suffer* wrong, they manufacture it, and worse still, they fail to see how their action undermines their eschatological pretensions.

---

[1] We saw above, pp. 15-16, that the verb "to judge" has a rather broad range of meanings in Jewish thought.

[2] My translation.

[3] See also Conzelmann, *Der erste Brief an die Korinther*, p. 125.

[4] See the only other appearance of this term in Rom. 11:12 where according to Robertson and Plummer, *A Critical and Exegetical Commentary on the First Epistle of St. Paul to the Corinthians*, p. 116, the word means "defeat." The NEB translation, "You already fall below your standard," is much too bland. Dinkler, "Zum Problem des Ethik bei Paulus, Rechtsname und Rechtsverzicht (I Kor. 6,1-11)," p. 209, rightly notes that the defeat is theological not juristic.

[5] "Kerygma and History in the New Testament," in *The Bible and Modern Scholarship*, ed. James Philip Hyatt (Nashville: The Abingdon Press, 1965), p. 130.

Now in verses 9-11 Paul seeks to restore what Käsemann calls the "eschatological reservation"[1] in two ways : (1) He challenges the eschatological certainty of the Corinthians. You do wrong, Paul says, and "you know, don't you, that wrongdoers will not inherit the Kingdom of God" (my translation of 6:8 f.). Paul thus underscores the point that apart from continued vigilance in Christ there is no guarantee of salvation. (2) He speaks of the Kingdom of God as a future inheritance not a present possession. In rapid succession there appear two of Paul's infrequent references to the Kingdom of God (6:9, 10), and both are coupled with a verb in the future tense ($\kappa\lambda\eta\rho\text{o}\nu\text{o}\mu\acute{\eta}\sigma\text{o}\nu\sigma\iota\nu$).

Finally, in 6:11 we have what is undoubtedly a reference to baptism : "You were washed, you were consecrated, you were justified in the name of the Lord Jesus."[2] To the Corinthian appeal to baptism as the gateway to the resurrected life in the present,[3] Paul juxtaposes the demand that comes with baptism. This imperative underscores the "eschatological reservation," and the need for continuing vigilance.

The emphasis on judging internal disputes by the community itself is not unique to Paul of course. Evidence abounds in the Old Testament priestly writings of judgment by the elect.[4] We know that the Qumran

---

[1] So now also Schweizer, "Dying and Rising with Christ," pp. 1-14; Robert C. Tannehill, *Dying and Rising with Christ* (Beiheft zur Zeitschrift für die neutestamentliche Wissenschaft und die Kunde der Älteren Kirche, vol. XXXII; Berlin : Töpelmann, 1967), and others.

[2] Robinson, "Kerygma and History," pp. 123-124, is perhaps correct in making a connection between these verses and I Cor. 1:13-17 where Paul minimizes his role as baptizer and thus disassociates himself from the Corinthian identification with mystagogues who mediate salvation (1:12). He sees 15:3-5 as a corrective, for here Paul speaks of our death with the perfect tense but our resurrection is described with the future tense. He concludes that the Corinthians saw baptism not as the *inauguration* of God's final battle, but as complete victory. Dinkler, "Zum Problem des Ethik bei Paulus," p. 226, fails to see the significance of this tension for Paul when he says, "Der Welt gegenüber *hat* der Christ bereits die $\dot{\epsilon}\lambda\epsilon\nu\theta\epsilon\rho\acute{\iota}\alpha$ (Gal 5,13; 1 Kor 10,29; 2 Kor 3,17), innerhalb der $\ddot{\alpha}\delta\iota\kappa\text{o}\iota$ *ist* der Christ bereits eine $\kappa\alpha\iota\nu\grave{\eta}$ $\kappa\tau\acute{\iota}\sigma\iota\varsigma$ (2 Kor 5,17)" (emphasis added). Moreover, Dinkler's statement that "in der kosmologischen Eschatologie eine existentiale Eschatologie sich ausspricht" (p. 225) is wide of the mark. Existentialized eschatology is at the root of the problem at Corinth; it is unlikely that it is a part of the solution.

[3] Julius Schniewind, "Die Leugner der Auferstehung in Korinth," in *Nachgelassene Reden und Aufsätze* (Berlin : Alfred Töpelmann, 1952), pp. 110-139, is followed here. Schniewind was the first to see that I Cor. 15:12 is a reference to those who claim eschatological fulfilment, and since death is behind them and the life of unmitigated glory is present they say there is no "resurrection of the dead."

[4] Lev. 20:11-18; 24:16, etc.

text, aptly named Manual of Discipline, outlines the judging procedure of the community.¹ In a passage of uncertain date, Midrash Rabbah Exodus calls Israel's judges superior to the heathen simply because Israel judges by Torah :

> Both the heathen and Israel have judges, and you do not know what difference there is between both. It can be compared to a sick man whose doctor paid him a visit and then said to the family : "Give him to eat whatever he wants." When he came to the other he left word : "Take care not to let him eat that and that thing." When he was asked, "The first thou didst allow to eat whatever he wishes, and the second, thou didst forbid certain things," his reply was : "The first has no chance of recovering; for this reason did I allow him to eat what he fancies; but the second will yet live, and therefore did I command strict caution in his diet." Similarly, the heathen have judges, but neither study the Torah nor fulfil it.²

Rabbi Tarphon (c.a. A.D. 100), on the other hand, admonishes Israel against using heathen courts because scripture commands it : "In any place where you find heathen law courts, even though their law is the same as the Israelite law, you must not resort to them since it says, *These are the judgments which thou shalt set before them*, that is to say, *before them* and not before heathen." ³ The Midrash, like Paul, expresses dismay at lawsuits among God's people : "All God's creatures borrow one from another, yet make no peace with one another without lawsuits." ⁴

We see, therefore, that judgment within the community and discouragement of lawsuits between brothers of the faith were common themes of contemporary Judaism. Paul, however, changes the tone of the judgment within the community when he places it in eschatological perspective. The coming judgment gives the present judgment special urgency and added significance. The church which now judges itself does so to keep itself in readiness for the eschatological Day. Then the elect will participate in God's victory and share in his judgment of the world and angels (6:2). It is noteworthy that for the present it is God, not the church, which judges those outside (5:12). In the eschatological Day, however, the victorious church will share in the judgment of those outside (6:2).

---

[1] *Supra*, pp. 43-44. CD 10:4-11; 14:6-12; I QS 6:8-9; 6:24-7:25.
[2] P. 371.
[3] BT, Giṭṭin, p. 430 (emphasis added). Cf. Mekilta, III, 2.
[4] MR Exodus, p. 396.

The participation of the saints in the final judgment and the ensuing rule is also a common theme of Jewish apocalyptic thought and early Christian tradition. Daniel 7:22 speaks of the judgment (דינא) which the Ancient of Days gave to the saints of the Most High.[1] Jubilees speaks of the judgment of the Philistines by the saints. All who escape the sword of the Gentiles which God sends against them will be rooted out in judgment by the righteous. While this reference to judging takes place within history, I Enoch contains allusions to the role of the saints in the Last Judgment. In the coming judgment "shall the kings and the mighty perish and be given into the hands of the righteous and holy" (I Enoch 38:5; cf. 48:9). The writer urges the suffering elect not to be afraid of the sinners, "For again will the Lord deliver them into your hands, That ye may execute judgment upon them according to your desires" (I Enoch 95:3). The elect will also accompany the Messiah when he comes for judgment : " And behold! He cometh with ten thousands of his holy ones / To execute judgment upon all, / And to destroy all the ungodly" (I Enoch 1:9).[2]

We see, therefore, that Paul draws on and reinterprets traditional materials in order to qualify the Corinthian eschatological enthusiasm. He recalls the believers to an existence within a framework of eschatological tension where the emphasis is less on rights than concern for the brother. By his emphasis on corporate responsibility Paul shows

---

[1] Note that the Revised Standard Version of the Bible translates לקדישי עליונין " for the saints of the Most High" which implies that Yahweh does the judging. In 7:22b, however, Yahweh gives the Kingdom to the Saints to rule. This may indicate that the translation should run " to the saints of the Most High." Francis Brown, S. R. Driver. Charles A. Briggs (eds.), *A Hebrew and English Lexicon of the Old Testament*, based on the lexicon of William Gesenius (Oxford : At the Clarendon Press, 1907), p. 1098, prefer "for" or "on behalf of." Cf., however, Gustaf Hermann Dalman, *Aramäisch-neuhebräisches Handwörterbuch zu Targum, Talmud und Midrash* (3d ed.; Göttingen : Verlag von Eduard Pfeiffer, 1938), p. 212, who lists "zu" as the preferred translation of the Aramaic preposition. I prefer to read "to the saints" with the King James Version, James Moffatt (trans.), *A New Translation of the Bible* (New York, London : Harper and Brothers, Publishers, 1922), and *The Bible : An American Translation*, trans. J. A. Powis Smith and Edgar J. Goodspeed (Chicago : The University of Chicago Press, 1931).

[2] See I Enoch 98:12 : "Woe to you who love the deeds of unrighteousness : Wherefore do ye hope for good hap unto yourselves? Know that ye shall be delivered into the hands of the righteous, and they shall cut off your necks and slay you, and have no mercy upon you."

On the absence of any rabbinic references to Israel's participation in the future judgment see p. 65 above.

that the strife of brother against brother is no mere private matter which each one in his own apocalyptic joy can ignore. Through his restoration of the eschatological tension to the church's life Paul also demonstrates that the lawsuit of Christian against Christian is no mere secular quarrel which those full of eschatological preoccupation can disdain. Such factuous behavior carries the gravest implications not only for the individuals concerned, but for the whole church. Consequently, Paul calls on the church to exercise its eschatological prerogative as an instrument of divine judgment. This judgment is to assume its full range of powers—forensic, restorative, mediating, and reconciling. Once again we see, therefore, that Paul forges a strong link between his eschatology and his ecclesiology.

3. In II Thessalonians 3:1-16 we see a milder reference to the community judgment. As in I Corinthians 5 and 6 Paul's view is bifocal. He commands the church to avoid lazy Christians who have deserted his traditions (II Thess. 3:6), and he orders the perpetually idle as well as the busybodies to devote themselves to quiet, constructive labor (II Thess. 3:12 f.). If the slothful reject his instruction then the church is to mark the offenders and ostracize them.[1] Here, as in I Corinthians 5, the prohibition refers to members of the Christian community, not the larger society. Here, as in I Corinthians 5, the prohibition is intended to discipline the irresponsible whose acts threaten the life of the community. We are compelled, therefore, to disagree with Ernst von Dobschütz who says, "... die Motiv dabei ist nicht das pharisäische sich selbst rein erhalten, oder das spätere kirchliche Prinzip der Heiligkeit der Gemeinde, sondern echt apostolisch die heilsame Wirkung auf den betreffenden Sünder." [2] Here, as in I Corinthians 5, we see that the judgment which the church effects is intended to lead to the restoration of the offenders as well as the health of the church. William Neil is entirely correct, therefore, when he says—

> ... it is plain that he regarded the social relationships of individual members as a matter of concern for the whole Church. A man no longer lives for himself once he has entered the fellowship : he is responsible to God and his brothers in Christ .... For the good name of Christ and the inner health of His body

---

[1] We note the similarity of the prohibitive μὴ συναναμίγνυσθαι to that in I Cor. 5:9, 11 : μὴ συναναμίγνυσθαι.

[2] *Die Thessalonicher-Briefe* (7th ed.; Kritisch-exegetischer Kommentar über das Neue Testament, vol. X; Göttingen : Vandenhoeck und Ruprecht, 1909), p. 316.

it is therefore essential that all should feel themselves equally obliged to maintain both.¹

Here, as in I Corinthians 5 and 6, the present judgment is held in tension with the future judgment. Although there are no references to the future judgment in the immediate context, there need be none. The purpose of the entire letter is to deal with the Thessalonian misunderstanding of Paul's earlier proclamation of the imminent Day. Elsewhere Paul aptly holds the need of the Thessalonian church before the light of the eschatological dawn. It is hardly an accident that after one of Paul's most vividly apocalyptic paragraphs (II Thess. 1:5-10), he expresses his hope that the Thessalonians "may *fulfil every good resolve and work of faith* by his power" (II Thess. 1:11; emphasis added). Paul's Gospel had led some not to watchfulness but to quietism. Throughout the letter he shows how this mood is inconsistent with "the traditions" he left and the eschatological imperative. Finally, against this placid manner which ill befits the urgency of the moment, Paul holds the threat of judgment in the present so the lazy may be "ashamed" now ($\dot{\epsilon}\nu\tau\rho\alpha\pi\hat{\eta}$; cf. I Cor. 6:5, $\dot{\epsilon}\nu\tau\rho o\pi\dot{\eta}\nu$). This present embarrassment may forestall the more awesome eschatological shame.

4. In II Corinthians 2:6-11 we see many of the same motifs that we have observed elsewhere in Paul's letters. The corporate dimension of the offense is obvious. The sinner has pained not just Paul but the whole church (2:5). The forensic language ² suggests that a judgment has been held, and a punishment inflicted by "the many." ³ Although it is not explicitly stated that this judgment was executed for the sake of the church, contextual references intimate that such is the case. In II Corinthians 7:11 the Corinthian church manifests a desire to clear itself: ⁴ " For see what earnestness this godly grief has produced in you, what eagerness to clear yourselves, what indignation, what alarm, what longing, what zeal, what punishment." It is probable that Paul's earlier sharp rebuke of the church (II Cor. 2:9) moved the church to take this action.

---

¹ William Neil, *The Epistle of Paul to the Thessalonians* (The Moffatt New Testament Commentary; New York: Harper & Brothers, Publishers, 1950), p. 196.

² Alfred Plummer, *A Critical and Exegetical Commentary on the Second Epistle of St Paul to the Corinthians* (The International Critical Commentary; New York: Charles Scribner's Sons, 1915), p. 57.

³ See I QS 7:20, 24, etc., reference to " the many."

⁴ Floyd V. Filson, " The Second Epistle to the Corinthians : Introduction and Exegesis," in *The Interpreter's Bible* (12 vols.; New York, Nashville : Abingdon Press 1953), X, 294.

As in other contexts, so here also, the chastisement is aimed at redeeming the individual. In this case, the exclusion has had the desired effect; the offender has returned to the church in repentance and Paul urges the church to forgive and restore him fully to the fellowship (2:6 f., 10).

As we have noted elsewhere, Paul here also refers to the discipline in reference to Christ (2:10). Likewise, the allusion to the struggle with Satan may indicate that Paul believes the final eschatological testing has now begun (2:11).

5. At first glance it might appear that Romans 14:1-23 contradicts what Paul says elsewhere. In this passage Paul commands the church not to judge. The verdict the weak have reached concerning the strong and the decision the strong have made concerning the weak threaten to divide and destroy the church. In the face of this contingency Paul asks in 14:10, "Why do you pass judgment on one another?" In 14:13 Paul commands, "Then let us no more pass judgment on one another." Is Paul asking the church to give up its judging function altogether? Apparently so, but re-examination makes this conclusion less certain. Paul is not so much arguing against the performance of the judgment function *per se;* from experience he knows that a broad and easy tolerance can follow the surrender of this function (I Cor. 5). More likely, Paul is discouraging a contemptuous judgment. The question in 14:10 —"Why do you pass judgment on your brother?"— is paralleled by the question that follows—"Or you, why do you despise your brother?" Paul's play on words in 14:13 shows what kind of judgment is needed : "Therefore, let us no longer pass judgment ($\kappa\rho\iota\nu\omega\mu\epsilon\nu$) but come to this judgment ($\kappa\rho\iota\nu\alpha\tau\epsilon$)—not to put (a stumbling block or) an offense in your brother's way." [1] The disdainful judgment of the weaker brother by the strong may lead to the ruin of "one for whom Christ died" (14:15). This judgment of scorn stands in marked contrast to a judgment which is to be given in the spirit of brotherhood (II Thess. 3:14f.) or to a judgment which, although severe, hopes for the salvation of the offender (I Cor. 5:5b). It appears, likewise, that Paul's intention in Romans 14 is not so much to discourage judgment altogether as it is to call for a new concern for the brother. This conclusion accords well with Paul's closing remarks to this section in Romans 15:1-6. There Paul aims for the upbuilding of the church : "let each

---

[1] My translation.

of us please his neighbor for his good to edify him." The judgment of the weak and the strong has been aimed at the ruin, not the salvation of the brother. This kind of judgment may lead to the division or even destruction of the church instead of its edification. Since the strong and the weak judge in their own interests, their judgment has lost its Christocentric focus (15:3). The judgment has been exercised by and for the moment, and, as such, has lost its eschatological perspective. Both parties have forgotten that "we shall all stand before the judgment seat of God" (14:10). We are led, therefore, to disagree with C.K. Barrett who thinks that in this section Paul is arguing against the execution of any kind of judgment. Only Christ's judgment is valid or permissible.[1] While the judgment is in Christ's name and, therefore, is in that sense Christ's judgment, the church is an instrument of that judgment in the present as well as the future.[2]

From I Corinthians we learn that Paul could oppose the misuse of the judging function while commanding its proper use. The apostles, for example, have been appointed directly by God and are judged by God. Paul realizes the necessity of evaluating the trustworthiness of God's stewards (I Cor. 4:2), but he thinks the church goes too far when it finally and irrevocably pronounces "judgment before the time, before the Lord comes" (4:5) on these apostles who are directly accountable before the Lord's judgment. The church oversteps her judicial limits when she seeks a verdict by a "human day" (I Cor. 4:3) against the Lord's apostles who have authority over the church. As such the apostles are accountable not to the church's judgment but to the Lord alone. In the following chapter (I Cor. 5) Paul encourages, even commands, the church to perform its proper judicial function.

Paul's teaching here may, as Dodd claims, apply to a strictly limited set of problems. Thus the general application of Paul's instruction to his thought about Judgment must be applied with care.[3] What is clear, however, is that certain motifs appear in this section which have a wider currency in Paul's judgment thought. Paul's advice to the "strong" in I Corinthians 8 parallels at many points the advice he gives here. He counsels the "strong" and "weak" to use their freedom for mutual upbuilding (14:19; 15:2). In I Corinthians 8:1 he advises the "strong" to use their "knowledge" to edify the church.

---

[1] *Romans*, p. 261.

[2] Cf. *supra*, pp. 115 ff.

[3] *The Epistle of Paul to the Romans*, p. 220.

Just as it is said that love must govern relationships in the church in Romans 14:15, the love of God appears also as a prominent theme in I Corinthians 8:1 f. In both letters, sin against the brother is equivalent to sinning against Christ (Rom. 14:15; I Cor. 8:12). In both passages the conduct of the brotherhood stands in a close relationship to judgment (I Cor. 10:1-12; Romans 14:10). So while it is true that Paul's discussion here may apply to a strictly limited set of problems, the fact remains that the eschatological impulses which generally inform Paul's thought about judgment are present here. While the case of the "strong" offending "the weak" may be an isolated one, the judgment is everywhere visited on those who, like the scornful, tear the fabric of the church itself, who crucify afresh the King of Glory and put him to open shame.

We conclude, therefore, that Paul is not committing a gross inconsistency here, but is merely directing the church in the proper use of its judicial powers. We can say, therefore, that Paul is not opposing judgment in Romans 14 in its entirety but its improper and selfish use.

In summary, we note that Paul sees the church as an instrument of judgment in the present and the future. Christ is the basis of this authority; its goal is the edification and purification of the church, and the redemption of the offenders. The judgment though commanded in some cases is forbidden in others. The church must not presume to judge the apostles who are directly responsible to the Lord, and it must not judge the brothers in a contemptuous way, for the church is not only the instrument of God's judgment, but also the object of his judgment. It will be held accountable for the proper use of its powers. It is to this consideration that we now turn.

B. The Church as an Object of Judgment

The judging church is judged. God's judgment is expressed in and on the church as well as through it. We see this judgment effected in two ways: by the Lord himself and through the apostolic office.

1. In I Corinthians 11:27-34 we see the church experiencing this judgment in the present. Paul brings an impressive array of judicial terms to bear on the Corinthian world-view and celebration of the Eucharist. Δοκιμάζειν (v. 28), κρίμα (v. 29), διακρίνειν (v. 29), κρίνειν (v. 31) and κατακρίνειν (v. 32) all appear in rapid, staccato fashion. Δοκιμάζειν

may refer to the testing of gold.¹ Κρίμα can mean a dispute, a lawsuit, a decision, a decree, or a verdict.² Διακρίνειν may refer to a correct judgment passed, discrimination, or a judicial decision.³ Κρίνειν means to judge in this context,⁴ and κατακρίνειν almost invariably means to condemn, whereas the noun κατάκριμα means doom or final eschatological punishment.⁵ The forensic shading of the passage is unmistakable. The reference is to a judicial event now taking place in the congregation assembled for worship.⁶

This anouncement may have come as a shocking surprise to the Corinthians. If the Corinthians believed that they already enjoyed fully the blessing of the eschatological age,⁷ then it seems likely that they would celebrate the Lord's Supper not as a foretaste of the eschatological feast but as the Messianic Banquet itself. The judgment, therefore, could be assigned a place in the past and the hard lessons of the crucifixion could be forgotten. This, added to the incipient tendency toward individualism, could have led each member of the congregation to eat only to satisfy his own desires. Such behavior was heedless of the needs of the members of the body and insensitive to the special character of the meal itself (I Cor. 11:20 f.). When Paul says the Christians were not "discerning the body" (11:29), he perhaps is speaking on two levels at once.⁸ They are heedless of their ties with and responsibility to the body of believers. At the same time they fail to discern the

---

¹ William F. Arndt and F. Wilbur Gingrich, *A Greek-English Lexicon of the New Testament and Other Early Christian Literature* (a translation and adaptation of Walter Bauer's *Griechisch-Deutsches Wörterbuch zu den Schriften des Neuen Testaments und der übrigen urchristlichen Literatur*; Chicago : The University of Chicago Press, 1957), p. 201

² *Ibid.*, pp. 451-452.

³ *Ibid.*, p. 184.

⁴ *Ibid.*, pp. 452 f.

⁵ *Ibid.*, pp. 413, 473.

⁶ Käsemann, *Essays*, p. 119, sees συνερχόμενοι as a forensic term since it "is the acknowledged term in antiquity for the official assembling of the *demos*, the 'people.' " This term, he believes, is taken over by the church to denote the gathering of the church for worship at the Lord's Supper. In this gathered church the judgment takes place.

⁷ *Supra*, pp. 109-112.

⁸ Lampe, " Church Discipline," p. 346, correctly says, " It is particularly hard to tell whether 'the body' which the unworthy do not 'discern' is the community as body of, or in, Christ, or the body of Christ whose death is proclaimed in the Supper, or, as is probable, the two are so closely interrelated as to be indistinguishable from each other in this context. A man who eats and drinks unworthily is guilty of the body and blood of Christ. This suggests that to violate the solemn fellowship of Christ's people ... is to become implicated in responsibility for the death of Christ."

nature of the "bread and cup of the *Lord*" (11:27; emphasis added). The Corinthian debauchery of the Eucharist can hardly be called the *Lord's* Supper (I Cor. 11:20).[1] Since the Eucharist is the means through which the Lord manifests himself—

> ... any worshipper is behaving himself inappropriately at the Eucharist who does not reckon with the self-manifestation of the Lord... Further, he is guilty of "the body and blood of the Lord"—which can have no other meaning than the death of Jesus. In the self-manifestation of the Christ there are only two possibilities open—either to unite with the Christian community in proclaiming the death of Jesus or to unite with the world in bringing it about.[2]

Paul's allusion to the judgment which is already anticipated in the Lord's Supper accords well with the nature of the eschatological Day itself. That Day, as often noted above, signals victory for those who have accepted the judgment of the cross and surrendered to it, but defeat for those who spurn God's righteous deed. If one grants the dynamic character of the Eucharist and the identification of the Christ with his community, and if the description of the offense against the "Body" of the Lord as both meal and church is at all accurate, then it is easy to understand the punishment that follows. Illnesses and even death attest to the *present* reality of the judgment (I Cor. 11:30). In light of I Corinthians 10:1-12, it seems unlikely that Paul believed the sacrament itself carried a special potency.[3] We agree with Lampe, who says—

---

[1] Moule, "The Judgment Theme in the Sacraments," p. 473, suggests that τὸ σῶμα includes both the Lord's body present in some sense in association with the sacraments and the church.

[2] Käsemann, *Essays*, p. 123.

[3] This position is against that of Allo, *Première*, pp. 282-283, who speaks of Paul's belief in a "présence Réelle" which accounts for the "réalisme terrible" of Paul's description of the frightful results of misusing the sacrament. Hans Lietzmann, *An die Korinther I-II* (4th ed.; Handbuch zum Neuen Testament; vol. IX; Tübingen : J.C.B, Mohr [Paul Siebeck] 1931), p. 59, takes a position similar to that of Allo when he says "v. 30 zeigt die Realität der Vorstellung : das φάρμακον ἀθανασίας, (Ignatius, Eph. 20:2) wird bei unwürdigem Gebrauch zum φάρμακον θανάτου." Hurd, *Origin*, p. 136, appears to agree : "Thus here in I Cor. may be a view which is more magical than von Soden allows." Bultmann, *Theology*, I, p. 313, notes two facts which he claims show "how little Paul consciously disavows the idea that the Supper has a magical effect." The above writers appear unmindful of the common belief in Judaism that offense against God or his community could bring illness or death (cf. BT, Shabbath, pp. 153-154; Acts 5:1-11).

It seems more probable that Paul is pointing to the sickness and death of some Corinthians as a divinely inflicted punishment for a grave offense against the Christian society, which implied a direct repudiation of its essential character in its relationship to the Lord whose death was proclaimed at every Eucharistic assembly.[1]

Although we cannot assume the church was free of superstition, Paul's point is that the gift "brings with it the Giver himself." [2] Consequently, it is the judging presence of the Lord and not some magical power of the sacrament which accounts for the illnesses and deaths.[3]

In light of the threatened judgment of the Lord in the present Paul exhorts the Corinthians to judge themselves voluntarily, to accept the judgment in the congregation, and to approach the sacraments with a plea of guilty in order to avoid the wrath of the Lord himself. If the Corinthians refuse to accept the indictment of the Lord's death then the salvation of the Lord becomes judgment. Paul, however, understands even this judgment as grace because its goal is salvation. Paul notes that the Lord will chasten his church so that it will not be condemned ($\kappa\alpha\tau\alpha\kappa\rho\iota\theta\hat{\omega}\mu\epsilon\nu$) with the rest of the world (11:32). If, however, in spite of the chastisement the church persists in its stubborn and defiant ways surely $\kappa\alpha\tau\acute{\alpha}\kappa\rho\iota\mu\alpha$ is a real possibility for the church. The sacraments do not guarantee salvation no matter how culpable the community may be. What C.F.D. Moule says of baptism applies as well to Holy Communion : " ... the baptized Christian is no safer in playing fast and loose with his privileges than were the Israelites who had been 'baptized' in the cloud and the sea."[4]

Three facts emerge from our discussion : (1) As was the case in our consideration of the judgment terminology and themes,[5] and the judging church,[6] so also here, the judgment is related to the Christ-event (cf. 11:26, 27, 32). The Spirit of the Lord himself is present to judge those who by their selfish and greedy manner violate the Lord's body. (2) The present judgment on the church anticipates and, if accepted, forestalls the final condemnation (11:28, 29, 32). (3) Although the judg-

---

[1] "Church Discipline," p. 346.

[2] Käsemann, *Essays*, pp. 124-125.

[3] Moule, "The Judgment Theme in the Sacraments," p. 472, takes essentially the same position taken here.

[4] *Ibid.*, p. 479. Cf. Schweitzer, *Mysticism*, p. 260.

[5] *Supra*, pp. 68-91, 94-108.

[6] *Supra*, pp. 112 ff.

ment affects individuals, it takes place *in* the gathered community and with special reference *to* that community. Käsemann underscores this point when he says—

> We do not by our own lack of reverence, render his gift ineffective, nor turn the presence of Christ into absence. We cannot paralyse God's eschatological action; salvation despised becomes judgment.... Wherever we do not truly partake of him ... according to 10:22 we are provoking the Kyrios to display his power of judgment and death and to meet us as the one stronger than we.[1]

Miss Mattern disagrees with our interpretation at two points. First, she maintains that the judgment manifest in the Eucharist is not a judgment of expiation as most exegetes claim. In a rather simple-minded way she says, "Ist der Mensch 'rein,' dann wird ein zukünftiges Gericht überflüssig, denn das jetzige Gericht hat die zukünftige Strafe vorweggenommen." [2]

Second, Miss Mattern argues that the present judgment does not anticipate the future judgment. Instead, the judgment of the church is juxtaposed to the judgment of the world. Paul, she claims, deals not with παιδεύεσθαι or κρίνεσθαι as anticipation of the κατακρίνεσθαι. The contrast between κρίνεσθαι and κατακρίνεσθαι, she maintains, rests not in the tension between the "Jetzt—Einst" but rather in the *distinction* between different kinds of judgment. She says, "der Zeitpunkt spielt hier nicht *die* Rolle, die beiden Gerichte sind grundsätzlich verschieden." [3] She continues by saying that, "Die Andersartigkeit der Gerichte wird an den verschiedenen Objekten deutlich : Es ist nicht das jetzige Gericht an der Gemeinde, das das künftige Gericht an der Gemeinde vorwegnimmt, *das Züchtigungsgericht* über die Gemeinde steht vielmehr *dem Vernichtungsgericht* über die Welt gegenüber." [4] According to this Zürich dissertation the present judgment points to the special position of the community. The church will be disciplined by its Lord while the world goes to its fate. Miss Mattern concludes by saying, "hier ist das Stafgericht nicht Vorwegnahme des Jüngsten Gerichtes, sondern die *einzige* Strafe für die Gerichten, während die andern dem Vernichtungsgericht entgegengehen." [5]

---

[1] *Essays*, p. 125.
[2] *Verständnis*, p. 102.
[3] *Ibid.*
[4] *Ibid.*, emphasis added.
[5] *Verständnis*, p. 103; emphasis added.

Three objections can be raised against Miss Mattern's position:

(1) Since she takes no cognizance of the problem in Corinth which evoked Paul's response, she can assume that the judgment passages were written to reassure the church. Unlike the world the penitent church looks forward to salvation at the Last Judgment. Although there are certain assurances to be drawn from God's gracious acts, the self-assured Corinthians did not need assurance. They were "puffed up" (I Cor. 4:6; φυσιοῦσθε). Instead of being assured of a special status at the Last Judgment which would lead to still more arrogance, they needed to hear of a judgment that "destroys the wisdom [and arrogance] of the wise" (I Cor. 1:19; cf. 3:19).

(2) Miss Mattern's removal of the temporal tension in Paul's doctrine of judgment is highly speculative. Even if one should grant that Paul contrasts here the victory of the Christian with the fate of the world and that no tension exists between the present and the future judgment, he would still need to reckon with the eschatological tension at other levels of Paul's thought. If this tension is as prominent in his thought and vocabulary as we have suggested above,[1] then it is difficult to understand why Paul would avoid such a theme in a section such as this, which is filled with judgment terminology and themes. Moreover, in I Corinthians 10:1-13 there is no possibility of applying Miss Mattern's schematization. Surely thought of the eschatological future predominates in chapter 10 where the present is tautly strung between a past judgment and the "end of the ages" (10:11).

(3) Miss Mattern ignores the importance of the tension between the cross and the *parousia* for understanding Paul's thought. When Paul speaks of the present judgment he frequently sets it in tension with the *parousia* (e.g., I Cor. 5:5; 11:32), and when he considers the future judgment he often does so in its relationship to the cross (I Cor. 1:18 f.). Moreover, from I Corinthians 11:26—"as often as you eat this bread and drink this cup, you proclaim the Lord's death until he comes"— it seems evident that the Eucharist is celebrated on a temporal plane in the time of the church wedged between the cross and *parousia*.

C.F.D. Moule speaks of the judgment present in baptism, and observes a difference between the judgment expressed in baptism and that experienced in the Eucharist. The forensic nature of the former is absolute and unrepeatable; the other is repeated.[2] The difficulty with

---

[1] *Supra*, pp. 68-91, 94-108.
[2] "The Judgment Theme in the Sacraments," pp. 464-468.

Moule's position is that Paul nowhere mentions judgment in relationship to baptism although for John the Baptist the connection was very close (Mt. 3:4-11). However, if God's wrath is revealed in the cross as we have argued,[1] it is perhaps accurate to say that in baptism one accepts the judgment of the cross and is baptized into Jesus' death. If this be so, then another part of the Corinthian puzzle, i.e., the problem concerning the presuppositions of the errorists, falls into place. The Christians at Corinth may have understood the absolute and unrepeatable judgment of baptism as the final judgment. Once that judgment was accepted the Corinthians could not grasp the reality of or the need for a continuing Judgment between the times. Since they had "died with Christ" they could not understand the Eucharist as a repeated proclamation of the Lord's death (judgment) until his coming again (victory). Rather, with the experience of death behind them, they mistakenly believed the victory was already fully realized. Thus it is easy to understand why Paul attempts to restore the emphasis on the Lord's judging and saving work as it is seen in the present as well as on the final eschatological Day.

2. The church also experiences the present judgment through the apostolic office. Our study will focus on I Corinthians 16:22 where perhaps most clearly we have a present judgment on the church through apostolic pronouncement. In our treatment of the expression, εἴ τις οὐ φιλεῖ τὸν κύριον, ἤτω ἀνάθεμα, μαράν αθά (16:22), we shall treat the questions regarding (a) background and (b) the broader and more immediate contexts. Our consideration necessarily must be confined to the points relevant to this study.

a. Central to any study of this passage is a consideration of the background of the word *anathema*. Used in the Septuagint as a translation for חרם, the noun ἀνάθεμα can designate that which is dedicated for holy or sacrificial use and thus set apart for destruction (Lev. 27:28-29), that which is forbidden (e.g., spoil; Deut. 13:17), or that which is "delivered up to divine wrath, dedicated to destruction and brought under a divine curse."[2] The verb ἀναθεματίζειν most often refers to the infliction of total destruction in holy war (Num. 21:2; Deut. 13:15;

---

[1] *Supra*, pp. 78-83.

[2] Johannes Behm, "The NT Term ἀνάθεμα" in *Theological Dictionary of the New Testament*, ed. Gerhard Kittel, trans. and ed. Geoffrey W. Bromiley (Grand Rapids, Mich.: Wm. B. Eerdmans Publishing Company, 1964), I, 354. Cf. Josh. 6:16 f.; 7:1-13; Jud. 1:17; Zech. 14:11.

20:17; Josh. 6:20; Jud. 1:17; I Sam. 15:3; II Kgs. 19:11, and I Macc. 5:5). Since the Septuagint uses ἀνάθεμα to translate חרם, it is obvious that for the translators ἀνάθεμα had a precise negative meaning, referring either to the execution of the guilty brother (e.g., Aachan in Josh. 7:1-13), or the death of the enemy (e.g., the Canaanites, Num 21:2).

חרם in the Qumran writings can refer to food banned from the altar (CD 16:15),[1] sacred objects polluted by unlawful contact (CD 6:15), or spoils which are taboo (I QM 18:5). Significantly, CD 9:1 refers to a man guilty of a capital offense who is devoted to destruction: כל אדם אשר יחרים.[2] Chaim Rabin correctly notes that this passage alludes to those anathematized by the community and handed over to the gentiles to be put to death.[3] On the Day of the Lord, however, the holy army itself will destroy (החרם) the enemy of God (I QM 9:7).

The late but nevertheless important rabbinic uses of חרם refer primarily to those banned from the synagogue.[4] In extraordinary cases, e.g., those involving heretics (מינים), the guilty were solemnly cursed in the service of worship and God's punishment was invoked upon them.[5] Levey thinks the ban known to Ezra (10:8)[6] was revived in the first century B.C. to punish cases of apostasy and religious insurrection which the Romans refused to prosecute. Schürer, likewise, believes the ban was used in the first century, although the death sentence had to be ratified by the procurator.[7] While not carrying definitive significance the judgment of both of these scholars has been given additional

---

[1] I.e., man cannot dedicate food for a sacred purpose if he needs the food to eat.

[2] "As for every man who shall be devoted to extermination from human society, a man who ceases to be among men, he is to be executed (להמית) according to the laws of the gentiles" (my translation).

[3] Chaim Rabin (trans. and ed.), *The Zadokite Documents* (2nd ed.; Oxford: At the Clarendon Press, 1958), p. 44, n. 8; Theodor H. Gaster (trans. and ed.), *The Scriptures of the Dead Sea Sect* (London: Secker & Warburg, 1957), p. 112, n. 45, notes Rabin's interpretation on p. 54 (1st ed.) and follows it.

[4] Strack-Billerbeck, "Der Synagogenbann," in *Kommentar*, IV, part 1, 293-333.

[5] Irving Levey, "Anathema," in *The Universal Jewish Encyclopedia*, ed. Isaac Landman (10 vols.; New York: Universal Jewish Encyclopedia Co., Inc., 1939), I, 295.

[6] If a returned exile ignored Ezra's summons to come to Jerusalem in three days his property would be destroyed and he "himself would be banned from the congregation of the exiles" *Ibid*. Lyder Brun, *Segen und Fluch im Urchristentum* (Oslo: Kommisjon hos Jacob Dybwad, 1932), unfortunately is of little help on this problem because he is imprecise in his treatment of different terms. Although he is aware of the need for careful study of the particular nuances a word may carry, the contribution of his work is minimized by his tendency to rationalize the negative implications of the "curse."

[7] Schürer, *History*, div. II, vol. II, pp. 60-62.

support by the Qumran materials to which we referred above. It seems safe, therefore, to conclude that in Paul's time the curse was applied in Jewish circles to persons guilty of serious offenses against the community or against God. Furthermore, while the ban or curse and exclusion from the community were not synonymous, being cursed necessarily entailed exclusion.[1] Whether at Qumran or among the rabbis חרם represented the most severe punishment inflicted on a person, and while its use (especially by the rabbis) did not necessarily involve death it allowed for that possibility. In any case the imposition of חרם was severe, meaning exclusion from the community, restrictions on religious, social, business, and scholarly activity, and possible confiscation of property.[2] In both instances the primary purpose of the curse is to preserve the integrity of the community, and the context in which the curse is pronounced is corporate, or perhaps even cultic. Given the Jewish use of the word in pre-Pauline materials and Paul's familiarity with that background, it is likely that the Jewish use of the word informed Paul's understanding of it. While some may wish to argue for a background in non-Jewish sources [3] or hellenistic Jewish materials, [4] the evidence leads us in another direction.[5]

---

[1] The ban and exclusion are not synonymous, although they are complementary. The Qumran sect followed Ezra in using חרם for the ban or curse (e.g., CD 9:11) but בדל for exclusion (I QS 2:16; 5:1; 5:10; 5:18; I QH 7:12, etc.).

[2] Schürer, *History*, div. II, vol. II, pp. 60-62.

[3] Interestingly enough, Adolf Deissmann, *Light from the Ancient Near East*, trans., Lionel R. M. Strachan (4th ed.; Grand Rapids, Mich.: Baker Book House, 1965), p. 302, sees a parallel between Jewish and "pagan" execrations. In both, the victim is committed to a dark figure of the underworld. From the epitaph of Halicarnassus he cites a grave inscription which reads, "if anyone attempt to take away a stone ... let him be accursed" (p. 303). One must note, however, that in content and purpose the "pagan" curses are strikingly different from the Jewish.

[4] Philo uses $\dot{\alpha}\nu\dot{\alpha}\theta\epsilon\mu\alpha$ twenty five times in all to mean a dedication or votive offering, a sacred object, or act of dedication (see Ioannes Leisegang, *Philonis Alexandrini Opera Qvae Supersunt*. [7 vols.; Berlin: Walter de Gruyter & Co., 1926], VII, part 1, 88-89). Typical of Philo is his statement that the "whole heaven, and the whole world is an offering ($\dot{\alpha}\nu\dot{\alpha}\theta\epsilon\mu\alpha$) dedicated to God" (On Dreams, V, 429). Nowhere does Philo use this term to refer to a sentence pronounced on an immoral act. For Philo $\kappa\alpha\tau\alpha\rho\hat{\alpha}\sigma\theta\alpha\iota$ or one of its compounds frequently designates the curse; however, even this word lacks the strong moral seriousness it has for Paul (Gal. 3:10, 13; Rom. 12:14) and the Septuagint (in over fifty places). Typical of Philo's usage is his commentary on the cursing of the snake in Gen. 3:14: "Let us see how appropriate the curses are which He pronounces upon it. He says that it is cursed from all cattle ... Our irrational faculty of sense-perception, then, is of the cattle kind, and each of our senses curses pleasure as a deadly enemy" (Allegorical Interpretation, I, 375, 377).

[5] In his commentary on Rom. 9:3, Michel, *Römerbrief*, p. 195 says flatly that $\dot{\alpha}\nu\dot{\alpha}\theta\epsilon\mu\alpha$

There is evidence within I Corinthians 16:22 itself which argues for the Jewish background of this term. We know that 16:22 is pre-Pauline from (1) the use of φιλεῖ only here by Paul to refer to love for the Lord,[1] and (2) Paul's use of μαράν αθά (or μαράνα θά) only here to denote Christ's presence or coming. Kuhn cogently argues that μαράν αθά probably arose

> in a congregation which spoke only Aramaic, and attained there such special significance and so fixed a form that it remained in the original Aramaic when adopted in Greek speaking congregations.[2]

The likely origin of this formula ("If anyone does not love the Lord...") in the Palestinian church adds further weight to our conclusion that ἀνάθεμα must be seen in light of its Jewish background.

If one grants that the more immediate background of I Corinthians 16:22 is in pre-Pauline Christian tradition the question emerges as to the structure and use of the formula in the primitive Christian community. This brings us then to the second part of our treatment.

b. Hans Lietzmann claims that both the pre-Pauline and Pauline *Sitz im Leben* of 16:22 is the Eucharist.[3] The appearance of μαράν αθά in eucharistic materials in Didache 10:6, he believes, parallels its use in I Corinthians. Although Lietzmann acknowledges the post-Pauline date of the Didache, the use of μαραναθά in *liturgical* materials, he believes, attests to the great age of this tradition, even pre-Pauline.[4] He sees μαραναθά in Didache 10:6 as an integral part of the litany prescribed by the rubric in 10:1 (" After you have finished your meal, say grace in this way :..."). The grace ends with the words :

---

is " prophetisch und spätjudisch." There is no reason to believe Michel would assess the reference in I Cor. 16:22 otherwise.

[1] Elsewhere Paul uses ἀγάπη (Rom. 8:28; I Cor. 2:9; 8:3, etc.). See Bornkamm, " Das Anathema," p. 124, who makes the same point.

[2] Karl Georg Kuhn, " The NT Term μαραναθά" in *Theological Dictionary of the New Testament*, ed. Gerhard Kittel, trans. and ed. Geoffrey W. Bromiley (Grand Rapids, Mich. : Wm. B. Eerdmans Publishing Company, 1964), IV, 470. Adolf Deissmann, *Die Urgeschichte des Christentums im Lichte der Sprachforschung* (Tübingen : J.C.B. Mohr, 1910), pp. 27-28.

[3] *Mass and the Lord's Supper, A Study of the History of the Liturgy*, trans. Dorothea H. G. Reeve (Leiden : E.J. Brill, 1953), pp. 186-194.

[4] Bornkamm, " Anathema," p. 125, also believes the post-Pauline Didache preserves pre-Pauline material in 10:6, following Martin Dibelius, " Die Mahl-Gebete der Didache," *Zeitschrift für die neutestamentliche Wissenschaft*, XXXVII (1938), 32-41.

> If anyone is holy let him come.
> If anyone is not [holy], let him repent.
> Maranatha.
> Amen.[1]

Lietzmann has difficulty, however, aligning this tradition with I Corinthians 16:22:

> If anyone does not love the Lord,
>   let him be anathema.
> Maranatha.

He would like to read I Corinthians 16:22 as an exclusion formula preceding the eucharist. In the Didache, however, the μαραναθά *follows* the Supper. Lietzmann argues, however, that the Didache formula is out of sequence; the antiphonal character of the passage, he believes, accounts for its location at the end of the service rather than after "the blessing of the elements and *before* communion." [2] Once he has been able to effect this rearrangement of materials the way is clear for drawing a parallel between I Corinthians 16:22 and Didache 10:6. Since the Didache elsewhere calls for confession of sin before the Eucharist (14:1-3), Lietzmann reads 10:6, "If anyone is not [holy], let him repent," as a call to confession. Drawing on this reconstruction, Lietzmann concludes that I Corinthians 16:22 is also an introduction to the Eucharist which the church begins immediately after the reading of the letter.[3]

Certain questions intrude on Lietzmann's generally accepted thesis. Given the explicit character of the rubrics elsewhere in the Didache (e.g., 10:1), one is puzzled by their silence here, if indeed the liturgy requires the saying of the response *before* rather than *after* the Eucharist. On the contrary, the rubic in 10:1 explicitly orders the saying of the grace "After you have finished your meal." A cursory reading will show

---

[1] My translation from Hans Lietzmann, *Die Didache mit kritischem Apparat* (Kleine Texte, no. 6; Berlin: Walter de Gruyter & Co., 1948), p. 11.

[2] *Mass*, p. 192. Emphasis added.

[3] *Mass*, p. 186, "We are among the assembled Christians at Corinth. A letter of the apostle is being read aloud—it is drawing to a conclusion—Another exhortation to amendment of life, to love and peace and unity. Then the solemn words ring out 'Salute one another with the holy kiss' ... and the Corinthians kiss one another. 'The grace of our Lord Jesus Christ and the love of God and the fellowship of the Holy Spirit be with you all!'—and with thy Spirit' is the response of the people. *The epistle is concluded and the Lord's Supper begins* " (emphasis added).

that the call to repentance is an integral part of the grace. Granting the Palestinian origin of *maranatha* one wonders if the versicle in 10:6 does not fit the Jewish pattern of reciting verses after the benediction in which Israel expresses her hope for future redemption. In support of this view we note that the Eucharist as eschatological prolepsis *ends* on a note of expectation in I Corinthians 11:26 ("... until he comes."). If Didache 10:6 thus remains where it is at the end of the Eucharist, then any attempt to read I Corinthians 16:22 as an exclusion formula patterned after the Didache is abortive. Furthermore, since the only significant word the two passages share is μαραναθά the similarity of the two passages is less than impressive. The presence of what is probably a Greek translation of *maranatha* in Revelation 22:30 (ἔρχου κύριε Ἰησοῦ) in a non-eucharistic context suggests that *maranatha* could be and was used in other ways. Even if the use of *maranatha* began in the Eucharist, there is nothing to prevent Paul from using these sacramental allusions for his dialectical purposes which take place outside the cultic context [1] Finally, the mention of the kiss in 16:20 cannot be read as an eucharistic allusion since the reference to the kiss is a normal part of the conclusion of other Pauline letters (II Cor. 13:12; I Thess. 5:26; Rom. 16:16). We conclude, therefore, that even if I Corinthians 16:22 did originate as a liturgical formula,[2] the evidence will not support the view that it was ever used as an eucharistic exclusion formula, or that the *Sitz im Leben Pauli* was the Lord's Supper.[3]

---

[1] Tannehill, *Dying and Rising with Christ*, showed how Paul uses sacramental materials for didactic (i.e., non-sacramental) purposes.

[2] C.F.D. Moule, "A Reconsideration of the Context of *Maranatha*," *New Testament Studies*, VI (1960), 307-310, argues that Rev. 22:20 may not be eucharistic at all but a sanction on anyone molesting the book itself. *Maranatha* in I Cor. 16:22, therefore, could be a sanction for the ban, and thus a basic reaffirmation of the message of the book itself. If Moule's interpretation stands, then *maranatha* may have been used in an eucharistic context, but there is nothing to restrict its use to such a context.

[3] W.F. Albright and C.F. Mann, "Two Texts in I Corinthians," *New Testament Studies*, XVI (1970), 271-276, conjecture that through crasis and haplography the once continuous text emerged into its present corrupted form. The original text read: *ANAAΘEEMAPMAPAN(A) MAPANAΘA*. Using Rev. 22:20 as a model, their reconstruction of the original reads:

εἴ τις φιλεῖ τὸν κύριον ἤτω If anyone loves the Lord, let it be (i.e. let him respond)—
ἀνὰ ἀθέ ἐμαρ μαρὰν I am coming, said our Lord.
μαρὰν ἀθά Come, O Lord (p. 273).

Ernst Käsemann includes I Corinthians 16:22 in his list of *Sätze heiligen Rechtes* spoken first by pre-Pauline charismatic Christian prophets and now by Paul.[1] These sentences, according to Käsemann, invoke the judgment of God on each man according to his works, follow the *jus talionis* pattern and, like Old Testament prophetic oracles, they are occasionally chiastic in form. The verb in the apodosis, which often repeats the verb in the protasis, is in the future tense. The subject of this future verb is the outstanding, though imminent, Day of the Lord proleptically experienced by the hearer. This Holy Law places the hearer in the sphere of the End of the Age thus allowing him to prepare for the outstanding Day, or to anticipate the fulfillment of the Day before it comes. The content of this Spirit-inspired law is curse and blessing, and thus serves as an eschatological sanction to keep the church on the "beaten track."[2] Only at this point, according to Käsemann, was it possible for the church to live by faith, or do without administrative, disciplinary, or canon law. The delay of the eschatological dénouement brought church law or a new casuistry which undermined holy or eschatological, divine law.[3] While Käsemann accepts the judgment of Lietzmann and Bornkamm that I Corinthians 16:22 is a part of a eucharistic setting, he goes beyond them calling it a sentence of Holy Law. Thus, Käsemann believes, I Corinthians 16:22 proclaims the already present power of the Judge, the anticipation of which stands in the service of grace by granting the subject space for repentance.[4] One should add, that although Käsemann's thesis draws on Lietzmann, its viability does not rest on the soundness

---

While the proposal of Albright and Mann is interesting, one wonders, nevertheless, if it is likely that a copyist could have read ἀνάθεμα (one word) for ἀνα ἀθέ (ἐμαρ) μαρὰν ἀθά (an entire phrase), then transposed what he read to the present form adding a negative. In the absence of any textual evidence for the conjecture of Albright and Mann, we would prefer to try to understand the passage in its present form. If this is possible then the proposal of Albright and Mann is superfluous.

[1] *New Testament Questions*, pp. 66-81. Also included in this category are Gal. 1:19; Rev. 22:18 f.; Lk. 12:18; Mk. 8:38; 4:24; Mt. 5:19; 6:14 f. Hans Conzelmann, *Der erste Brief an die Korinther*, speaks of " sakralen Rechtstil," in his commentary on I Cor. 3:17 (p. 97), and of "Rechtssatz" in his remarks on 14:38 (p. 291). Bornkamm, " Anathema," p. 125, calls I Cor. 16:22 a formula belonging to the sphere of " heiligen Rechts."

[2] *New Testament Questions*, p. 89.

[3] *Ibid.*, pp. 78-81.

[4] *Ibid.*, p. 70.

of Lietzmann's conclusion. For that reason it requires separate treatment.

Although Ernst Fuchs and Rudolf Bultmann have challenged Käsemann's thesis that apocalyptic was the mother of Christianity,[1] until recently Käsemann's thesis concerning the *Sätze heiligen Rechtes* needed a careful assessment. Now, thanks to Klaus Berger, we have a form critical study of New Testament (mostly synoptic Gospel) sentences dealing with reward and punishment.[2] Taking his cue from the introduction to the *Sätze*, the author finds four types of conditional sentences dealing with reward and punishment : (1) those beginning with ὅς *(γὰρ) ἐάν* or ὅς ἄν,[3] (2) those introduced with πᾶς ὁ +present participle,[4] or πᾶς ὅσ(τις) with an apodosis in the future tense, (3) those with ὅταν in the introduction + an imperative or a demand,[5] and (4) those sentences with ἐάν in the protasis + a command.[6] In discussing the content of the forms Berger challenges Käsemann's thesis at every critical point. Types three and four deal repectively with religious behavior and the ordering of community life. Their aim is parenesis, not eschatological anticipation. Although he cannot deny that future references occur, Berger contends that their primary purpose is to match reward with behaviour quite independent of any imminent expectation. The background of these sentences he locates not in prophecy but in wisdom materials. For example, the same logic that rules Mat-

---

[1] " Über die Aufgabe einer christlichen Theologie," *Zeitschrift für Theologie und Kirche*, LVIII (1961), 245-267; Rudolf Bultmann, " Ist die Apokalyptik die Mutter der christlichen Theologie ? Eine Auseinandersetzung mit Ernst Käsemann," in *Apophoreta, Festschrift für Ernst Haenchen* (Beiheft zur Zeitschrift für die neutestamentliche Wissenschaft und die Kunde der alteren Kirche, vol. XXX; Berlin : Alfred Töpelmann, 1964), 64-69.

[2] " Zu den sogenannten Sätzen heiligen Rechtes," *New Testament Studies*, XVII (1970), 10-40. We can do no more than sketch the outline of Berger's thesis here. For supporting evidence see the article itself.

[3] E.g., Mt. 5:19, ὃς ἐὰν οὖν λύσῃ μίαν τῶν ἐντολῶν τούτων τῶν ἐλαχίστων... ἐλάχιστος κληθήσεται ἐν τῇ βασιλείᾳ... Cf. 5:31; 15:5; 23:16.

[4] Especially characteristic of Q : πᾶς ὃς ἀπολύων τὴν γυναῖκα αὐτοῦ παρεκτὸς λόγου πορνείας ποιεῖ αὐτὴν μοιχευθῆναι (Mt. 5:32 = Lk. 16:18; cf., Mt. 7:8 = Lk. 11:10, etc.).

[5] ὅταν προσεύχησθε, οὐκ ἔσεσθε... (Mt. 6:5; cf., Mk. 9:25; Lk. 9:2, etc.). Berger believes this type of sentence parallels the Septuagintal law style.

[6] ἐὰν δὲ ἁμαρτήσῃ ὁ ἀδελφός σου ὕπαγε ἔλεγξον αὐτὸν μεταξὺ σοῦ καὶ αὐτοῦ μόνου (Mt. 18:15 = Lk. 17:3; cf., Mt. 18:16-17; 5:23-24; Mk. 10:10). Curiously, Berger attributes Mark's deviation from the pattern to *later redaction* (p. 17).

thew 10:41 (ὁ δεχόμενος προφήτην εἰς ὄνομα προφήτου μισθὸν προφήτου λήμψεται) he sees also in Proverbs 13:20 (ὁ συμπορευόμενος σοφοῖς σοφὸς ἔσται). Furthermore, he thinks a direct link is probable between Luke 14:11 ("Whoever exalts himself will be humbled and he who humbles himself will be exalted") and the saying of Ahiḳar 149-150 ("If you want to be exalted, my son, humble yourself before God who humbles the exalted and exalts the humble ").[1] Apocalyptic, Berger believes, grew out of wisdom thought and consequently shifted the judgment more and more into God's hands.[2] Nevertheless, the fundamental purpose of the apocalyptic judgment is the same as that of wisdom, namely to effect "einen Ausgleich im Glück und Unglück."[3] Thus, we see, according to Berger, God does not vindicate his righteousness in the judgment so much as he reverses the status man occupies in this world. Berger contends that even the eschatological *Sätze* serve the parenetic function by setting present behavior in a broader context; the concept of imminent expectation may be present but it is incidental to their character. Consequently, he renames the sentences of Holy Law "*Sätzen weisheitlicher Belehrung.*"[4] Since the logic of wisdom teaching is self contained, any contact with early Christian prophets becomes superfluous. It is not the authority of the speaker which obligates, he argues against Käsemann, but the results which are described in the sentence. It is an inward logic, not a powerful eschatological figure, which forms the basis of early Christian parenesis.[5] Of course, if Berger's thesis stands the nerve of Käsemann's position would be cut, and it could have far reaching effects on our reading of I Corinthians 16:22.

Although Berger's article initiated an overdue discussion, it may prove to be of limited value. At four points we find his thesis less than satisfying. (1) By introducing conditional sentences of every description into the sentence category, he reveals a basic failure in logic. Saying all *Sätze* match punishment with deed is hardly the same as saying that all sentences which match punishment and deed are *Sätze*. (2)

---

[1] "Sätzen," p. 22, n. 2.

[2] *Ibid.*, pp. 23-25.

[3] *Ibid.*, p. 31.

[4] *Ibid.*, p. 24.

[5] *Ibid.*, pp. 32-33. Berger allows that the " Amen-Worte " are linked to Jesus as an authoritative seer or apocalyptic wisdom teacher but somewhat incongruously he disallows any such connection with other charismatic figures, e.g., Paul.

Berger assumes too quickly that apocalyptic developed out of wisdom which, as Russell shows, remains an open question.[1] Whether or not one subscribes to Russell's thesis that apocalyptic developed out of prophecy, one must admit that the background of apocalyptic is disputed and uncertain, It seems hazardous, therefore, to build one's entire thesis on such a shaky presupposition. If for any reason that assumption falls then Berger's whole thesis miscarries. (3) By ignoring the context of his materials the author has missed basic checks on the workability of his thesis. For example, if it is the inward logic of these sentences not the authority of the speaker and his Gospel which obligates, why is Paul's insistence on and defence of his apostolic authority so vigorous ? Can the position really be sustained that imminent expectation is incidental to the basic meaning of Paul's sentences in light of the whole of I Thessalonians, Romans 16:20, etc. ? (4) One wonders on what grounds Berger omitted a consideration of prophetic pronouncements made in the name and power of the Lord when they match the punishment with the deeds.[2] For example, in Joshua 7:25 the charismatic leader of Israel pronounces the verdict over Aachan who violates the ban on booty in the conquest of Ai : "How you troubled us; now Yahweh will trouble you." [3] The sentence corresponds to the warning in 7:15 spoken by no less an authoritative figure than the Lord himself. The structure of the warning conforms perfectly to Berger's first category with ὃς ἂν in the protasis + the apodosis : ἐνδειχθῇ, κατακαυθήσεται ἐν πυρὶ καὶ πάντα, ὅσα ἐστὶν αὐτῷ (" Whoever is caught with the accursed thing shall be burned with fire, he and everything he owns "). Note that in the mind of the writer the punishment matches the deed—he who takes the accursed thing is accursed (Josh. 6:18). The introduction of the conditional protasis appears then as a natural result of the shift of judgment to a future beyond history, but the concept of judgment itself is integral to all of Israel's experience and thus appears at all levels. The future judgment necessitates the coupling of the warning with "whoever", "he who," "if anyone" etc., and this adjustment is reflected in all levels of apocalyptic. It is erroneous, therefore, to locate the origin of this type of saying in aphoristic wisdom

---

[1] *Supra*, pp. 28-29.

[2] See, Zech. 7:13; II Chron. 24:20; 34:24 f.; Josh. 7:25.

[3] MT : מה עכרתנו יעכרך יהוה ביום הזה LXX : τί ὠλέθρευσας ἡμᾶς ἐξολεθρεύσαι σε κύριος καθὰ καὶ σήμερον.

materials, though one does not wish to deny the presence of wisdom in apocalyptic thought.

While one may find Berger's conclusions to be of limited value, his article, nevertheless, raises two important questions : (1) What, after all, *is the form* of the sentences of Holy Law ? (2) What is the relationship of the *Sätze* to early Christian prophecy ?[1] While Käsemann nowhere systematically lists his criteria for isolating the sentences of Holy Law, one of his principal guides is the *lex talionis*. One must ask, however, if in using this criterion it is really possible to isolate I Corinthians 16:22 since only in the broadest possible sense does the punishment ($\dot{\alpha}\nu\dot{\alpha}\theta\epsilon\mu\alpha$) match the misdeed (lovelessness).[2] One can hardly use chiasm as a criteria, as Käsemann appears to do in his discussion of I Corinthians 3:17a, since of the sentences he lists only the Pauline ones are chiastic. Given this fact, one might wonder if the use of chiasm is more of a characteristic of Paul's literary style than of early Christian prophetic utterances.[3] On the other hand, according to Käsemann, the parenetic character of II Corinthians 9:6 disqualifies it as a *Satz* even though it is chiastically constructed and future oriented.[4] Now we have the problem of distinguishing clearly between future oriented parenesis and sentences of Holy Law. How can we tell, or can we, whether Matthew 5:19 is parenesis motivitated by Matthew's struggle against antinomianism, or Holy Law directed against libertines ? Even though I Corinthians 16:22 is not chiastic, and does not conform to the *lex talionis* model, it is a better candidate than most for the title " sentence of Holy Law." It's non-Pauline character is clear; it is disjointed in the context; it deals with an apodictic pronouncement; and its juridical character is evident. Whether it originated in early

---

[1] The fact that Käsemann's thesis needs modification at points in no way discredits his work which by his own admission was intended to provoke lively discussion and useful debate. In this regard one must say his work has been eminently successful.

[2] I Cor. 3:17a and 14:38 conform while I Cor. 16:22 and Gal. 1:19 do not.

[3] J.J. Collins, "Chiasmus, the 'ABA' Pattern and the Text of Paul," in *Analecta Biblica*, XVII-XVIII (2 vols.; "Studiorum Paulinorum Congressus Internationalis Catholicus"; Rome : Pontificio Instituto Biblico, 1963,) II, 575-583, shows how Paul can arrange whole blocks of material on the chiastic pattern. See p. 577 for a brief survey of scholarship. Joachim Jeremias, "Chiasmus in den Paulusbriefen," *Zeitschrift für die neutestamentliche Wissenschaft*, XLIX (1958), 145-156, shows this tendency in individual verses in Paul.

[4] *New Testament Questions*, p. 73.

Christian prophecy is uncertain,[1] and whether Paul conceived of himself as a prophet is, as yet, undecided. It is to that issue that we now turn.

If Paul, as Käsemann claims, draws from a tradition of eschatological prophecy, one must ask : to what extent is he representative of that tradition and how does eschatological prophecy inform Paul's understanding of his mission ? The answer to that question will have a direct bearing on how one is to read I Corinthians 16:22.[2] The best place to begin such an investigation is in the letters themselves.

Many of Paul's own remarks seem to suggest a prophetic self-understanding. Munck has claimed that the Apostle's references to "being set apart from my mother's womb," "being called," and "being sent" (Gal. 1:15; Rom. 1:1, 5) parallel the prophetic call.[3] We know also that at many points Paul's activity and experience correspond to those of the prophet. Like the prophet he can both foretell (I Thess. 3:4; Gal. 5:21; Rom. 11 : 25f.; I Cor. 15:51 f.) and forthtell (I Cor. 16:22). He too speaks in the power of the Spirit (I Cor. 5:3) and receives revelations (II Cor. 12:1-5). He does sings and mighty works (II Cor. 12:12). Like Jeremiah he calls himself a fool (II Cor. 11:17), and like the prophets Paul expects to suffer for his message (II Cor. 4:10-11; 6:5-6; 11:24-33). In light of this evidence the question is, did Paul understand himself as an eschatological prophet called to perform a crucial role in the unfolding drama of salvation ? The answer to that question, at least in part, lies hidden within Paul's own explicit allusions to prophecy.

Paul's references to prophecy come in two classes : (1) quotations of or allusions to the prophets of old, and (2) statements about current prophecy. In the first class Paul names the "prophets" of old five times,[4] and either alludes to or quotes from them directly over forty times.[5]

---

[1] At Qumran (I QS 2:4, 11) the priest pronounces the curse and all the initiates say " Amen."

[2] Because of the limited scope of this work we must confine our remarks to Paul's concept of eschatological prophecy.

[3] *Paul*, pp. 11-35.

[4] Rom. 1:2; 3:21; 11:3; 16:26; I Thess. 2:15.

[5] Rom. 1:17=Hab. 2:4; Rom. 2:24=Isa. 52:5; Rom. 2:25=Jer. 9:25-26; Rom. 3:15-17=Isa. 59:7-8; Rom. 3:29=Jer. 4:4; Rom. 9:13=Mal. 1:2-3; Rom. 9:19-21=Isa. 29:16; 45:9; 64:8; Jer. 18:6; Rom. 9:25-26=Hos. 2:23; 1:10; Rom, 9:27-29=Isa. 10:22; 1:9; Rom. 9:33=Isa. 28:16; 8:14-15; Rom. 10:11=Isa. 28:16; Rom. 10:13=Joel 2:32; Rom. 10:15=Isa. 52:7; Rom. 10:16=Isa. 53:1;Rom. 10:20-21=Isa. 65:1-2; Rom. 11:

An examination of these references shows that for Paul almost all the prophets of old did and said pertained to the present.[1] The prophets predicted the coming of the eschatological age which is now dawning (Rom. 1:2; 3:21; 16:26, etc.). They foresaw the rejection of Jesus as the Christ by most of the Jews and the inclusion of the gentiles which is now being realized in Paul's ministry (Rom. 3:29; 9:25-26; 10:20; 15:12). They anticipated the laying of a new cornerstone in the person of Jesus the Christ (Rom. 9:33), and they promised a covenant which is now established in Jesus (II Cor. 3:14-18). They spoke of the present manifestation of God's righteousness (Rom. 3:21), and they wrote about the present.[2] Their murder foreshadowed the death of the Lord (I Thess. 2:15), and their suffering his suffering. In examining these allusions, one is impressed by the preponderance of their predicative or anticipatory character, as well as the absence of any reference to the prophetic pronouncements or sentences of Holy Law. If Paul does see the *Sätze heiligen Rechtes* as prophetic pronouncements, and if he does see the prophet of old as a model for his own ministry, is not this omission surprising? In the Gospels, on the other hand, the prediction *and* pronouncement of the eschatological prophet, John the Baptist, clearly corresponds to the old prophetic model (Mt. 3:4-12). If Paul sees himself as a prophet one would expect here also such a connection between his own pronouncements and those of the prophets. Nowhere, however, does such a connection exist. Could it be that Paul does not view I Corinthians 16:22 as a *prophetic* pronouncement at all?

Of equal importance for our investigation are Paul's allusions to prophecy in his own time. Significantly, all of the references except

---

8=Isa. 29:10; Rom. 11:26-27=Isa. 59:20-21; 27:9; Rom. 11:34=Isa. 40:13; Rom. 14:11=Isa. 45:23; Rom. 15:12=Isa. 11:10; Rom. 15:21=Isa. 52:15; I Cor. 1:19=Isa. 29:14; I Cor. 1:31=Jer. 9:24; I Cor. 2:9=Isa. 64:4; I Cor. 2:16=Isa. 40:13; I Cor. 14:16= Neh. 8:6; I Cor. 14:21=Isa. 28:11-12; I Cor. 15:32=Isa. 22:13; I Cor. 15:54-55=Isa. 25:8; Hos. 13:14; II Cor. 3:14-18=Jer. 31:31; IICor. 6:2=Isa. 49:8; II Cor. 6: 16-18=Ez. 37:27; Isa. 52:11; II Cor. 10:17=Jer. 9:24; Gal. 3:11=Hab. 2:4; Gal. 4:27=Isa. 54:1; I Thess. 5:3=Isa. 13:8 or Jer. 6:24; Phil. 2:10-11=Isa. 45:23, etc.

[1] We see the same exegetical principle in operation at Qumran except that there the eschatological age is still outstanding. Therefore, the prophets speak of the *future* eschatological events.

[2] Even if Rom. 16:25-26 be judged non-Pauline, this passage, nevertheless, reflects a Pauline view.

two appear in I Corinthians.[1] Paul views Christian prophecy[2] as one of the χαρίσματα (12:4). As a rational exercise (14:13-19) this gift of the Spirit remains under the control of the prophet rather than the reverse (14:32). The Christian prophet comforts, encourages, edifies and exhorts the church (14:4,31), interprets the Gospel to the congregation (14:5, 8-9),[3] convicts and/or judges the unbeliever who comes to the service (14:24-25), evaluates the words of other prophets (14:29), and receives and shares revelations (14:30), mysteries and knowledge (i.e., eschatological knowledge, 13:2). Prophecy promotes the wellbeing (εἰρήνη) of the congregation over against disorder. Prophecy belongs to the whole church and, as the Spirit wills, all *may* prophesy "one by one" (14:31). Although all are urged to aspire to prophesy (14:5), as a matter of fact not all are now or ever will be prophets (12: 29-31). Although prophecy ranks second in the list of χαρίσματα (12: 28), it is, nevertheless, provisional. Its apprehension is fragmentary (13:9) and temporary (13:8), and it is so subject to misunderstanding or misuse that it requires testing (14:38). From I Corinthians we get the distinct impression that these modern prophets differ from the prophets of old. The contemporary prophets are local figures who work within and are responsible for the local congregation,[4] whereas the

---

[1] The exceptions are Rom. 12:6 and I Thess. 5:20. The references in I Cor. are : προφήτης—12:28, 29; 14:29, 32, 37; προφητεία—12:10; 13:2, 8; 14:6, 22; προφητεύω—11:4, 5; 13:9; 14:1, 3, 4, 5, 24, 31, 39.

[2] I am aware of a certain inappropriateness in using the adjective "Christian" here since Paul nowhere uses the term. Yet for the sake of convenience I use it nevertheless.

[3] Eduard Schweizer, "The Service of Worship," in *Neotestamentica* (Zürich/Stuttgart : Zwingli Verlag, 1963), pp. 333-343, esp. 340, unduly restricts prophecy to the interpretive function. Günther Bornkamm, "Faith and Reason in Paul's Epistles," *New Testament Studies*, IV (1958), 93-100, makes the interesting suggestion that the Corinthians combined "pneumatic ecstasy" and "rational speech." To counteract the excesses caused by this combination Paul interprets prophecy as rational speech and draws a sharp line between ecstatic speech and prophecy. While Bornkamm's suggestion is fascinating, it is highly speculative; there is little evidence in the text to support or disprove the theory.

[4] Campenhausen, *Amt*, pp. 66-67; Barrett, *Commentary*, p. 295; Heinrich Greeven, "Propheten, Lehrer, Vorsteher bei Paulus," *Zeitschrift für die neutestamentliche Wissenschaft*, XLIV (1952/53), 1-43; Wolfgang Schrage, *Die konkreten Einzelgebote in der paulinischen Paränese* (Güttersloh : Gerhard Mohn, 1961), pp. 183-184, support the position taken here against Adolf Harnack, *Die Lehre der Zwölf Apostel* (Texte und Untersuchungen; Leipzig : J.C. Hinrichs'sche Buchhandlung, 1884), II, 96-97, who saw the prophets as teachers wandering from place to place. In the Didache, but not in Paul, prophets are seen as wandering missionaries.

ancient prophets served primarily to anticipate the present eschatological drama.[1]

Paul clearly distinguishes between apostolic and prophetic activity. In I Corinthians 12:28 Paul says, "God has appointed in the church πρῶτον ἀποστόλους, δεύτερον προφήτας..." The distinction is underscored in 12:29 by means of questions with implied answers : "Not all are apostles, are they ? Not all are prophets, are they ?"[2] Paul also makes a functional distinction between his apostleship and Corinthian prophecy. For Paul, apostolic activity is primarily missionary activity (II Cor. 10:16; Rom. 15:18-24); prophecy is local in character.[3] The apostle founded the Corinthian church (I Cor. 3:5, 10), the prophets build up the church. The apostle is over the church, giving standards by which prophecy is measured, and serving as a model for eschatological behavior.[4] The prophet is within the church giving important guidance. His work is subordinate (though not necessarily inferior) to that of the apostle. Prophecy is an occasional gift which all members

---

[1] Since the eschatological age anticipated by the prophets of old is now arriving the Christian prophet need not forecast but rather interpret the claims of that age for his own time. See E. Fascher, ΠΡΟΦΗΤΗΣ. Eine sprach- und religionsgeschichtliche Untersuchung (Giessen : Alfred Töpelmann, 1927), p. 170; Weiss, Der erste Korintherbrief, p. 322.

[2] Paul assumes these distinctions are common knowledge to his readers. This verse, therefore, goes against Schmithals, Die Gnosis, pp. 268-270, who says the Corinthian Gnostics make no distinction between "speaking in tongues" and "prophesying in the spirit." According to Schmithals, Paul's distinction between the two charismata and his emphasis on the corporate and edifying function of the spiritual gifts is a polemic against the Gnostics. See, Bornkamm, "Faith and Reason," 93-100.

[3] Schmithals, Die Gnosis, p. 268, says, "Apostel und Propheten haben in der Gnosis dieselbe Funktion. Ihr... Unterschied ist lediglich der, dass die zur Mission ausgesandten Propheten den Titel ἀπόστολος tragen können." While Schmithals observation would be true for a later period, in the absence of supporting evidence it cannot be assumed for Paul's time.

[4] Cf., I Cor. 14:37, "If anyone thinks himself to be a prophet or a pneumatic let him recognize that what I write to you is a commandment of the Lord : And if anyone ignores (this command), he is ignored (by God)." Manuscripts P[46] B K pe sy have the imperative ἀγνοείτω for the equally well attested passive ἀγνοεῖται (A G lat or). We agree with Nestle and Aland in reading the more difficult passive in Novum Testamentum Graece (25th ed.; Stuttgart : Württembergische Bibelanstalt, 1964), p. 451. Since the passive is frequently used as a circumlocution to avoid direct mention of the divine name, 14:38 could be translated, "God will not recognize (or, will reject) whoever does not recognize (or, rejects) this" (cf., Käsemann, New Testament Questions, p. 68 ff). Herbert Chanan Brichto, The Problem of the "Curse" in the Hebrew Bible (Journal of Biblical Literature, Monograph Series, vol. XIII; Philadelphia : Society of Biblical Literature, 1963), p. 214,

of the church may possess "one by one."¹ The apostle's mission continues uninterrupted. The apostle is called and sent through a personal meeting with Christ (Gal. 1:1, 16; I Cor. 9:1); the Spirit empowers the prophet (I Cor. 12-14).

The separation of prophecy from apostleship, however, is far from absolute. Since both operate in the power of the Spirit there is overlap. Paul, like the prophet, shares in and interprets mysteries (I Cor. 15:51), and prophets like apostles are instruments of God's judgment. The apostle may prophesy² and he may speak in tongues, but his function, call, commission and position of authority distinguish him from the charismatic prophet. Käsemann is surely right, therefore, when he says, "Selbst der Apostel steht in der Reihe der Charismatiker, durch seinen Auftrag ausgezeichnet, aber einzig mit der Autorität seines Dienstes begabt."³ The prominence his apostolic mission assumes in the arriving Kingdom shows that Paul sees himself as a powerful eschatological figure.⁴ However, given the distinction Paul makes between his own function and authority and that of the Christian prophets, and given the fact that Paul nowhere emphasizes his pro-

---

says the passive form may indicate the automatic self-fulfilling power of the word. This passage, then, should be seen as a judgment pronouncement on a church which has come perilously close to losing its respect for the Lord.

¹ "You can all ($\pi \acute{a} \nu \tau \epsilon \varsigma$), prophesy, one by one, that all ($\pi \acute{a} \nu \tau \epsilon \varsigma$) may learn and all ($\pi \acute{a} \nu \tau \epsilon \varsigma$) receive exhortation" (my translation). Greeven, "Propheten," pp. 4-8, thinks that the first $\pi \acute{a} \nu \tau \epsilon \varsigma$, in 14:31 refers to "alle Propheten" while the second and third $\pi \acute{a} \nu \tau \epsilon \varsigma$ refer to the entire "Gemeinde." While Greeven's conclusion would support our position, the text will not bear the burden he places on it. We side, therefore, with Barrett, *Commentary*, p. 329, who takes "all" in each case to refer to the entire congregation, i.e., "you all." See the clear precedent for occasional prophecy in I Sam. 10:6-13, which speaks of the prophetic activity of Saul in the power of the Spirit. In 10:13 Saul's prophetic activity comes to an end.

² I Cor. 14:6 seems to allow for prophetic activity by Paul: "Now, brethren, if I come to you speaking in tongues, how shall I benefit you unless I bring you some revelation or knowledge or prophecy or teaching?" The $\dot{\epsilon} \acute{a} \nu$ followed by the subjunctive seems to suggest that this is a hypothetical case which Paul introduces for didactic reasons. Being hypothetical, however, does not mean that it is impossible. Note that in 14:18 Paul refers to his ability to speak in tongues. Could it be that the apostle possesses a broader range of charismatic gifts than other believers?

³ "Geist und Geistesgaben im NT," in *Die Religion in Geschichte und Gegenwart* (6 vols.; 3rd ed.; Tübingen: J.C.B. Mohr [Paul Siebeck], 1958), II, cols. 1272-1279.

⁴ Munck, *Paul*, surely established this much, even if one cannot accept the thesis that Paul was the "restrainer" of II Thess. 2:7.

phetic gifts or defends his prophetic call and mission, it is anachronistic if not erroneous to call Paul a Latter Day Jeremiah.[1]

To summarize, our study has shown that I Corinthians 16:22 should be read neither as an eucharistic exclusion formula (Lietzmann), nor as a sentence of Holy Wisdom whose logic is self contained (Berger). Although Käsemann is right that the sentence is a judgment pronouncement, its relationship to early Christian prophecy is unclear. What is clear is that it is Paul's apostolic mission, not his prophetic gifts, which authorizes him to make judgment pronouncements. I Corinthians 16:22, therefore, should be read in its *present* context as an *apostolic* pronouncement of judgment carrying special power to convict the church. Whatever its background, when spoken by Paul the sentence assumes normative and powerful dimensions, because the apostle does in effect re-present the Lord in his Power to judge and to heal.

Given the use of the curse in the conclusion, one must ask what significance can be attached to its location there. If we take our cue from the other letters and read I Corinthians 16:22 as a major concern which briefly surfaces in the conclusion,[2] then we see why the apostle places the formula in this location. It focuses on a major problem in the church, namely lack of love expressed in an individualistic appropriation of the gifts of the Spirit, a selfish use of freedom, and an arrogant boasting of eschatological knowledge or wisdom.

---

[1] Judging from the preferences he shows in his quotations (*supra*, p. 153, n. 5), if Paul does have a favorite prophet he would appear to be not Jeremiah but Isaiah whom he quotes more than three times as often. Note, furthermore, that Paul nowhere mentions Jeremiah by name. Moreover, the birth parallel is not compelling since tradition ascribes special phenomena to the birth of most key *heilsgeschichtliche* figures (e.g., Moses in Ex. 2:1-7).

[2] This tendency is quite obvious in II Thess. where as early as 3:6 Paul commands the church to "keep away from any brother who is living in idleness," followed by the apostolic command in the conclusion to ostracize him (3:14). Likewise, II Cor. 13:10 focuses on the question of authority which dominates chapters 10-13. In Gal. 6:17 it is possible that Paul intends to show that circumcision or the "good showing in the flesh" used to avoid persecution for the cross of Christ (6:12) compares unfavorably with the στίγματα of Jesus which he himself bears on his body. If that be so, Gal. 6:17 is not so unrelated to the central thrust of the letter as it first appears. Erhard Güttgemanns, *Der leidende Apostel und sein Herr, Studien zur paulinischen Christologie* (Forschungen zur Religion und Literatur, vol. XC; Göttingen: Vandenhoeck & Ruprecht, 1966), p. 134, argues that there is a "Realpräsenz" of Christ crucified in the sufferings of the apostle; therefore, to mistreat the apostle is to harm the Lord himself.

Long before this conclusion Paul checks the enthusiasm of the Corinthians with statements about love and the action it requires. Already in 8:1 Paul qualifies the slogan of the Corinthians, "We know that we all have knowledge," by belittling knowledge which "puffs up,"[1] and praising love which "builds up." The statement in 8:2, "If anyone thinks he knows anything, he still does not know what he ought to know," is followed by a reference to what man ought to know : εἰ δέ τις ἀγαπᾷ τὸν θεόν, οὗτος ἔγνωσται ὑπ᾽ αὐτοῦ.[2] The similarity of the protasis in 8:3 to that of 16:22 is often overlooked : εἴ τις οὐ φιλεῖ τὸν κύριον. Here in one letter we have both (all) of Paul's conditional statements referring to love for the deity. Ceslans Spicq taught us that τις οὐ φιλεῖ in 16:22 is a litotes built on the model of Matthew 25:12 and means οὐκ οἶδα ὑμᾶς, "I do not want anything to do with you," or "I do not want to be related to you."[3] If one accepts Spicq's suggestion that failure to love is the rejection of a relationship or refusal "to know" one readily sees a parallel in the protasis, as well as in the apodosis of 8:3 and 16:22. To be anathematized is equivalent to being unrelated to, or cut off from the Lord (cf., Rom. 9:3), or, in the language of 8:3, to being unkown. The *anathema* removes those from the Lord's community who have repudiated their relationship with each other and the Lord. To be anathematized is to be unknown, or to suffer a broken relationship. Conversely, to be known by the Lord is the functional opposite of *anathema*. One means exclusion and ruin; the other means inclusion and salvation. I Corinthians 16:22 and 8:3 are, therefore, the convex and concave of the same lens—one is positive in character, the other negative; one is from pre-Pauline Christian tradition, the other is a creation of Paul. We see, therefore, that "knowing" for Paul was inescapably relational in character and love was endemic to its true expression. Consequently, this interpretation radically qualified the Corinthian tendency to view the possession of wisdom as an individualistic, esoteric experience.[4]

I Corinthians 14:38, "If anyone does not know [this], he is not

---

[1] We recall, of course, the relationship of γνῶσις and φυσιοῖ in 1:17-2:16; 3:18-23 and the special reference to φυσιοῦσθε in 4:6. See also 5:2 where being " puffed up " is synonymous with boasting in 5:6.

[2] "If anyone loves God, he is known by him" (i.e., God).

[3] "Comment comprendre *ΦΙΛΕΙΝ* dans 1 Cor. XVI, 22 ?" *Novum Testamentum*, I (1956), 200-204.

[4] Cf., James M. Robinson, "Kerygma and History," pp. 124-125.

known [by the Lord]," must be viewed in a similar way. It stands at the close of chapters 12-14 to which the chapter on love serves as a fulcrum.[1] Paul tells the prophets that rejection of his instruction as a command of the Lord is tantamount to a repudiation of the Lord himself. Such a renunciation brings renunciation in return. To refuse to "know" is to be "unknown." [2] And to be unknown is to suffer the judgment in the here and now, or is to realize the presence of God through the terror of his absence, or is to experience grace through the wrath.[3]

According to I Corinthians 13:1-13, love qualifies, directs and outlasts all of the *charismata* which the Corinthians claim as evidence of complete eschatological absorption. Sandwiched between Paul's discussion of spiritual gifts in chapters twelve and fourteen, Paul's chapter on love forms the nucleus of this entire section. Likewise, love, not the *charismata*, should serve as the organizing center of all eschatological behavior. Contrary to the Corinthian view, the gifts of the Spirit are provisional and temporary; *agape* is ultimate.[4] Moreover, when Paul describes how love acts toward the brother (13:4-7), not how it feels to love, he underscores the relational character of the love itself.

As a part of his final eschatological instruction to the church, Paul says, "Watch! Stand fast in the faith! Be strong ($\dot{\alpha}\nu\delta\rho\iota\zeta\epsilon\sigma\theta\epsilon$, lit. "be men!") ! Overcome! Let all that you do be *done in love*" (16:13-14).[5] Here, struggle and love are enjoined for a church which in its

---

[1] Lietzmann, *An die Korinther*, p. 75, rightly sees 14:37-40 as the conclusion of an entire section, chapters 12-14.

[2] Lietzmann, *An die Korinther*, p. 75, "den kennt der Herr nicht, von dem will er nicht wissen." Also, Weiss, *Der erste Korintherbrief*, p. 343. Barrett, *Commentary*, p. 334, is in error in thinking 14:38 merely refers to the lack of inspiration of the man who does not recognize the divine origin of what Paul writes. Against this view see *supra*, p. 156, n. 4.

[3] Weiss, *Der erste Korintherbrief*, p. 387, is perhaps correct in linking 16:22 with 10:1-22 which deals with idolatry and its by-products, i.e., grumbling, immorality and tempting God. Note that idolatry and loveless behavior are linked in both chapter eight and 10:23 ff., and both lead to judgment and possible ruin (10:5, 6, 12, 22). If Weiss' judgment is sound, then our own position is strengthened.

[4] Helmut Koester, *ΓΝΩΜΑΙ ΔΙΑΦΟΡΟΙ*. The Origin and Nature of Diversification in the History of Early Christianity," *Harvard Theological Review*, LVIII (1965), p. 312, says, "*Agape* is the only phenomenon in which the eschatological future is directly present in the Church (I Cor. 13:8-13). *Agape* controls the exercise of any other religious qualities and leaves no room for the demonstration of eschatological fulfilment."

[5] My translation with emphasis.

eschatological bliss had lost a sense of tension that comes from the awareness of living between the times. The church had ostensibly outgrown the need for the basic constituent of Christian community, i.e. love. Love as a fruit of the Spirit (Gal. 5:22) is for Paul fundamentally eschatological; therefore, he viewed the claim of the Corinthians to an eschatological fulfilment without love as a contradiction.

Finally, there is here, as elsewhere, the command to show love toward the brother with the φιλήματι ἁγίω (16:20), followed by Paul's assurance of his own love. Given the situation in Corinth one need not assume this closing admonition and assurance is a mere gratuitous gesture.

It seems clear from the frequency and character of these references that the absence of love or corporate concern is a grave problem at Corinth. The claims of eschatological completion had led to arrogant pretentions of wisdom. The misuse of freedom had hurt other people. The dangerous elevation of ecstatic speech threatened to split the church. Paul interpreted such behavior as an offense against the Lord himself. To fail to love the brother is in effect to refuse to love the Lord (11:27). The apostle thus enjoined struggle and love (16:13-14) for a church which through its eschatological pretensions had lost a sense of living between the times. By making love the basic *charisma* and emphasizing its eschatological character, Paul qualifies the claim of the Corinthians to heavenly bliss. Finally, Paul proclaims the inextricable relationship between knowing God (relational) and loving God (also, relational), and that knowing (i.e., possessing wisdom) without loving is impossible.

I Corinthians 16:22, therefore, is an integral part of an attempt by Paul to address the total situation at Corinth. In this concluding traditional formula, Paul neither singles out a particular adversary,[1] nor addresses *only* those who by accident or design curse Jesus (12:3),[2] nor warns teachers who are misleading the church,[3] nor excludes the unbeliever from the Eucharist,[4] but adresses "believers" whose

---

[1] Spicq, "Comment comprendre ΦΙΛΕΙΝ dans 1 Cor XVI, 22 ?" p. 201, n. 1.

[2] Against Schmithals, *Die Gnosis*, p. 119, stands Birger Pearson, "Did the Gnostics Curse Jesus ?" *Journal of Biblical Literature*, LXXXVI (1967), 301-305.

[3] Against Adolf Schlatter, *Paulus der Bote Jesu, eine Deutung seiner Briefe an die Korinther* (2nd ed.; Stuttgart : Calwer Verlag, 1956), p. 460, who says, "jetzt war das Anathema mehr als eine Drohung; schon jetzt kündete es den neuen Lehrern die Gemeinschaft aus."

[4] Against Bornkamm, "Anathema," pp. 125-126, stands Barrett, *Commentary*, p. 397, who notes that there is nothing "in the limitation *If anyone does not love the*

loveless behavior threatens the very existence of the church (3:17; 11: 27). The *anathema* falls on but is not restricted to those profaning the body in the Eucharist; it includes but is not limited to those who anathematize Jesus; [1] it encompasses but is not confined to those who in their arrogant display of their ecstatic arts hurt the brother and fragment the body of Christ. On these loveless ones the curse brings exclusion from the community and commitment to the realm of the wrath of God.

One must briefly note that Paul frequently links the closing eschatological warning with a reference to the power of his apostolic commission. In II Thessalonians 3:12-13, for example, comes the call to heed the epistolary instruction of the apostle; anyone who disobeys is to be excluded from the church. II Corinthians, likewise, ends with a reference to the authority which the apostle has received from the Lord, and Paul expresses the hope that when he comes he can use this power for "building up" and not for "tearing down" (13:10). Also in I Corinthians immediately before the *anathema* Paul reminds the Corinthians that he writes the final greeting "with my own hand" (16:21). It is possible that the coupling of this verse with 16:22 is intended to forge the same link between the figure speaking and his utterance that we see in other closings. If such is the intention, the importance and power of the utterance are underscored. The force of the judgment pronouncement is further emphasized by the concluding cry, *maranatha*. The Lord has come in the proclamation of the apostle; [2] the Lord will come in his *parousia* to establish and rule over his church.[3] In this judgment pronouncement we see once again how Paul's own eschatological outlook informs his understanding of and his relationship to the church.[4]

Lord that would exclude 'unbelieving outsiders', who, through prophecy, have been led to the confession *God truly is among you* ..."

[1] Cursing God and slander in Ex. 22:27 and Lev. 24:16 were capital offenses.

[2] Käsemann, *New Testament Questions*, p. 70, correctly says, " The charismatic does not merely warn, but proclaims the already present power of the Judge." Our investigation also finds support in Käsemann's statement that here the apostle "as a representative of his heavenly Lord, possesses the authoritative power of blessing and cursing."

[3] One need not go all the way with Kuhn, "μαραναθά," 472, who says מרן אתא meant *either* the confession of the exalted Christ in the community, *or* the cry of the waiting church for its Lord. For Paul, the word could mean *both* "the Lord has come" *and* "the Lord will come " both of which are linguistically defensible.

[4] Note the threat in I Cor. 4:21 : "Shall I come to you with a rod ... ?" Similarly in I Cor. 4:19 Paul says, "I will come to you soon ... and I will find out not the talk

3. This judgment on the church also has a future dimension. In I Corinthians 3:10-17 Paul speaks of the future test and what it portends for the church, but this judgment section is dynamically related to what precedes it as well as to that which follows.

Upon reading chapters 1 and 2 one is struck by the dispatch with which Paul moves to the substantive issue. Over against the Corinthian tendency to subordinate Christ and the cross to a trans-historical *Sophia* Paul places the radically historical proclamation.[1] Gerhard Krodel properly notes how Paul reverses the emphasis in the Corinthian church:

> When in Corinth the gospel was interpreted in terms of divine wisdom which bypassed the revelation of God in history in the cross of Christ, then Paul sets forth the cross of Christ as the criterion of divine wisdom. The question for Paul was not whether, for instance, the golden rule could be interpreted as a regulation of divine wisdom; the problem is rather whether the cross can be accepted as the manifestation of the wisdom of God.[2]

In I Corinthians 3:10-17 Paul sets the wisdom and party loyalties of the Corinthians in eschatological perspective. The command, ἕκαστος δὲ βλεπέτω πῶς ἐποικοδομεῖ may well be an injunction to eschatological watchfulness.[3] Verses 10 and 11 speak of the judgment of man's work that will take place in relationship to the foundation, Jesus Christ. The true measure of authentic works, wisdom, or leadership, Paul says, is not present popularity or success but whether or not they are centered on the Christ of the cross. If they are built on any other foundation they will perish like stubble in the final test of fire (v. 13).[4] No longer is

---

of these arrogant people but their power." It is possible that these passages also assume the power of the apostle to judge just as he also has the power to perform signs and wonders (*supra*, pp. 114-115). See Acts 5:1-11 where Peter pronounces judgment in the power of the Spirit. Schlier, *Der Brief an die Galater*, p. 40, rightly reads Gal. 1:8-9 as a judgment spoken by the Apostle. He observes that Paul's repetition of the curse coupled with the indicative mood of the main verb, proves that Paul had "einen wirklichen Fall im Auge" (p. 40), and " die Vollmacht des Apostels ... das Gericht Gottes nicht nur zu verkündigen, sondern auch zu verhängen (ἔστω und nicht ἐστιν)" (p. 41).

[1] Funk, *Language*, p. 295.

[2] "The Gospel According to Paul," *Dialog*, VI (1967), 102.

[3] Weiss, *Der erste Korintherbrief*, p. 254. Cf. I Cor. 16:13; Rom. 11:21 ff.; Mt. 24:42; 24:43; 25:13, etc.

[4] Jean Héring, *The First Epistle of Saint Paul to the Corinthians*, trans. A.W. Heathcote and P.J. Allcock (London : The Epworth Press, 1962), p. 23, is overly sensitive to the suggestion that Paul speaks here of a purging. Héring objects that there is no purgatory here, but rather a destruction of worthless materials.

wisdom the measure by which Christ is judged, but Christ is the measure by which the community and all wisdom are judged.

It may appear to some as if Paul is speaking only to individuals in this section when he says in verse 15, "If any man's work is burned up, he will suffer loss, though he himself will be saved, but only as through fire." The individual judgment, however, is staged within the framework of the church. Notice, for example, that the judgment section, 3:10-15, is bracketed by references to the church. In verse 9 Paul says, "[Y]ou are God's field, God's building." In verse 16 Paul asks rhetorically, "Do you not know that you are God's temple and that God's Spirit dwells in you?" The foundation which Paul laid, even Jesus Christ, is obviously meant to refer to the foundation of the church (v.11). It is the building, i.e., the church, that will be tested and purged at the last judgment. Each man's reward or loss will stand in direct proportion to the quality of materials he places in the building. Shoddy materials will still allow salvation while suffering loss, but those who seek to destroy "God's temple, God will destroy" (3:17). Judgment of the individual, therefore, takes place with respect to the corporate body.

Certain illuminating parallels to this section of Corinthians appear in the Manual of Discipline. Like Paul, the Qumran community condemned arrogance and praised humility. This praise and blame are especially evident in Brownlee's translations:

> ... none shall walk in the stubbornness of his heart to go astray after his own heart and his own eyes and his own impulsive desire; but EAM is to circumcise in the Community the uncircumcision of desire and the stiff neck, to lay a foundation of truth for Israel (for the Community of the eternal covenant) (5:4-5).[1]

In 4:2-4 the covenanters praise humility:

> The way of the Spirit of truth is to enlighten the heart of man, and to make straight before him all the ways of true righteousness, and to make his heart tremble with the judgments of God, and a spirit of humility and slowness to anger, and great compassion and eternal goodness, and understanding and insight and mighty wisdom which believes in all God's works and leans upon His abundant mercy.[2]

The Manual of Discipline also contains references to the cleansing at the End Time:

---

[1] *The Dead Sea Manual of Discipline*, p. 18
[2] *Ibid.*, p. 14.

> And then God will purge by His truth all the deeds of man, refining for himself some of mankind in order to abolish every evil spirit from the midst of his flesh and to cleanse him through a Holy Spirit from all wicked practices, sprinkling upon him a Spirit of truth as purifying water to cleanse from all untrue abominations and from wallowing in [or, being defiled by] the Spirit of impurity (4:20 f.).[1]

While the Qumran materials do not account for the Corinthian passage, they do illumine it. The manual of the sect fixes its attention with respect to the judgment on the sovereignty of the Most High. Before Him there is room only for humility and obedience. Likewise Paul warns the "wise" Corinthians that they must accept in humility what the judgment portends or face future humiliation and loss. This must have been a shocking announcement to the Corinthians who believed the judgment for them was now in the past.

Since the context of this passage affects its interpretation, we now turn to its consideration. The references to Apollos both preceding and following this passage pose a problem for its exegesis (3:4-9; 3:22; 4:6). How is Apollos related to the problem at Corinth? Even if Apollos' presence in Corinth is not needed to *explain* the problem in the church, given Paul's reference to his presence, how are we to interpret it? In what sense was Apollos in Paul's purview in 3:10-16? The answers to these questions influence to some degree the interpretation of 3:10-16.

Judging from the Acts account, Johannes Weiss concludes that after Paul had broken away from the synagogue in Corinth—

> Apollos was able to approach the Jews once more and to unfold the Gospel in such a way to his adherents that they gained the impression they had something different and higher than they could have received from Paul. The secret of this attraction was the "wisdom" of Apollos, for Paul attempted to justify himself when he renounced "wisdom" in his preaching.[2]

With his superior rhetorical skill and Alexandrian-type scriptural exegesis Apollos could have made his spiritualized message more attractive. One might gather from I Corinthians 4:8 ff. that Apollos' wisdom promised an eschatological blessedness and a transcendent vision with God *hic et nunc*.

If Apollos' influence on the Corinthian church was as pronounced as Weiss believes, Paul does not respond by attacking or belittling

---

[1] *Ibid.*, p. 16.
[2] *Earliest Christianity*, I, 335.

Apollos.[1] Instead, he subordinates both Apollos and himself to the Lordship of Christ. He says, "We are fellow workmen *under God*" (3:9; emphasis added). In this same vein he adds, "[O]ne should regard us as servants *of Christ* and stewards of the mysteries *of God*" (4:1; emphasis added). Paul says, "I have applied all of this to myself and Apollos for your benefit, brethren, that you may learn by us *not to live above scripture*" (4:6; emphasis added). The clear implication of Paul's remark is that the Corinthians are to live *under* scripture as he does. It is obvious from Paul's rebuke of his own supporters (3:5), that he did not attempt to resolve the problems in the Corinthian congregation through a contest of personalities but at the more basic theological level.

If this is a sound appraisal of Paul's response to the threat posed by Apollos' popularity and teaching in the Corinthian church, then 3:10-17 applies quite well to the loyal adherents of Apollos. One need not contend, as does Weiss, that 3:10-17 is addressed to the Peter group, whereas that which precedes and follows applies to the Apollos group. Weiss's position is weakened by the absence of a single reference in 3:10-17 to Peter or his followers. It is more likely, therefore, that this passage refers to the enthusiasts who indeed may be representative of Apollos' position. To these adherents of a "realized eschatology," Paul brings a fresh word of judgment. When Yahweh bares his mighty arm all things will be put under his feet. In the light of that Day special relationships to mystagogues who have replaced Christ will not suffice. For those who submit themselves to anyone less than the Lord of history the Day can only mean threat and loss. Paul stops short of saying the Day means destruction for the baptized, but if they persist in their false loyalties to the point of destroying the church they will be destroyed themselves (3:17). They will share the fate of the enemy of the church (Phil. 1:28), or the enemy of the cross (Phil. 3:18).

Miss Mattern believes that the situation described in 3:15 ff. is different from that in chapters 1 and 2. She claims that the earlier chapters relate the sin of Christians to salvation; chapters 3 and 4 emphasize the usefulness of works in relation to salvation. In Chapters 1 and 2 Paul promises salvation in spite of sin; in 3:15 ff. he promises salvation independent of works. The emphasis in 3:13, she claims,

---

[1] *Ibid.*, p. 337.

is not on the future judgment but rather on the salvation of the Christian in spite of a negative judgment. Since the future judgment is over the *works* of the Christian and not over the *person* himself, it follows that faulty works do not endanger salvation. Since faulty works do not jeopardize salvation, we can infer that the central message of this passage is that man is justified not by works but *sola gratia*.[1]

This biblical scholar further explicates her position by contrasting Paul's position with that of the rabbinic tradition and apocalyptic thought. To the rabbinate the last judgment consisted of weighing good against bad works to see where the sentence would fall; to the apocalyptists the last judgment was concerned with separating the righteous from the condemned. For Paul, however, the judgment decides *what kind* of work the Christian has produced. Therefore, she concludes, any possibility of human anticipation of this judgment is excluded because the Christian cannot know ahead of time if any work is good or bad. Since the Christian cannot know this, he is thrown back on grace for his support.[2]

Several questions can be raised about this position. First, is it permissible to divide neatly chapters 1-4 into two conceptual blocks? The close relationship between chapters 2 and 3 seems assured by the contrast between πνευματικοῖς and ψυχικὸς in 2:14-15 which in turn is tied to a similar contrast in 3:1 between the πνευματικοῖς and the σαρκίνοις. That some natural progression of thought carries forward from chapter 2 into chapter 3 seems assured by the resurfacing of the wisdom discussion in 3:18-20 which last appeared in 2:13.

Robert W. Funk argues, as do we, that chapters 1-4 are to be seen as a basic unity and that 4:1-5 stands in a close relationship to what precedes. Verse 1 is transitional; it restates the unity of the apostles under the lordship of Christ and thus rejects the judgment of the Corinthians.[3] In 4:2-5 it becomes obvious that the Corinthians are disputing Paul's apostolic authority. Paul's reply renews the theme of 2:14-16 and anticipates the ἀπολογία in 9:3. Verse 5 serves as a kind of eschatological climax and conclusion to 4:1-5 while verse 6 summarizes 4:1-5 and may reach as far back as chapter 1.[4] Funk's observations,

---

[1] *Verständnis*, pp. 109 ff.
[2] *Ibid.*, pp. 168 ff.
[3] *Language*, p. 285.
[4] *Ibid.*, p. 286.

therefore, give us added reason for dissenting from Miss Mattern's division of chapters 1-4 into two independent blocks.

In her discussion of 4:1-5, Lieselotte Mattern makes a distinction between judging sin and work. The judgment of sin, she says, must take place in the present to protect the Christian from the future judgment. The judgment of work, however, must wait until the last judgment because the work is not finished. Therefore, she concludes, it would be premature to judge the work in the present. She says—

> Das Gericht über das Werk des Christen, seine Partizipation am Werk Gottes, kann darum erst am Jüngsten Gericht stattfinden, weil auch das präsentische Gericht des Herrn keine eschatologische Bedeutung hätte. Diese Antwort klingt wie eine Blasphemie, aber sie trifft den Kern des paulinischen Gerichtsverständnisses : Ob der Diener seinen Dienst treu und gut ausgeübt hat, kann, wenn der freie verantwortungsvolle Dienst des Christen von Gott ernst genommen wird, jetzt noch nicht beurteilt werden, weil der Diener noch dient und Gott ihm noch Zeit zu diesem Dienst gewährt hat.[1]

This statement ignores the context of Paul's remarks. Paul is not polemicizing against the Corinthians for prematurely judging his works because the final tally of them is incomplete; rather, he is opposing an arrogant and presumptuous attitude which calls into question his apostolic authority.[2] It is also questionable if one can find a neat distinction in this passage between the judgment of sin (present) and the judgment of works (future). Her position that the future judgment decides the relative goodness of the Christian's works, not his salvation or damnation, will not stand (cf. 3:16-17; 9:27).

Second, is it possible except in the broadest possible sense to say that Paul discusses the relationship of sin and salvation in chapters 1 and 2? The word $\dot{\alpha}\mu\alpha\rho\tau\acute{\iota}\alpha$ does not appear at all in these chapters; $\sigma\dot{\omega}\zeta\omega$ appears only in 1:18 ($\sigma\omega\zeta o\mu\acute{\epsilon}\nu o\iota\varsigma$). Surely if Paul were making such a contrast he would have introduced the relevant terms. The discussion in these chapters is not so much on the relation of sin to salvation as it is on the relationship of a false doctrine of salvation to a true one, or on the contrast between wisdom salvation and salvation by the cross.

Third, is the central emphasis of 3:15 ff. the assurance that faulty Christian work does not endanger salvation? In a general sense that

---

[1] *Verständnis*, pp. 185-186.
[2] Nils A. Dahl, "Paul and the Church at Corinth according to I Corinthians 1-4," in *Christian History and Interpretation : Studies Presented to John Knox*, ed. W.R. Farmer, C.F.D. Moule and R.R. Niebuhr (Cambridge : At the University Press, 1967), pp. 333-334.

statement is consistent with the Chistian proclamation and Pauline theology; however, in the present context the statement overlooks the the situation in Corinth which required Paul's immediate attention. Paul did not write this passage to reassure those who feared their salvation was in jeopardy, but he wrote to unnerve those who believed their salvation was assured. What Paul says in 10:12 could apply as well to his argument here. Those who presumed too much were warned : "[L]et any one who thinks that he stands take heed lest he fall."

Fourth, is it true that apocalyptic literature is concerned only with the separation of the righteous from the unrighteous? While it is generally true that after the exile the Jews shifted the purging and condemnatory judgment more and more toward the heathen, in certain circles judgment retained its harsh relevance for the sinners among the elect. As noted above, the Manual of Discipline envisioned a time of cleansing even for God's people.[1] The Damascus Document, likewise, expresses the belief that unfaithful members of the community would be destroyed along with the great mass of perdition : "But as for all those of the members of the covenant who have broken through the boundary of the law : when the glory of God will appear unto Israel they shall be cut off from the midst of the camp" (20:25f.). II Baruch 42:2-3 speaks of the punishment to be visited on Israel : "For lo! I see many of Thy people who have withdrawn from Thy law... To those who have believed there shall be good which was spoken aforetime, and to those who despised there shall be the contrary of these things." IV Ezra 8:55-59 carries a similar theme : " Therefore, ask no more concerning the multitude of them that perish; for having received liberty they despised the Most High; scorned his Law, and forsook his ways... Therefore..."[2] Miss Mattern cannot use the apocalyptic literature, therefore, to argue that the future purging does not apply to the elect.

---

[1] *Supra.*, p. 45.

[2] BT, Rosh Hashanah, p. 64, says, "It has been taught : Beth Shammai says, There will be three groups at the Day of Judgment—one of thoroughly righteous, one of thoroughly wicked, and one of intermediate. The thoroughly righteous will forthwith be inscribed definitively as entitled to everlasting life; the thoroughly wicked will forthwith be inscribed definitively as doomed to Gehinnom.... The intermediate will go down to Gehinnom and squeal and rise again, as it says, and I will bring the third part through the fire, and will refine them as silver is refined, and will try them as gold is tried. They shall call on my name and I will answer them."

In light of the above discussion we find it impossible to accept Lieselotte Mattern's position that chapters 1 and 2 deal with salvation in spite of sin, whereas chapters 3 and 4 deal with salvation independent of works. We have argued instead that, considering the spiritual enthusiasm of the Corinthian church, Paul calls upon them to judge their own work and the work of the apostles in light of the future judgment. Our earlier observation holds, therefore, that in 3:10-17 the same eschatological tension characterizes Paul's doctrine of judgment that we have noticed elsewhere. The wisdom of the cross and the judgment which will be held at the *parousia* are clearly the dominant themes of chapters 1-4.

A long-standing disagreement persists over what prompted Paul to write I Corinthians 10:1-13. The integrity of I Corinthians hinges on how one resolves this issue. A convenient summary of the arguments used to separate 10:1-22 from its context is given by John C. Hurd, Jr.[1] It is argued by many scholars that in 8:1-13 and 10:23-33 Paul is more permissive about eating idol meat than he is in 10:1-22. Paul makes his appeal to conscience on a high ethical plane, allowing that "all of us possess knowledge" (8:1), that "an idol has no real existence" (8:4), and that the Corinthians are to "eat whatever is sold in the meat market without raising any question on the ground of conscience" (10:24). In 10:1-22, on the other hand, Paul's argument reflects a superstitious belief in demons, and a magical concept of the sacraments. The above discrepancies, these scholars conclude, show that Paul wrote these passages at different times favoring different groups in the church. A part of the letter favoring the "strong," or "wise," Gentile Christians is seen in 8:1-13 and 10:23-33 while 10:1-22 favors the more scrupulous Jewish Christians.[2]

Hurd raises some weighty objections to this partition theory. He notes the lack of any manuscript support for such a division.[3] He disallows the belief that different premises stand behind 8:1-13 and 10:1-22 by showing that such statements as "all of us possess knowledge" (8:1) and "an idol has no real existence" (9:4) may be Corinthian slogans which Paul modifies. Paul repeats the first slogan and then qualifies it : "We know that 'all of us possess knowledge.'

---

[1] *Origin*, p. 131.
[2] *Ibid.*, 131-133.
[3] *Ibid.*, p. 132.

'Knowledge' puffs up, but love builds up." Likewise in 8:4 Paul says, "We know that 'an idol has no real existence,' and 'there is no God but one,'" and then adds "however, not all possess this knowledge." [1] Hurd notes that Paul's qualifications of the Corinthians' slogans are wholly consistent with his argument in 10:1-22. Hurd also objects to a second argument, that Paul's use of the Old Testament in 10:1-22 seems "awkward and superfluous" in the present position. He perceptively notes that in Romans 14-15 Paul couples his plea for a brotherly concern for the "weaker brother" with an appeal to the Old Testament for support (15:3). Paul makes the same connection in 8:1-13 and 10:1-22. Moreover, the same eschatological note is sounded in both (I Cor. 10:6, 11; Rom. 15:4).[2]

Hurd seeks to refute the claim that eating idol meat in 8:1-13 and 10:23-33 is a matter of indifference but forbidden in 10:1-22. In both, he argues, the *eating* is a matter of indifference (8:8; 10:19). In the former, however, eating which is injurious to Christian fellowship is forbidden while in the latter eating which establishes fellowship with demons is prohibited (10:20), because it destroys fellowship with God (10:21). Hurd correctly notes that "idolatry and disregard for the 'brother for whom Christ died' (8:11) are co-ordinate sins against God (8:12; 10:22)." [3] It seems accurate, therefore, to say that Paul's arguments in 8:1-13, 10:23-33 and 10:1-22 do not contradict but complement each other.

If Hurd's position is sound, then we gain new insight into the conditions which prompted Paul's statement on judgment in I Corinthians 10:1-13. In I Corinthians 8:1-13 Paul centers on the abuse of freedom which ignores the needs of the weaker Christian. With fine tact, by applying love's imperative to himself, Paul shows the Corinthians what is required of them in this situation: "Therefore, if food is a cause of my brother's falling, I will never eat meat lest I cause my brother to fall" (8:13). Sinning against a newborn Christian, Paul says, is equivalent to sinning against Christ himself (8:12). Later in chapter 9 Paul confesses that it is possible that even an apostle might be disqualified (9:27). Implicit in this admission may be a warning for the "puffed up" (8:1), over-enlightened Christians.

In 10:1-13 Paul forbids the ritualistic eating of idol meat that might

---

[1] *Origin*, pp. 132-133.
[2] *Ibid.*, pp. 133-134.
[3] *Ibid.*, pp. 134-135

lead to fellowship with demons and even to idolatry. In 8:1-13 the proud Corinthians are heedless of the effect their eating might have on the weak brother. In 10:1-22 the Corinthians appear as foolhardy men who believe that they can participate in the pagan feasts and yet avoid fellowship with demons. Perhaps the Corinthian church had appealed to its status as a sacramental community to silence any or all objections. How could those who already shared in the fruits of the Messianic Age be intimidated by the warnings of apostasy?

If this be a reasonably accurate description of the situation in the Corinthian congregation, then Paul's remarks sound especially appropriate. In 10:1-13 he reminds the church that just as her life as the sacramental community is prefigured in Israel's wilderness wandering, so also may the punishment for her malfeasance be anticipated in Israel's judgment.[1] Israel's status as the sacramental family of God did not exempt her from the judgment of her Lord. Her murmuring brought capital punishment (cf. Num. 14:36-38; 16:11-35, 41-49). Her immorality and idolatry brought the fall of 23,000 (24,000 according to Num. 25:9) in a single day. Her tempting the Lord brought destruction by serpents (Num. 21:5-9).

Israel's judgment forms the basis for Paul's warning to the church. The Corinthians are commanded $\mu\eta\delta\grave{\epsilon}$ $\pi o \rho \nu \epsilon \acute{\nu} \omega \mu \epsilon \nu$ in 10:8.[2] The church, Paul warns, cannot take salvation for granted.[3] Israel's example should offer sufficient evidence of this presumption to lead to amendment of life and vigilance of faith. The imperative in 10:12 [4] to watch ($\beta\lambda\epsilon\pi\acute{\epsilon}\tau\omega$) has eschatological connotations. $\pi\acute{\epsilon}\sigma\eta$ in 10:12 means more than falling into sin or unbelief; it refers to the danger of falling out of grace (Gal. 5:4) or into eschatological ruin (Rom. 11:22).[5] The Corinthians are forewarned that the end of the age(s) [6] is imminent when

---

[1] Lietzmann, *An die Korinther*, p. 45, says, the Old Testament events have not happened, in Paul's mind, for their own sake but their purpose is to anticipate the Messianic Age.

[2] Since harlotry and idolatry are often linked in the Old Testament (e.g., Num. 25:1-9 where bowing down to the gods of Moab is called whoredom), Paul's command "do not be immoral" is entirely apposite to the Corinthian situation.

[3] Weiss, *Der erste Korintherbrief*, p. 254.

[4] Cf. 3:10; 16:13; Rom. 11:22.

[5] Weiss, *Der erste Korintherbrief*, p. 254.

[6] *Ibid*. Weiss sees τῶν αἰώνων (v. 11) as plural—the end of one age and the beginning of another. Lietzmann, *An die Korinther*, p. 47, believes the plural refers to all world ages preceding the end.

the judgment will be manifest (10:11). The πειρασμοί may not represent merely human temptations but enticements by demons at the pagan cultic feasts and by Satan (7:5; II Cor. 2:11; I Thess. 3:5). We see in Revelation 3:10 that the πειρασμός can even be associated with the messianic trials which accompany the end of the age. Paul's somber eschatological language is offered as a solemn pastoral counsel to a church that is in danger of losing its life. Thus we see that Paul's purpose in this whole section is—

> ... to refute the opinion of the Corinthian enthusiasts that the sacramental *opus operatum* is a pledge of the impossibility of damnation now or in the future. On this side the Apostle stresses with unmistakable sharpness that the sacrament does *not* provide insurance against apostasy or against the divine rejection. A guarantee is just what it is *not*; on the contrary it is ... a call to obedience, the possibility of a decision for faith and against the temptation to disobedience.[1]

The theology which Paul propounds here is a *theologia viatorum* which sees the church traveling toward the *parousia*, a theology opposed to a "realized eschatology" which has lost its sense of living between the times.[2] Paul stands this church before the judgment and shows the congregation how the judgment impinges sharply on its present life.

In II Corinthians 5:9-10 Paul makes a short but important allusion to the future judgment: "So whether we are at home or away, we make it our aim to please him. For we must all appear before the judgment seat of Christ, so that each may receive good or evil, according to what he has done in the body." When Paul says πάντας ἡμᾶς φανερωθῆναι δεῖ ἔμπροσθεν τοῦ βήματος τοῦ Χριστοῦ he means that the whole church (πάντας ἡμᾶς) must meet the judgment.[3] Although the warning applies to all Christians this does not allow us to conclude that the judgment applies only to Christians.[4]

A consensus is developing which requires an understanding of this

---

[1] Käsemann, *Essays*, pp. 116-117.

[2] *Ibid.*, p. 123.

[3] This is borne out by Paul's emphasis on πάντας in verse 10. Cf. Filson, "The Second Epistle to the Corinthians," p. 331.

[4] Lietzmann, *An die Korinther*, p. 122, accurately notes that although Paul only speaks of a judgment over the Christians, we cannot conclude that this is a judgment separate from the judgment of the world (Rom. 3:6; 1:18 ff., 2:5-12; I Cor. 6:2, 3; II Cor. 2:16; 7:10; Gal. 6:8). This fate meets non-Christians clearly in I Cor. 1:18; II Cor. 2:15; 4:3; Phil. 1:28; Rom. 9:22; 14:11.

passage in its polemical context.[1] This section (5:1-10) stands in a close relationship to Paul's defense of his apostleship in II Corinthians 4:1-18 and 5:11; 6:1-10. Paul's outward appearance is weak and unimposing (4:7-11). Persecution has weakened his body (4:9). His external nature is wasting away (4:16). The heavy odor of death hangs over him (4:12). Hardships, beatings, imprisonments, poverty, hunger, ridicule, and false accusations dog his steps (6:3-10). For some in Corinth [2] the power of these frailties over Paul places his apostleship in question. Perhaps for others, Paul's weakness vitiates his apostleship entirely. If Paul were indeed an emissary of God, he would radiate the power of God in his entire being. If his physical appearance contradicts the Gospel he claims to "re-present," one must conclude that he is an impostor (6:8). Paul contends, however, that his Gospel is veiled to those perishing (4:3). The proof of the Gospel, Paul counters, is not in himself, his works or appearance, but in the death of Jesus through which God's power is manifest (4:6). Moreover, Paul argues, the cuts, bruises, personal abuse, and natural perils which he suffers do indeed raise the stench of death around him. Far from contradicting the Gospel, these unpleasant odors are wholly consistent with it,[3] because another death, the death of Jesus, stands at the center of the Gospel message. Always he carries in his body "the death of Jesus" (4:11), but, he reminds his accusers, through that death new life is manifested (4:11). For this reason, Paul is afflicted, but not crushed (4:8), perplexed but not despairing (4:8), persecuted but not forsaken (4:9), etc. His groan-

---

[1] Schmithals, *Die Gnosis*, and Georgi, *Die Gegner*, in their own respective ways made this point well. They were not, however, the first to see the polemical cast of this correspondence. See Ernst Käsemann, "Die Legitimität des Apostles," *Zeitschrift für die neutestamentliche Wissenschaft*, XLI (1942), 33-71, available in book form (Libelli, vol. XXXIII; Darmstadt : Wissenschaftliche Buchgesellschaft, 1956); Rudolf Bultmann, "Exegetische Probleme des zweiten Korintherbriefs," in *Exegetica, Aufsätze zur Erforschung des Neuen Testaments* (Tübingen : J.C.B. Mohr [Paul Siebeck], 1967), pp. 298-322; Helmut Köster, "Häretiker im Urchristentum," in *Die Religion in Geschichte und Gegenwart* (6 vols.; 3rd ed.; Tübingen : J.C.B. Mohr [Paul Siebeck], 1958), III, 17-21, and Günther Bornkamm, *Die Vorgeschichte des sogenannten zweiten Korintherbriefs* (Sitzungsberichte der Heidelberger Akademie der Wissenschafter; Heidelberg : Carl Winter Universitätsverlag, 1961). For a good survey of the respective positions, see C.K. Barrett, "Paul's Opponents in II Corinthians," *New Testament Studies*, XVII (1971), 233-254.

[2] The position of Georgi I take to be substantially correct.

[3] Käsemann, "Die Legitimität," 62 f., rightly sees that Paul places "signs and mighty works" in the context of obedient service and suffering.

ing, therefore, is rooted in hope, not eschatological disappointment (5:4). He does not bemoan his personal tragedies; rather, he yearns for the vindication of God's righteousness. Paul, consequently, can admonish his readers not to misinterpret the external signs. It is in light of this polemic that II Corinthians 5:10 must be read. Paul warns those who would challenge the apostolic character of his mission as well as the integrity of his Gospel, that the judgment is outstanding. It is before the divine tribunal that the final test will be made. It is at the judgment seat of Christ, not before the collective judgment of men, that the reward will be given. There Paul's Gospel will receive its vindication, and those who oppose him and his Gospel can expect eschatological ruin ($\phi a\hat{v}\lambda o\nu$).[1] Even if the Christological character of his suffering is veiled from the accusers, it is clear to God (5:11) in whose hand the final outcome rests. In the face of that ultimate judgment, not before the weak and vascillating estimation of men, the apostle carries on his work and lays the claim of his Gospel upon his hearers. Paul urges the Corinthians to join him in this theological outlook (5:11).

To summarize, we have seen in this chapter that Paul's doctrine of the judgment is vitally related to his ecclesiology.[2] Empowered by

---

[1] Mattern, *Verständnis*, pp. 151-158, argues that the judgment in this context applies only to Christians, and the judgment is limited to the works of the believers. God's judicial act does not decide *if* the Christians have pleased the Lord, but *how* they have pleased the Lord, more or less. The hope of eternal life, she contends, is independent of the outcome of this judgment : if this were not so, the strong hopeful element in II Corinthians 5:1-8 would be absurd. Miss Mattern's argument (1) ignores the polemical cast of vss. 1-8 which are not so hopeful as she contends. To those who believe they are already in Christ Paul speaks of being "at home with the Lord" in the future (v. 8). To those who think they already see, Paul speaks of walking by faith (v.7). To the libertines Paul speaks of deeds done in the body (v. 10). To those claiming eschatological bliss, Paul speaks of the coming judgment (v.10). (2) She makes an artificial distinction between the universal judgment and the more limited judgment over the *works* of individual Christians. Here Paul is emphasizing the fact that the whole church must stand before the judgment seat of Christ, not that the judgment will be restricted to them and different in character from the judgment over the world. In Rom. 14:10f. Paul uses an almost identical phrase which clearly sets the judgment of the church in a universal context : "For we shall all stand before the judgment seat of God." (3) She incorrectly assumes that a dark prediction adjacent to a hopeful aspiration makes the latter absurd. The fear of God's judgment in Judaism is frequently coupled with implicit trust and hope in his mercy (cf., I QH 7:28-30; also, I Cor. 10:13 [hope] vs. 10:1-12 [judgment]).

[2] It is noteworthy that a number of authors who treat Paul's doctrine of the church give little or no space to the relationship of Paul's eschatology to his ecclesiology. Weiss,

her Lord, the church already performs her judging tasks while awaiting a judgment to come. Disciplined by her Lord, directly or through the apostolic office, the church is purified for participation in the future eschatological victory. Both Paul's ecclesiology and eschatology stand in a dynamic relationship to and are thoroughly informed by his Christology. It is perhaps erroneous, then, to restrict one's discussion of judgment in Paul's letters to its relationship to justification by faith. Such an emphasis ignores the broader sweep of Paul's theology, focuses much too exclusively on the individual, and distorts Paul's doctrine of grace. We have concluded that Paul's understanding of judgment and his doctrine of the church are seen in the closest possible relationship.

Earliest Christianity, II, 629-650; 559-563, deals with the eschatological motif in Paul's ethics and the sacraments, but his discussion of the church contains no treatment of its eschatological dimension.

Lucien Cerfaux, *The Church in the Theology of Paul*, trans. Geoffrey Webb and Adrian Walker (New York : Herder and Herder, 1959), gives little evidence that his study has been informed by a grasp of Paul's eschatology.

Bruce M. Metzger, "The Teaching of the New Testament Concerning the Church," *Theology Today*, XIX (1962), 369-380, mentions the relationship between Paul's ecclesiology and his Christology, but omits any discussion of eschatology and the church.

George Johnston, *The Doctrine of the Church in the New Testament* (Cambridge : At the University Press, 1943), p. 76, says, "The *Ecclesia* of God is eschatologically conditioned," but does not show how this is true for Paul.

Shedd, *Man in Community*, rightly emphasizes the corporate nature of Paul's theology but fails to mention any way Paul's eschatology influences his understanding of the church.

Bultmann, *Theology*, I, 308-311, however, believes, as we do, that the church was for Paul an eschatological congregation through and through.

As we noted in Chapter I, a few significant works stress the importance of understanding Paul's eschatology for grasping his theology of the church.

CHAPTER FIVE

CONCLUSION

The foregoing study allows us to draw certain conclusions. 1. The background of Paul's judgment outlook lies in Jewish apocalyptic thought. Paul freely shares with the apocalyptic writers the eschatological framework, a vital grasp of the covenant concept, a sense of Salvation History, and a wealth of forensic language. While at points Paul's understanding of judgment reflects that of the rabbinic materials, the differences are striking. Much of Paul's judgment terminology is missing altogether or plays an insignificant role in the rabbinic materials. Other concepts such as the covenant or *Heilsgeschichte* mean something quite different for the Tannaim than for Paul. Although some concessions are made to Jewish nationalism, the judgment for the rabbis was primarily a future, stationary event which each man meets after death. In Jewish apocalyptic and Paul's letters, on the other hand, the judgment was dynamic, coming to meet man in the imminent future. It looms on the horizon, impinging sharply on the present. While for the rabbis the judgment is one concern among many, for the apocalypticists and Paul eschatology provides the framework in which the entire message is conveyed.

As in apocalyptic thought, Paul's judgment allusions focus primarily on God's vindication of his righteousness rather than on how the individual "gets right" with God. In a way characteristic of Old Testament prophetic and Jewish apocalyptic thought, God vindicates himself on behalf of the oppressed or poor. As judge he is no mere objective, unbiased authority who decides *cases* by abstract norms. He acts to establish his justice, or to vindicate his righteous will through the salvation of the oppressed and helpless. It is precisely in the salvific deed manifest in the cross of Christ that judgment and vindication has already begun. It is no accident, therefore, that Paul calls the eschatological community the poor (Rom. 15:26; cf. I Cor. 1:26-31). Our study of the judgment allusions in the Corinthian correspondence shows, moreover, that Paul, like the apocalyptic writers, can and often does speak of the judgment in contexts where justification by faith is unmentioned. These two observations led us to conclude that while justification by faith is an important motif in

Pauline theology, and has special relevance for the contemporary man, it is a distortion of Paul's thought to view justification by faith and judgment in a dialectical relationship. Any attempt to reconcile these motifs may be more of a concern of the western theologian for consistency than a concern of Paul's.

As in apocalyptic thought, Paul's emphasis falls on the corporate aspects of judgment. This tendency is apparent in the prominent role the church plays in Paul's judgment allusions. In both the present and the future, the church stands at the center of Pauls thought about the Day of the Lord. The church is an instrument of God's judgment both now and in the future, and she is judged by her Lord both now and in the future. As she accepts this judgment of the Lord in the present, her future condemnation is forestalled, and she can face the future judgment in confidence. While the church may trust God's power to establish his righteousness, and while the elect may expect to share in the promised future salvation, she cannot trade on her status as the sacramental community as insurance against eschatological loss or ruin. It is her response in believing obedience that ratifies God's offer of salvation. If the church attempts to take the fruits of salvation without assuming the responsibilities that go with them then the judgment portends loss and possible ruin. God's indicative carries with it an imperative for eschatological watchfulness. This watchfulness has a definite content; it is more than passive waiting.

While Paul, like the apocalyptic writers, is not unmindful of the individual believer, the individual member of the church is first and foremost a social being. The implications of membership in the Body of Christ reach far beyond the individual himself. If the old dominion governs the Christian's style of life, the whole church is implicated by his malfeasance. On the other hand, if one member of the church betrays his calling the whole church is responsible for his restoration.

2. While Paul's judgment thought parallels that of Jewish apocalyptic at points, his Christocentric emphasis distinguishes his outlook from that of his background. God's judgment—his wrath as well as his saving work—is *now* being realized. The tension between the present and the future judgment is rooted in the crucifixion of the Christ and his *parousia*. The cross signals the beginning and delineates the character of the final judgment. The *parousia* signals its completion. It is this span between the death of Christ and his return which forms the bridge between Paul's ecclesiology and his eschatology. As the eschatological community, the church must order her life accord-

ingly, accepting the present judgment in repentance, exercising it with love, and thus anticipating the ultimate triumph of God's righteousness.

For Paul as for the authors of the synoptic Gospels judgment begins at the house of God. In this sense Paul differs from most (but not all) of his Jewish contemporaries for whom judgment meant condemnation for gentiles and apostate Jews but salvation for faithful Israel. While Paul allows that God will judge those outside, in his letters he addresses himself to the ways the coming and present judgment impinges on those inside. The purpose of this judgment is multifaceted. It aims at the edification of the church through the protection and nurture of the weak, the discipline of the loveless, the reproof of false teachers, and the warning of the vascillating. It aims to encourage the helpless without power, and to warn the strong with power. It envisions the salvation of the whole inhabited world which includes both Jews and gentiles. It forms the basis of a hope for the future and an ethical imperative for the present. The threat of judgment is not so much a moral sanction which serves as the efficient cause of obedience as it is a result of Paul's belief that Jesus is the Messiah of God. Jesus Christ remains the heart and center of Paul's theology, and Paul's doctrine is illumined and informed by the Gospel he preaches.

We recall that the message of apocalyptic was forged in the fires of crisis and suffering. This mode of thought and faith evolved in periods of great environmental and social stress, in times when all human experience was threatened by the banalization, superficiality and emptiness of society, in periods when the dimensions and intensity of suffering seemed unbearable, in times when heroic men were murdered and the triumph of demonic powers seemed assured, and in times of total alienation between the world of oppression and fear and the world of justice and peace. It requires little imagination to draw certain parallels between that first century world and our own. Once again the threat of the "end of the world" is a part of our corporate consciousness. Dire predictions come from the lips of respected environmental and social scientists. Given these similarities of social context perhaps the way is clear for an imaginative appropriation of this eschatological model to inform and guide the life of the church today. For even if this study has shown in some measure what *krisis* in the church meant for Paul, it remains the more difficult task to show what *krisis* in the church means for the community of faith today. What are the implications of Paul's statement that judgment begins at the house of God? How are we to understand the fact that the Spirit comes for our discomfort as well as our comfort? How are we to understand and practice Paul's call for corporate responsibility carried on in love? How is the church to identify with those whom God vindicates in his judgment, i.e. the poor, the defenseless, the powerless, and suffering? What are the implications for a Christian style of life governed by a sense of living "between the times"? How is the church to live without claiming too much... or too little?

SELECTED BIBLIOGRAPHY

Achtemeier, Elizabeth R. "Righteousness in the OT," *The Interpreter's Dictionary of the Bible*. Edited by George Arthur Buttrick. 4 vols. New York, Nashville : The Abingdon Press, 1962, IV, 80-85.

Albright, William Foxwell and C.F. Mann. "Two Texts in I Corinthians," *New Testament Studies*, XVI (1970), 271-276.

Allo, Ernest-Bernard. *Saint Paul, Première épître aux Corinthiens*. 2d ed. (Etudes Bibliques) Paris : Librairie Lecoffre, 1934.

Althaus, Paul. *Die Letzten Dinge*. 6th ed. Gütersloh : Carl Bertelsmann Verlag, 1956.

The Babylonian Talmud. Edited by Lazarus Goldschmidt. 8 vols. Berlin und Wien : Benjamin Harz Verlag, 1925.

Baeck, Leo. *The Pharisees and Other Essays*. Translated from the German. New York : Schocken Books, 1947.

Baird, Joseph Arthur. *The Justice of God in the Teaching of Jesus*. Philadelphia : The Westminster Press, 1963.

Baird, William. "Among the Mature : The Idea of Wisdom in I Cor. 2-6," *Interpretation*, XIII (1959), 433-443.

Barrett, Charles Kingsley. "Christianity at Corinth," *Bulletin of the John Rylands Library*, XLVI (1946), 269-297.

——. *A Commentary on the First Epistle to the Corinthians*. (Black's New Testament Commentaries) London : Adam & Charles Black, 1968.

——. "New Testament Eschatology," *Scottish Journal of Theology*, VI (1953), 136-155.

——. "Paul's Opponents in II Corinthians," *New Testament Studies*, XVII (1971), 233-254.

——. "Things Sacrificed to Idols," *New Testament Studies*, XI (1965), 138-153.

Barth, Karl. *Christ and Adam*. Translated by T.A. Smail. New York : Harper & Brothers, Publishers, 1956, 1957.

Bauer, Walter. *A Greek-English Lexicon of the New Testament and Other Early Christian Literature*. Translated and adapted by William F. Arndt and F. Wilbur Gingrich. Chicago : The University of Chicago Press, 1957.

Beare, Francis Wright. *St. Paul and His Letters*. New York, Nashville : The Abingdon Press, 1962.

——. "St. Paul as Spiritual Director," *Studia Evangelica*. Edited by F.L. Cross. 2 vols. (Texte und Untersuchungen zur Geschichte der altchristlichen Literatur, vol. LXXXVII.) Berlin : Akademie-Verlag, 1964, II, 303-314.

Behm, Johannes. "The NT Term ἀνάθεμα," *Theological Dictionary of the New Testament*. Edited in the German by Gerhard Kittel. Translated and edited by Geoffrey W. Bromiley. Grand Rapids, Mich.: Wm. B. Eerdmans Publishing Company, 1964, I, 354-356.

——. "The NT Term διαθήκη," *Theological Dictionary of the New Testament*. Edited in the German by Gerhard Kittel. Translated and edited by Geoffrey W. Bromiley. Grand Rapids, Mich. : Wm. B. Eerdmans Publishing Company, 1964, II, 129-134.

Berger, Klaus. "Zu den sogenannten Sätzen heiligen Rechtes," *New Testament Studies*, XVII (1970), 10-40.

Bernard, John Henry. *Studia Sacra*. London : Hodder and Stoughton, 1917. *N.V.*
Betz, Hans Dieter. "Zum Problem des religionsgeschichtlichen Verständnisses der Apokalyptik," *Zeitschrift für Theologie und Kirche*, LXIII (1966), 391-409.
Betz, Otto. "The Dichotomized Servant and the End of Judas Iscariot," *Revue de Qumran*, V (1964), 43-58.
The Bible : An American Translation. Translated by J.M. Powis Smith and Edgar J. Goodspeed. Chicago : The University of Chicago Press, 1931.
Biblica Hebraica. Edited by Rudolf Kittel. Stuttgart : Privileg. Würt. Bibelanstalt, 1954.
Bonsirven, Joseph. *L'Évangile de Paul*. Paris : Éditions Montaigne, 1948.
——. *Palestinian Judaism in the Time of Jesus Christ*. Translated by William Wolf. New York, Chicago, San Francisco : Holt, Rinehart and Winston, 1964.
Bornkamm, Günther. "Das Anathema in der urchristlichen Abendmahlsliturgie," *Das Ende des Gesetzes*. (Beiträge zur evangelischen Theologie, vol. XVI.) München : Chr. Kaiser Verlag, 1952, 123-132.
——. "Faith and Reason in Paul's Epistles," *New Testament Studies*, IV (1958), 93-100.
——. "Die Frage nach der Gerechtigkeit Gottes (Theodizee und Rechtfertigung)," *Das Ende des Gesetzes*. (Beiträge zur evangelischen Theologie, vol. XVI.) München : Chr. Kaiser Verlag, 1952, 196-209.
——. "The History of the Origin of the So-called Second Letter to the Corinthians," *New Testament Studies*, VIII (1962), 258-264.
——. "Die Offenbarung des Zornes Gottes," *Das Ende des Gesetzes*. (Beiträge zur evangelischen Theologie, vol. XVI.) München : Chr. Kaiser Verlag, 1952, 9-33.
——. *Die Vorgeschichte des sogenannten zweiten Korintherbriefs* (Sitzungsberichte der Heidelberger Akademie der Wissenschafter) Heidelberg : Carl Winter Universitätsverlag, 1961.
Bousset, Wilhelm. *Der Erste Brief an die Korinther*. Herausgegeben von Johannes Weiss. (Die Schriften des Neuen Testaments, vol. II.) Göttingen : Vandenhoeck & Ruprecht, 1908.
——. *Die Religion des Judentums im späthellenistischen Zeitalter*. Herausgegeben von Hugo Gressmann. 3rd ed. (Handbuch zum Neuen Testament, vol. XXI.) Tübingen : J.C.B. Mohr (Paul Siebeck), 1926.
Bouttier, Michel. *Christianity According to Paul*. Translated by Frank Clarke. (Studies in Biblical Theology, no. 49.) Naperville, Ill.: Alec R. Allenson, Inc., 1966.
Braun, Herbert. *Gerichtsgedanke und Rechtfertigungslehre bei Paulus*. (Untersuchungen zum Neuen Testament, vol. XIX.) Leipzig : J.C. Hinrichs'sche Buchhandlung, 1930.
——. *Qumran und das Neue Testament*. 2 vols. Tübingen : J.C.B. Mohr (Paul Siebeck), 1966.
Brichto, Herbert Chanan. *The Problem of the "Curse" in the Hebrew Bible*. (Journal of Biblical Literature, Monograph Series, vol. XIII.) Philadelphia : Society of Biblical Literature, 1963.
Brown, Francis, Samuel R. Driver, and Charles A. Briggs. *A Hebrew and English Lexicon of the Old Testament*. Based on the lexicon of William Gesenius as translated by Edward Robinson. Oxford : At the Clarendon Press, 1907.
Brownlee, William Hugh. "A Comparison of the Covenanters of the Dead Sea Scrolls with Pre-Christian Jewish Sects," *The Biblical Archeologist*, XIII (1950), 50-72.
—— (trans.). *The Dead Sea Manual of Discipline*. (Bulletin of the American Schools of Oriental Research, Supplementary Studies, vols. X-XII.) New Haven, Conn.: American Schools of Oriental Research, 1951.

Brun, Lyder. *Segen und Fluch im Urchristentum.* Oslo : Kommisjon hos Jacob Dybwad, 1932.

Brunner, Heinrich Emil. *The Letter to the Romans.* Translated by H.A. Kennedy. Philadelphia : The Westminster Press, 1959.

Büchler, Adolf. *Studies in Sin and Atonement in the Rabbinic Literature of the First Century.* Translated from the German. (Reissued in Library of Biblical Studies) New York : KTAV Publishing House, Inc., 1967.

Bultmann, Rudolf. "Adam and Christ According to Romans 5," *Current Issues in New Testament Interpretation : Essays in Honor of Otto A. Piper.* Edited by William Klassen and Graydon F. Snyder. New York : Harper & Brothers, Publishers, 1962, 143-165.

―――. "ΔΙΚΑΙΟΣΥΝΗ ΘΕΟΥ" *Journal of Biblical Literature,* LXXXIII (1964), 12-15.

―――. "Exegetische Probleme des Zweiten Korintherbriefs," *Exegetica, Aufsätze zur Erforschung des Neuen Testaments.* Tübingen : J.C.B. Mohr (Paul Siebeck), 1967, 298-322.

―――. *Existence and Faith.* (Living Age Books, no. 29.) New York : Meridian Books, Inc., 1960.

―――. "Faith," *Bible Key Words.* Translated and edited by Dorothea M. Barton, P.R. Ackroyd and A.E. Harvey. (From G. Kittel's *Theologisches Wörterbuch zum Neuen Testament.*) New York : Harper and Brothers, 1960, IV, 1-56.

―――. *Glauben und Verstehen.* Tübingen : J.C.B. Mohr (Paul Siebeck), 1933.

―――. *History and Eschatology.* (Gifford Lectures, 1955.) Edinburgh : The University Press, 1957.

―――. "Ist die Apokalyptik die Mutter der christlichen Theologie ? Eine Auseinandersetzung mit Ernst Käsemann," *Apophoreta, Festschrift für Ernst Haenchen.* (Beiheft zur Zeitschrift für die neutestamentliche Wissenschaft und die Kunde der alteren Kirche, vol. XXX.) Berlin : Alfred Töpelmann, 1964, 64-69.

―――. "Das Problem der Ethik bei Paulus," *Zeitschrift für die neutestamentliche Wissenschaft,* XXIII (1924), 123-140.

―――. *Theology of the New Testament.* Translated by Kendrick Grobel. 2 vols. New York : Charles Scribner's Sons, 1951-1955.

Buri, Fritz. "Das Selbstverständnis des christlichen Glaubens als Prinzip der Dogmatik," *Theologische Zeitschrift,* X (1954), 355-376.

Burrows, Millar. *More Light on the Dead Sea Scrolls.* New York : The Viking Press, 1958.

Caird, George Bradford. "Everything to Everyone : The Theology of the Corinthian Epistles," *Interpretation,* XIII (1959), 387-399.

Campenhausen, Hans Freiherr von. *Kirchliches Amt und geistliche Vollmacht in den ersten drei Jahrhunderten.* (Beiträge zur historischen Theologie, vol. XIV.) Tübingen : J.C.B. Mohr (Paul Siebeck), 1953.

Cerfaux, Lucien. *The Church in the Theology of Paul.* Translated by Geoffrey Webb and Adrian Walker. New York : Herder and Herder, 1959.

Černy̆, Ladislav. *The Day of Yahweh and Some Relevant Problems.* Prague : Universita Karlova, 1948.

Charles, Robert Henry (trans. and ed.). *The Apocrypha and Pseudepigrapha of the Old Testament.* 2 vols. Oxford : At the Clarendon Press, 1913.

―――. *A Critical History of the Doctrine of the Future Life.* London : Adam and Charles Black, 1899.

——. *Eschatology : The Doctrine of the Future Life in Israel, Judaism, and Christianity*. 3rd. ed. New York: Shocken Books, 1963.
Cohen, Abraham. *Everyman's Talmud*. London : J.M. Dent & Sons, Ltd., 1932.
Collins, J.J. "Chiasmus, the 'ABA' Pattern and the Text of Paul," *Analecta Biblica*. 2 vols. (Studiorum Paulinorum Congressus Internationalis Catholicus.) Rome : Pontificio Instituto Biblico, 1963, II, 575-583.
Conzelmann, Hans. *Der erste Brief an die Korinther*. 11th ed. (Kritisch-exegetischer Kommentar über das Neue Testament, vol. V.) Göttingen : Vandenhoeck & Ruprecht, 1969.
——."On the Analysis of the Confessional Formula in I Corinthians 15:3-5," *Interpretation*, XX (1966), 15-25.
Craig, Clarence Tucker. "The First Epistle to the Corinthians : Introduction and Exegesis," *The Interpreter's Bible*. 12 vols. New York, Nashville : The Abingdon Press, 1953, X, 3-262.
Cross, Frank Moore, Jr. *The Ancient Library of Qumran and Modern Biblical Studies*. Rev. ed. (The Haskell Lectures, 1956-1957.) New York : Anchor Books, 1961.
Cullmann, Oscar. "The Proleptic Deliverance of the Body According to the New Testament," *The Early Church*. Edited by A.J.B. Higgins. Philadelphia : The Westminster Press, 1956, 166-173.
——. *Salvation in History*. Translated by Sidney G. Sowers and the staff of the S.C.M. Press. (New Testament Library.) London : S.C.M. Press, Ltd., 1965.
Dahl, Nils A. "Paul and the Church at Corinth according to I Corinthians 1-4," *Christian History and Interpretation : Studies Presented to John Knox*. Edited by W.R. Farmer, C.F.D. Moule and R.R. Niebuhr. Cambridge : At the University Press, 1967, 313-335.
Dalman, Gustaf Hermann. *Aramäisch-neuhebräisches Handwörterbuch zu Targum, Talmud und Midrash*. 3rd ed. Göttingen : Verlag von Eduard Pfeiffer, 1938.
Daniélou, Jean. "Eschatologie Sadocite et eschatologie Chrétienne," *Les manuscrits de la Mer Morte*. Paris : Presses Universitaires de France, 1957, 111-125.
——. *The Lord of History*. Translated by Nigel Abercrombie. Chicago : Henry Regnery, 1958.
Daube, David. "The Interpretation of a Generic Singular in Galatians 3:16," *Jewish Quarterly Review*, XXXV (1944), 227-230.
——. *The New Testament and Rabbinic Judaism*. (The Jordan Lectures, 1952.) London : The Athlone Press, 1956.
Davies, William David. *Christian Origins and Judaism*. Philadelphia : The Westminster Press, 1962.
——. *Introduction to Pharisaism*. (The W.M. Llewelyn Lecture, 1954.) Brecon : J. Colwell and Sons, 1954.
——. *Invitation to the New Testament*. Garden City, N.Y.: Doubleday & Company, Inc., 1966.
——. "The Jewish Background of the Teaching of Jesus : Apocalyptic and Pharisaism," *The Expository Times*, LXI (1948), 233-237.
——. "Paul and the Dead Sea Scrolls : Flesh and Spirit," *The Scrolls and the New Testament*. Edited by Krister Stendahl. New York : Harper & Brothers, Publishers, 1957, 157-182.
——. "Paul and Judaism," *The Bible and Modern Scholarship*. Edited by J. Philip Hyatt. New York, Nashville : The Abingdon Press, 1965, 178-186.
——. *Paul and Rabbinic Judaism*. 2d ed. New York : Harper Torchbooks, 1967.

The Dead Sea Scrolls of St. Mark's Monastery. Edited by Miller Burrows with the assistance of John C. Trever, and William H. Brownlee. 2 vols. New Haven : The American Schools of Oriental Research, 1950.

Deissmann, Adolf. *Light from the Ancient Near East*. Translated by R.M. Strachan. 4th ed. Grand Rapids, Michigan : Baker Book House, 1965.

——. *Die Urgeschichte des Christentums im Lichte der Sprachforschung*. Tübingen : J.C.B. Mohr, 1910.

Delcor, Mathias. "The Courts of the Church of Corinth and the Courts of Qumran," *Paul and Qumran, Studies in New Testament Exegesis*. Edited by Jerome Murphy-O'Connor. London : Geoffrey Chapman, 1968.

——. "L'eschatologie des documents de Khirbet Qumran," *Revue des sciences religieuses*, XXVI (1952), 363-386.

Devor, Richard Campbell. "The Concept of Judgment in the Epistles of Paul." Unpublished Ph. D. dissertation, Drew University, 1959.

Dibelius, Martin. *Die Geisterwelt im Glauben des Paulus*. Göttingen : Vandenhoeck & Ruprecht, 1909.

——. "Die Mahl-Gebete der Didache," *Zeitschrift für die neutestamentliche Wissenschaft*, XXXVII (1938), 32-41.

——. *An die Thessalonicher I-II, an die Philipper*. 3rd ed. (Handbuch zum neuen Testament, vol. XL.) Tübingen : J.C.B. Mohr (Paul Siebeck), 1937.

——. *Paul*. Edited and completed by Werner Georg Kümmel. Translated by Frank Clarke. London : Longmans, Green and Co., 1953.

Dietzfelbinger, Christian. *Heilsgeschichte bei Paulus?* (Theologische Existenz Heute.) München : Chr. Kaiser Verlag, 1965.

Dinkler, Erich. "The Historical and the Eschatological Israel in Romans, Chapters 9-11," *Journal of Religion*, XXXVI (1956), 109-127.

——. "Zum Problem der Ethik bei Paulus," *Zeitschrift für Theologie und Kirche*, XLIX (1952), 167-199.

Döbschutz, Ernst von. *Die Thessalonicher-Briefe*. 7th ed. (Kritisch-exegetischer Kommentar über das Neue Testament, vol. X.) Göttingen : Vandenhoeck & Ruprecht, 1909.

Dodd, Charles Harold. *The Apostolic Preaching*. New York : Harper & Brothers, Publishers, 1962.

——. *The Bible and the Greeks*. London : Hodder & Stoughton, 1935.

——. *The Epistle of Paul to the Romans*. (The Moffatt New Testament Commentary.) London : Hodder & Stoughton, Limited, 1932.

——. *New Testament Studies*. Manchester : At the University Press, 1953.

Dupont-Sommer, André. *The Essene Writings from Qumran*. Translated by G. Vermes. Oxford : Basil Blackwell, 1961.

Eichrodt, Walther, *Krisis der Gemeinschaft in Israel*. (Basler Universitätsreden, vol. XXXIII.) Basel : Verlag Helbing & Lichtenhahn, 1953.

——. *Theology of the Old Testament*. Vol. I. Translated by J.A. Baker. 2 vols. (The Old Testament Library.) Philadelphia : The Westminster Press, 1961.

Eissfeldt, Otto. *The Old Testament : An Introduction*. Translated from the 3rd German edition by Peter R. Ackroyd. New York, Evanston : Harper and Row, Publishers, 1965.

Ellis, Edward Earle. *Paul's Use of the Old Testament*. Edinburgh, London : Oliver and Boyd, 1957.

Fascher, E. *ΠΡΟΦΗΤΗΣ. Eine sprach- und religionsgeschichtliche Untersuchung.* Giessen : Alfred Töpelmann, 1927.

Feuillet, André. "L'explication 'typologique' des événements du désert en 1 Co 10, 1-4," *Studia Montis Regii*, VIII (1965), 115-135.

Fichtner, Johannes. "ὀργή," *Theologisches Wörterbuch zum Neuen Testament.* Edited by Gerhard Kittel. Stuttgart : W. Kohlhammer Verlag, 1954, V, 392-410.

Filson, Floyd Vivian. "The Second Epistle to the Corinthians : Introduction and Exegesis," *The Interpreter's Bible.* 12 vols. New York, Nashville : The Abingdon Press, 1953, X, 265-425.

——. *St. Paul's Conception of Recompense.* Herausgegeben von Hans Windisch. (Untersuchungen zum Neuen Testament, vol. XXI) Leipzig : J.C. Hinrichs'sche Buchhandlung, 1931.

Fuchs, Ernst. "Die Theologie des Neuen Testaments und der historische Jesus," *Zeitschrift für Theologie und Kirche*, LVII (1960), 296-301.

——."Über die Aufgabe einer christlichen Theologie," *Zeitschrift für Theologie und Kirche*, LVIII (1961), 245-267.

Funk, Robert Walter. *Language, Hermeneutic, and the Word of God.* New York : Harper and Row, 1966.

Galley, Klaus. *Altes und neues Heilsgeschehen bei Paulus.* (Arbeiten zur Theologie, ser. I. vol. XXII.) Stuttgart : Calwer Verlag, 1965.

Gaster, Theodor H. (trans. and ed.). *The Scriptures of the Dead Sea Sect.* London : Secker & Warburg, 1957.

Geoltrain, Pierre. "Une vision de l'histoire dans le Judaïsme intertestamentaire," *Oikonomia : Heilsgeschichte als Thema der Theologie. Oscar Cullmann zum 65. Geburtstag gewidmet.* Herausgegeben von Felix Christ. Hamburg-Bergstedt : Herbert Reich evang. Verlag, 1967, 26-31.

Georgi, Dieter. *Die Gegner des Paulus im 2. Korintherbrief.* (Wissenschaftliche Monographien zum Alten und Neuen Testament, Vol. XI.) Neukirchen : Neukirchener Verlag, 1964.

Glatzer, Nahum Norbert. "Hillel the Elder in the Light of the Dead Sea Scrolls," *The Scrolls and the New Testament.* Edited by Krister Stendahl. New York : Harper and Brothers, Publishers, 1957, 232-244.

Goguel, Maurice. "Le caractère, à la fois actuel et future, du salut dans la théologie paulinienne," *The Background of the New Testament and its Eschatology : In Honour of Charles Harold Dodd.* Edited by W.D. Davies and D. Daube. Cambridge : At the University Press, 1956, 322-341.

Goodenough, Erwin Ramsdell. *Jewish Symbols in the Graeco-Roman Period.* 12 vols. New York : Pantheon Books, 1953-1965.

Goppelt, Leonhard. "Paul and Heilsgeschichte," translated by Matthias Rissi, *Interpretation*, XXI (1967), 315-326.

Greeven, Heinrich. "Propheten, Lehrer, Vorsteher bei Paulus," *Zeitschrift für die neutestamentliche Wissenschaft*, XLIV (1952/53), 1-43.

Grønbaek, Johannes. "Zur Frage der Eschatologie der Verkundigung der Gerichtspropheten," *Svensk exegetisk årsbok*, XXIV (1959), 5-21.

Güttgemanns, Erhard. *Der leidende Apostel und sein Herr, Studien zur paulinischen Christologie.* (Forschungen zur Religion und Literatur, vol. XC.) Göttingen : Vandenhoeck & Ruprecht, 1966.

Hamilton, Neill Quinn. *Holy Spirit and Eschatology in Paul.* (Scottish Journal of Theology, Occasional Papers, no. 6.) Edinburgh : Oliver and Boyd, Ltd., 1957.
Hammershaimb, Erling. *Amos.* Copenhagen : Nyt nordisk forlag, 1946.
Hanson, Anthony Tyrell. *The Wrath of the Lamb.* London : S.P.C.K., 1957.
Hanson, Richard Patrick Crosland. *II Corinthians.* (Torch Bible Commentaries.) London : S.C.M. Press, Ltd., 1954.
——. "Qumran and the Essenes," *A Guide to the Scrolls.* Edited by Alfred Robert Clare Leaney (Nottingham Studies on the Qumran Discoveries.) London : S.C.M. Press, 1958, 58-64.
Harnack, Adolf. *Die Lehre der Zwölf Apostel.* (Texte und Untersuchungen zur Geschichte der altchristlichen Literatur, vol. II.) Leipzig : J.C. Hinrichs'sche Buchhandlung, 1884.
Heaton, Eric William. "The Root š'r and the Doctrine of the Remnant," *Journal of Theological Studies, III* (1952), 27-39.
Herford, Robert Travers. *Pirkē Aboth.* New York : Jewish Institute of Religion, 1945.
——. *Talmud and Apocrypha.* London : The Soncino Press, 1933.
Héring, Jean. *The First Epistle of Saint Paul to the Corinthians.* Translated by A.W. Heathcote and P.J. Allcock. London : Epworth Press, 1962.
——. *Le Royaume de Dieu et sa Venue.* Paris : Libraire Felix Alcan, 1937.
Higgins, Angus John Brockhurst. *The Lord's Supper.* (Studies in Biblical Theology, no. 6.) London : S.C.M. Press, 1953.
Hirsch, Emanuel. "Das Gericht Gottes," *Zeitschrift für systematische Theologie,* I (1923), 199-226.
The Holy Bible. Revised Standard Version. New York : Thomas Nelson and Sons, 1952.
[Homer.] *The Iliad.* Translated by A.T. Murray. 2 vols. (The Loeb Classical Library.) Cambridge, Mass.: Harvard University Press, 1960.
Huby, Joseph. *Saint Paul Épître aux Romains.* Rev. ed. (Verbum Salutis, vol. X.) Paris : Beauchesne, 1957.
Hunter, Archibald Macbride. *The Epistle to the Romans.* London : S.C.M. Press, 1955.
Hurd, John Coolidge, Jr. *The Origin of I Corinthians.* New York : Seabury Press, 1965.
Jaubert, Annie. *La notion d'alliance dans le Judaïsme.* (Patristica Sorbonensia, vol. VI.) Paris : Éditions du Seuil, 1963.
Jeremias, Joachim. "Chiasmus in den Paulusbriefen," *Zeitschrift für die neutestamentliche Wissenschaft,* XLIX (1958), 145-156.
——. *Eucharistic Words of Jesus.* Translated from the 3rd German edition by Arnold Ehrhardt. New York : The Macmillan Co., 1955.
The Jewish Encyclopedia. Edited by Isidore Singer, et al. 12 vols. New York, London : Funk and Wagnalls Company. 1902, III, 114-115.
Johnson, Sherman Elbridge. "The Jerusalem Church in Acts," *The Scrolls and the New Testament,* Edited by Krister Stendahl. New York : Harper & Brothers, Publishers, 1957, 129-142.
——. "Paul and the Manual of Discipline," *Harvard Theological Review,* XLVIII (1955), 157-165.
Johnston, George. *The Doctrine of the Church in the New Testament.* Cambridge : At the University Press, 1943.
Jüngel, Eberhard. *Paulus und Jesus, eine Untersuchung zur Präzisierung der Frage nach dem Ursprung der Christologie.* (Hermeneutische Untersuchungen zur Theologie, vol. II.) Tübingen : J.C.B. Mohr (Paul Siebeck), 1967.

Junker, Hubert. "Der alttestamentliche Bann gegen heidnische Völker als morals-theologisches und offenbarungsgeschichtliches Problem," *Aus Theologie und Philosophie : Festschrift für Fritz Tillmann*. Herausgegeben von Theodor Steinbüchel und Theodor Müncker. Düsseldorf : Patmos Verlag, 1950, 164-179.

Kabisch, Richard. *Die Eschatologie des Paulus*. Göttingen : Vandenhoeck & Ruprecht, 1893.

Käsemann, Ernst. "The Beginnings of Christian Theology," *New Testament Questions of Today*. Translated by W.J. Montague. London : S.C.M. Press, Ltd., 1969, 82-107.

——. *Essays on New Testament Themes*. Translated by W.J. Montague. (Studies in Biblical Theology, no. 41.) London : S.C.M. Press, Ltd., 1964.

——. "Geist und Geistesgaben im NT," *Die Religion in Geschichte und Gegenwart*. 6 vols. 3rd ed. Tübingen : J.C.B. Mohr (Paul Siebeck), 1958, II, 1272-1279.

——. "God's Righteousness in Paul." Translated by Wilfred F. Bunge. *The Bultmann School of Biblical Interpretation : New Directions ?* (Journal for Theology and the Church, vol. I.) New York : Harper Torchbooks, 1965, 100-110.

——. "Die Legitimität des Apostels," *Zeitschrift für die neutestamentliche Wissenschaft*, XLI (1942), 33-71.

——. "Paulus und Israel," *Exegetische Versuche und Besinnungen*. Göttingen : Vandenhoeck & Ruprecht, 1964, II, 194-197.

——."Primitive Christian Apocalyptic," *New Testament Questions of Today*. Translated by W.J. Montague. London : S.C.M. Press, Ltd., 1969, 108-137.

——. "Sentences of Holy Law in the New Testament," *New Testament Questions of Today*. Translated by W.J. Montague. London : S.C.M. Press, Ltd., 1969, 66-81.

——. "Zum Verständnis von Röm. 3, 24-26," *Exegetische Versuche und Besinnungen*. 2 vols. Göttingen : Vandenhoeck & Ruprecht, 1960, I, 96-100.

Kee, Howard Clark, Franklin W. Young and Karlfried Froehlich. *Understanding the New Testament*. 2d ed. Englewood Cliffs, N.J. : Prentice-Hall, Inc., 1965.

Klassen, William. "Vengeance in the Apocalypse of John," *Catholic Biblical Quarterly*, XXVIII (1966), 300-311.

Klein, Günter. "Individualgeschichte und Weltgeschichte bei Paulus," *Evangelische Theologie*, XXIV (1964), 126-165.

——. "Römer 4 und die Idee der Heilsgeschichte," *Evangelische Theologie*, XXIII (1963), 424-447.

Kleinknecht, Hermann, et al. "Wrath," *Bible Key Words*. Translated and edited by Dorothea M. Barton and P.R. Ackroyd. (From G. Kittel's *Theologisches Wörterbuch zum Neuen Testament*.) New York and Evanston : Harper and Row, Publishers, 1964, IV, 1-134.

Knox, John. *Chapters in a Life of Paul*. New York, Nashville : The Abingdon Press, 1950.

——. "The Epistle to the Romans : Introduction and Exegesis," *The Interpreter's Bible*. 12 vols. New York, Nashville : The Abingdon Press, 1954, IX, 354-668.

Knox, Wilfred Lawrence. *St. Paul and the Church of the Gentiles*. Cambridge : At the University Press, 1939.

Koester, Helmut, "ΓΝΩΜΑΙ ΔΙΑΦΟΡΟΙ. The Origin and Nature of Diversivication in the History of Early Christianity," *Harvard Theological Review*, LVIII (1965), 279-318.

——."Häretiker im Urchristentum," *Die Religion in Geschichte und Gegenwart*. 6 vols. 3rd ed. Tübingen : J.C.B. Mohr (Paul Siebeck), 1958, III, 17-21.

——. "The Role of Myth in the New Testament," *Andover Newton Quarterly*, VIII (1968), 180-195.

Kümmel, Werner Georg. "Die Bedeutung der Enderwartung für die Lehre des Paulus," *Heilsgeschehen und Geschichte*. Herausgegeben von Erich Grässer, Otto Merk, und Adolf Fritz. (Marburger theologische Studien, vol. II.) Marburg : N.G. Elwert Verlag, 1965, 36-47.

——. *Introduction to the New Testament*. Founded by Paul Feine and Johannes Behm; completly reedited by Kümmel; and translated by A.J. Mattil, Jr. 14th rev. ed. New York, Nashville : The Abingdon Press, 1966.

——. "Jesus und Paulus," *Heilsgeschehen und Geschichte*. Herausgegeben von Erich Grässer, Otto Merk und Adolf Fritz. (Marburger theologische Studien, Vol. III.) Marburg : N.G. Elwert Verlag, 1965, 81-106.

Kuhn, Karl Georg. *Konkordanz zu den Qumrantexten*. Göttingen : Vandenhoeck & Ruprecht, 1960.

——. "The NT Term μαρανaθά," *Theological Dictionary of the New Testament*. Edited by Gerhard Kittel. Translated from the German and edited by Geoffrey W. Bromiley. Grand Rapids, Mich. : Wm. B. Eerdmans Publishing Company, 1964, 466-472.

——. "Röm. 6:7," *Zeitschrift für die neutestamentliche Wissenschaft*, XXX (1931), 305-310.

Lampe, George William Hugo. "Church Discipline and the Interpretation of the Epistles to the Corinthians," *Christian History and Interpretation : Studies Presented to John Knox*. Edited by W.R. Farmer, C.F.D. Moule and R.R. Niebuhr. Cambridge : At the University Press, 1967, 337-361.

Leaney, Alfred Robert Clare. "The Righteous Community in St. Paul," *Studia Evangelica*. Edited by F.L. Cross. 2 vols. (Texte und Untersuchungen, vol. LXXXVII.), II, 441-446.

Leenhardt, Franz J. *The Epistle to the Romans*. Translated by Harold Knight. London : Lutterworth Press, 1961.

——. *Le sacrement de la sainte Cène*. (Série théologique de l'Actualité Protestante.) Neuchâtel, Paris : Delachaux & Niestlé, 1948.

Leisegang, Ioannes. *Philonis Alexandrini Opera Quae Supersunt*. 7 vols. Berlin : Walter de Gruyter & Co., 1926, VII.

Levey, Irving. "Anathema," *The Universal Jewish Encyclopedia*. Edited by Isaac Landman. 10 vols. New York : Universal Jewish Encyclopedia Co., Inc., 1939, I, 295.

Lietzmann, Hans. *The Beginnings of the Christian Church*. Translated by Bertram Lee Wolf. 3rd ed. rev. London : The Lutterworth Press, 1953.

——. *Die Didache mit kritischem Apparat*. (Kleine Texte, no. 6. Berlin : Walter de Gruyter & Co., 1948.

——. *Einführung in die Textgeschichte der Paulusbriefe, an die Römer*. 4th ed. (Handbuch zum Neuen Testament, vol. VIII.) Tübingen : J.C.B. Mohr (Paul Siebeck), 1933.

——. *An die Korinther I-II*. 4th ed. (Handbuch zum Neuen Testament, vol. IX.) Tübingen : J.C.B. Mohr (Paul Siebeck), 1949.

——. *Mass and the Lord's Supper, A Study of the History of the Liturgy*. Translated by Dorothea H.G. Reeve. Leiden : E.J. Brill, 1953.

Lindblom, Johannes. "Gibt es eine Eschatologie bei den alttestamentlichen Propheten ? " *Studia Theologica*, VI (1952), 79-114.

——. *Prophecy in Ancient Israel*. Philadelphia : The Westminster Press, 1965.

Lohmeyer, Ernst. *Die Briefe an die Philipper, an die Kolosser, und an Philemon.* 9th ed. (Kritisch-exegetischer Kommentar über das Neuen Testament, series I, vol. IX.) Göttingen : Vandenhoeck & Ruprecht, 1930.

Lohse, Eduard. *Märtyrer und Gottesknecht.* 2d ed. (Forschungen zur Religion und Literatur des Alten und Neuen Testaments, New series, vol. XLVI.) Göttingen : Vandenhoeck & Ruprecht, 1963.

Lyonnet, Stanislas. *Les épîtres de saint Paul aux Galates aux Romains.* Paris : Les éditions du Cerf, 1953.

———. "Gratuité de la justification et gratuité du salut," *Analecta Biblica.* 2 vols. (Studiorum Paulinorum Congressus Internationalis Catholicus.) Rome : Pontificio Instituto Biblico, 1963, I, 95-110.

———. "Justification, jugement, rédemption, principalement dans l'épître aux Romains," *Recherches Bibliques,* V (1960), 166-184.

MacGorman, John William "An Analysis of the Factors which Relate to the Possibility of Tracing Development in Pauline Eschatology." Unpublished Ph. D. dissertation, Duke University, 1965.

MacGregor, George Hogarth Carnaby. " The Concept of the Wrath of God in the New Testament," *New Testament Studies,* VII (1961), 101-109.

Manson, Thomas Walter. *On Paul and John.* Edited by Matthew Black. (Studies in Biblical Theology, no. 38.) Naperville, Ill. : Alec R. Allenson, Inc., 1963.

———. "Reflections on Apocalyptic," *Aux sources de la tradition chrétienne, Mélanges offerts à M. Maurice Goguel.* (Bibliothèque Théologique. Neuchâtel, Paris : Delachaux & Niestlé S.A., 1950, 138-145.

———. "St. Paul in Greece : The Letters to the Thessalonians," *Bulletin of the John Rylands Library,* XXXV (1953), 428-447.

———. *Studies in the Gospels and Epistles.* Edited by Matthew Black. Philadelphia : The Westminster Press, 1962.

Manson, William. "Mission and Eschatology," *International Review of Missions,* XLII (1953), 257-265.

Martyn, James Louis. "Epistemology at the Turn of the Ages : 2 Corinthians 5:16," *Christian History and Interpretation : Studies Presented to John Knox.* Edited by W.R. Farmer, C.F.D. Moule and R.R. Niebuhr. Cambridge : At the University Press, 1967, 269-287.

Mattern, Lieselotte. *Das Verständnis des Gerichtes bei Paulus.* (Abhandlungen zur Theologie des Alten und Neuen Testaments, vol. XLVII.) Zürich/Stuttgart : Zwingli Verlag, 1966.

Mekilta de-Rabbi Ishmael. Translated and edited by Jacob Z. Lauterbach. 3 vols. Philadelphia : The Jewish Publication Society of America, 1933.

Metzger, Bruce Manning. "The Teaching of the New Testament Concerning the Church," *Theology Today,* XIX (1962), 369-380.

Meyer, Arnold. *Das Rätsel des Jacobusbriefes.* Giessen : Alfred Töpelmann, 1930.

Meyer, Heinrich August Wilhelm. *A Critical and Exegetical Handbook to the Epistles to the Corinthians.* Translated from the 5 th German edition by Douglas Bannerman. Revised by William D. Dickson. New York : Funk & Wagnalls, Publishers, 1884.

Meyer, Werner. *Der erste Korintherbrief.* 2 vols. (Prophezei : Scweizerisches Bibelwerk für die Gemeinde.) Zürich : Zwingli Verlag, 1947, 1945.

Michaelis, Wilhelm. "Rechtfertigung aus Glauben bei Paulus," *Festgabe für Adolf Deissmann.* Tübingen : J.C.B. Mohr (Paul Siebeck), 1927, 116-138.

Michel, Otto. *Der Brief an die Römer.* (Kritisch-exegetischer Kommentar über das Neue Testament.) Göttingen : Vandenhoeck & Ruprecht, 1955.

——. *Paulus und seine Bibel.* (Beiträge zur Forderung christlicher Theologie.) Güttersloh : Druck und Verlag von C. Bertelsmann, 1929.

Midrash Rabbah. Translated under the editorship of H. Freedman and Maurice Simon. 13 vols. in 10. London : Soncino Press, 1939.

Minear, Paul Sevier. *And Great Shall Be Your Reward.* New Haven : Yale University Press, 1941.

The Mishnah. Translated and edited by Herbert Danby. Oxford : At the Clarendon Press, 1933.

Moffatt, James. *The First Epistle of Paul to the Corinthians.* (The Moffatt New Testament Commentary.) New York, London : Harper and Brothers, Publishers, 1938.

Montefiore, Claude Joseph Goldsmid and Herbert Martin James Lowe (ed. and trans.). *A Rabbinic Anthology.* London : Macmillan and Co., Ltd., 1938.

Moore, Arthur Lewis. *The Parousia in the New Testament.* (Supplements to Novum Testamentum, vol. XIII.) Leiden : E.J. Brill, 1966.

Moore, George Foot. *Judaism in the First Centuries of the Christian Era : The Age of the Tannaim.* 3 vols. Cambridge, Mass.: Harvard University Press, 1946.

Morrison, Clinton. *The Powers that Be.* (Studies in Biblical Theology, no. 29.) London : S.C.M. Press, Ltd., 1960.

Moule, Charles Francis Digby. "The Judgment Theme in the Sacraments," *The Background of the New Testament and Its Eschatology : In Honour of Charles Harold Dodd.* Edited by W.D. Davies and D. Daube. Cambridge : At the University Press, 1956, 464-481.

——. "Punishment and Retribution : an Attempt to Delimit Their Scope in New Testament Thought," *Svensk exegetisk årsbok,* XXX (1965), 21-36.

——."A Reconsideration of the Context of Maranatha," *New Testament Studies,* VI (1960), 307-310.

Moulton, William Fiddian, and Alfred Shenington Geden. *A Concordance to the Greek Testament.* 3rd ed. revised by H.K. Moulton. Edinburgh : T. & T. Clark, 1926.

Mowinckel, Sigmund Olaf Plyat. *Psalmenstudien II : Das Thronbesteigungsfest Jahwäs und der Ursprung der Eschatologie.* Kristiana : Dybwad, 1922-1924.

Munck, Johannes. *Christus und Israel.* (Aarsskrift for Aarhus Universitet, vol. XXVIII.) København : Universitetsforlaget Aarhus, 1956.

——. *Paul and the Salvation of Mankind.* Translated by Frank Clarke. Richmond, Va.: John Knox Press, 1959.

Murphy, Roland Edward. *The Dead Sea Scrolls and the Bible.* Westminster, Md.: The Newman Press, 1956.

Neil, William. *The Epistle of Paul to the Thessalonians.* (The Moffatt New Testament Commentary.) New York : Harper & Brothers, Publishers, 1950.

A New Translation of the Bible. Translated by James Moffatt. New York, London : Harper and Brothers, Publishers, 1922.

Nickle, Keith Fullerton. *The Collection.* (Studies in Biblical Theology, no. 48.) London : S.C.M. Press, Ltd., 1966.

Nock, Arthur Darby. *St. Paul.* New York : Harper Torchbooks, 1966.

Noth, Martin. *The Laws in the Pentateuch and Other Studies.* Translated by D.R. Ap-Thomas. Edinburgh, London : Oliver & Boyd, 1966.

Novum Testamentum Graece. Edited by Eberhard Nestle ; revised by Erwin Nestle and Kurt Aland. 25th ed. Stuttgart : Privileg. Württ. Bibelanstalt, 1964.

Nygren, Anders. *Commentary on Romans.* Translated by Carl C. Rasmussen. Philadelphia : Muhlenberg Press, 1949.

Odeberg, Hugo. *Pharisaism and Christianity.* Translated by J.M. Moe. St. Louis : Concordia Publishing House, 1962.

Pannenberg, Wolfhart. *Theology and the Kingdom of God.* Philadelphia : The Westminster Press, 1969.

Pearson, Birger. "Did the Gnostics Curse Jesus ?" *Journal of Biblical Literature,* LXXXVI (1967), 301-305.

[Philo.] "On Rewards and Punishments," *Philo.* Translated by F.H. Colson. 10 vols. (The Loeb Classical Library.) Cambridge, Mass.: Harvard University Press, 1939, VIII, 309-422.

Piper, Otto A. "The 'Book of Mysteries' (Qumran 27), A Study in Eschatology," *Journal of Religion,* XXXVII (1958), 95-106.

Plöger, Otto. "Das 4. Esrabuch," *Die Religion in Geschichte und Gegenwart.* 6 vols. 3rd ed. Tübingen : J.C.B. Mohr (Paul Siebeck), 1958, II, 697-699.

——. *Theokratie und Eschatologie.* 2d ed. (Wissenschaftliche Monographien zum Alten und Neuen Testament, vol. II.) Neukirchen : Neukirchener Verlag, 1962.

Plummer, Alfred. *A Critical and Exegetical Commentary on the Second Epistle of St. Paul to the Corinthians.* (The International Critical Commentary.) New York : Charles Scribner's Sons, 1915.

Price, James Ligon. *Interpreting the New Testament.* New York : Holt, Rinehart and Winston, 1961.

Rabin, Chaim (trans and ed.). *The Zadokite Documents.* 2nd ed. Oxford : At the Clarendon Press, 1958.

Rad, Gerhard von. "$\dot{\eta}\mu\dot{\epsilon}\rho\alpha$," *Theological Dictionary of the New Testament.* Edited in the German by Gerhard Kittel. Translated and edited by Geoffrey M. Bromiley. Grand Rapids, Michigan : Wm. B. Eerdmans Publishing Company, 1965, II, 943-953.

——. *Old Testament Theology.* Vol. II. Translated by D.M.G. Stalker. 2 vols. New York : Harper and Row, 1965.

Rengstorf, Karl Heinrich. "$\dot{\alpha}\pi\acute{o}\sigma\tau o\lambda o\varsigma$," *Theological Dictionary of the New Testament.* Edited in the German by Gerhard Kittel. Translated and edited by Geoffrey W. Bromiley. Grand Rapids, Michigan : Wm. B. Eerdmans Publishing Company, 1964, I, 407-451.

Reumann, John. "The Gospel of the Righteousness of God," *Interpretation,* XX (1966), 432-452.

Rhys, Howard. *The Epistle to the Romans.* New York : The Macmillan Company, 1961.

Ringgren, Helmer. *The Faith of Qumran.* Translated by Emilie T. Sander. Philadelphia : Fortress Press, 1963.

——. *Israelite Religion.* Translated by David E. Green. Philadelphia : Fortress Press, 1963.

Robertson, Archibald, and Alfred Plummer. *A Critical and Exegetical Commentary on the First Epistle of St. Paul to the Corinthians* (The International Critical Commentary.) New York : Charles Scribner's Sons, 1911.

Robinson, Henry Wheeler. " The Hebrew Conception of Corporate Personality," *Werden und Wesen des Alten Testaments.* Herausgegeben von Paul Volz, Friedrich Stummer, and Johannes Hempel. (Zeitschrift für die alttestamentliche Wissenschaft, Beiheft LXVI.) Berlin : Alfred Töpelmann, 1936, 49-62.

——. *Inspiration and Revelation in the Old Testament.* Oxford : At the Clarendon Press, 1946.

Robinson, James M. "The Dismantling and Reassembling of the Categories of New Testament Scholarship," *Interpretation,* XXV (1971), 63-77.

——. "Kerygma and History in the New Testament," *The Bible and Modern Scholarship.* Edited by James Philip Hyatt. Nashville : The Abingdon Press, 1965, 114-150.

Rössler, Dietrich. *Gesetz und Geschichte.* (Wissenschaftliche Monographien zum Alten und Neuen Testament, vol. III.) Neukirchen : Neukirchener Verlag, 1960.

Roetzel, Calvin J. "$\Delta\iota\alpha\theta\hat{\eta}\kappa\alpha\iota$ in Romans 9,4," *Biblica,* LI (1970), 377-390.

Rowley, Harold Henry. *Jewish Apocalyptic and the Dead Sea Scrolls.* (The Ethel M. Wood Lecture, 1957.) London : The Athlone Press, 1957.

——. *The Relevance of Apocalyptic.* 3rd ed. rev. New York : The Association Press, 1963.

——. *The Zadokite Fragments and the Dead Sea Scrolls.* Oxford : Basil Blackwell, 1952.

Russell, David Syme. *The Method and Message of Jewish Apocalyptic.* Philadelphia : The Westminster Press, 1964.

Sanday, William, and Arthur Cayley Headlam. *A Critical and Exegetical Commentary on the Epistle to the Romans.* (The International Critical Commentary.) New York : Charles Scribner's Sons, 1895.

Sasse, Hermann. "$\alpha\iota\acute{\omega}\nu$," *Theological Dictionary of the New Testament.* Edited in the German by Gerhard Kittel. Translated and edited by Geoffrey W. Bromiley. Grand Rapids, Mich. : Wm. B. Eerdmans Publishing Company, 1964, I, 197-208.

Schechter, Solomon. *Aspects of Rabbinic Theology.* New York : Shocken Books, 1961.

Schlatter, Adolf, *Der Glaube im Neuen Testament.* 4th ed. Stuttgart : Calwer Vereinsbuchhandlung, 1927.

——. *Gottes Gerechtigkeit : Ein Kommentar zum Römerbrief.* 2nd ed. Stuttgart : Calwer Verlag, 1952.

——. *Paulus der Bote Jesu, eine Deutung seiner Briefe an die Korinther.* 2nd ed. Stuttgart : Calwer Verlag, 1956.

Schlier, Heinrich. *Der Brief an die Galater.* (Kritisch-exegetischer Kommentar über das Neuen Testament.) Göttingen : Vandenhoeck & Ruprecht, 1949.

Schmithals, Walter. *Die Gnosis in Korinth.* 2d ed. (Forschungen zur Religion und Literatur des Alten und Neuen Testaments, new series, vol. XLVIII.) Göttingen : Vandenhoeck & Ruprecht, 1965.

Schnackenburg, Rudolf. "Kirche und Parusie," *Gott in Welt : Festgabe für Karl Rahner.* Herausgegeben von Johannes Baptist Metz, *et al.* 2 vols. Freiburg, Basel, Wien : Herder, 1964, I, 551-578.

——. *New Testament Theology Today.* Translated by David Askew. New York : Herder and Herder, 1963.

——. *Die sittliche Botschaft des Neuen Testaments.* (Handbuch der Moraltheologie, vol. VI.) München : Max Hueber Verlag, 1954.

Schneemelcher, Wilhelm. "Apostle and Apostolic," *New Testament Apocrypha.* Edited in the German by Edgar Hennecke and Wilhelm Schneemelcher. Translated by R. McL. Wilson. 2 vols. Philadelphia : The Westminster Press, 1965, II, 25-34.

Schniewind, Julius. "Die Leugner der Auferstehung in Korinth," *Nachgelassene Reden und Aufsätze*. Berlin : Alfred Töpelmann, 1952, 110-139.

Schoeps, Hans Joachim. *Paul : The Theology of the Apostle in the Light of Jewish Religious History*. Translated by Harold Knight. Philadelphia : The Westminster Press, 1961.

Schoonhoven, Calvin Robert. *The Wrath of Heaven*. Grand Rapids, Mich.: Wm. B. Eerdmans Publishing Company, 1966.

Schrage, Wolfgang. *Die konkreten Einzelgebote in der paulinischen Paränese*. Güttersloh: Gerhard Mohn, 1961.

Schrenk, Gottlob. "Righteousness in the New Testament," *Bible Key Words*. Translated by J.R. Coates. (From G. Kittel's *Theologisches Wörterbuch zum Neuen Testament*.) New York : Harper & Brothers, Publishers, 1951, IV, 26-55.

——. *Studien zu Paulus*. Zürich : Zwingli Verlag, 1954.

Schubert, Kurt. *The Dead Sea Community*. Translated by John W. Doberstein. London : Adam & Charles Black, 1959.

——. *Die Religion des nachbiblischen Jüdentums*. Freiburg-Wien : Herder, 1955.

Schubert, Paul. "Paul and the New Testament Ethic in the Thought of John Knox" *Christian History and Interpretation : Studies Presented to John Knox*. Edited by W.R. Farmer, C.F.D. Moule, and R.R. Niebuhr. Cambridge : At the University Press, 1967, 363-388.

Schulz, Siegfried. "Zur Rechtfertigung aus Gnaden in Qumran und bei Paulus," *Zeitschrift für Theologie und Kirche*, LVI (1959), 155-185.

Schürer, Emil. *A History of the Jewish People*. Translated by M. Macpherson and S. Taylor. 2 divs., 5 vols. Edinburgh : T. & T. Clark, 1924.

Schweitzer, Albert. *The Mysticism of Paul the Apostle*. Translated by William Montgomery. New York : The Macmillan Company, 1955.

——. *Paul and His Interpreters*. Translated by William Montgomery. London : Adam and Charles Black, 1912.

Schweizer, Eduard. *Church Order in the New Testament* (Studies in Biblical Theology, no. 32.) London : S.C.M. Press, 1961.

——. "Dying and Rising with Christ," *New Testament Studies*, XIV (1967), 1-14.

——. " The Service of Worship," *Neotestamentica*. Zürich/Stuttgart : Zwingli Verlag, 1963, 333-343.

——. "Spirit of God," *Bible Key Words*. Translated by A.E. Harvey (from G. Kittel's *Theologisches Wörterbuch zum Neuen Testament*.) New York : Harper and Brothers, Publishers, 1960, III, 24-88.

Scroggs, Robin. "The Exaltation of the Spirit by some Early Christians," *Journal of Biblical Literature*, LXXXIV (1965),359-373.

——. *The Last Adam*. Philadelphia : The Fortress Press, 1966.

——. " Paul : Σοφός and πνευματικός," *New Testament Studies*, XIV (1967), 33-55.

Septuaginta. Edited by Alfred Rahlfs. 2. vols. Stuttgart : Privilegierte Württembergisches Bibelanstalt, 1935.

Shedd, Russell Philip. *Man in Community : A Study of St. Paul's Application of Old Testament and Early Jewish Conceptions of Human Solidarity*. London : The Epworth Press, 1958.

Shires, Henry M. *The Eschatology of Paul in the Light of Modern Scholarship*. Philadelphia : The Westminster Press, 1966.

Smith, Dwight Moody, Jr. "*Ο ΔΕ ΔΙΚΑΙΟΣ ΕΚ ΠΙΣΤΕΩΣ ΖΗΣΕΤΑΙ*" *Studies in the History and Text of the New Testament : In Honor of Kenneth Willis Clark*. Edited by Boyd Daniels and M. Jack Suggs. (Studies and Documents, vol. XXIX.) Salt Lake City : University of Utah Press, 1967, 13-25.

Smith, Morton. *Tannaitic Parallels to the Gospels*. (Journal of Biblical Literature, Monograph Series, vol. VI.) Philadelphia : Society of Biblical Literature, 1951.

Spicq, Ceslans. " Comment comprendre *ΦΙΛΕΙΝ* dans 1 Cor. XVI, 22 ?" *Novum Testamentum*, I (1956), 200-204.

Stein, Albert. "Wo trugen die korinthischen Christen ihre Rechtshändel aus ?" *Zeitschrift für die neutestamentliche Wissenschaft*, LIX (1968), 86-90.

Stendahl, Krister. "The Apostle Paul and the Introspective Conscience of the West," *Harvard Theological Review*, XXIX (1963), 199-215.

——. "Hate, Non-Retaliation, and Love," *Harvard Theological Review*, LV (1962), 343-355.

Stinespring, William Franklin. "Hosea, Prophet of Doom," *Crozer Quarterly*, XXVII (1950), 200-207.

——. "Talmud." *Dictionary of the Bible*. Edited by James Hastings. Rev. ed. by Frederick C. Grant and H.H. Rowley. New York : Charles Scribner's Sons, 1963, 954-956.

Strachan, Robert Harvey. *The Second Epistle of Paul to the Corinthians*. (The Moffatt New Testament Commentary.) New York and London : Harper and Brothers, Publishers, 1935.

Strack, Herman Leberecht. *Introduction to the Talmud and Midrash*. New York : Harper Torchbooks, 1965.

Strack, Herman Leberecht, and Paul Billerbeck. *Kommentar zum Neuen Testament aus Talmud und Midrash*. 5 vols. München : C.H. Becksche Verlagsbuchhandlung Oskar Beck, 1922.

Strobel, August. *Untersuchungen zum eschatologischen Verzögerungsproblem*. (Supplements to Novum Testamentum, vol. II.) Leiden, Köln : E.J. Brill, 1961.

Stuhlmacher, Peter. "Erwägungen zum Problem von Gegenwart und Zukunft in der paulinischen Eschatologie," *Zeitschrift für Theologie und Kirche*, LXIV (1967), 423-450.

——. *Gottes Gerechtigkeit bei Paulus*. (Forschungen zur Religion und Literatur des Alten und Neuen Testaments, vol. LXXXVII.) Göttingen : Vandenhoeck & Ruprecht, 1965.

Talbert, Charles H. "A Non-Pauline Fragment at Romans 3:24-26 ?" *Journal of Biblical Literature*, LXXV (1966), 287-296.

Le Talmud de Jerusalem. Translated and edited by Moise Schwab. 6 vols. Paris : Maisonneuve, 1960.

Tannaitsche Midrashim : Sifre zu Deuteronomium. Translated and edited by Henrik Ljungmann. Stuttgart : W. Kohlhammer, 1964.

Tannehill, Robert C. *Dying and Rising with Christ*. (Beiheft zur Zeitschrift für die neutestamentliche Wissenschaft und die Kunde der Älteren Kirche, vol. XXXII.) Berlin : Töpelmann, 1967.

The Targums of Onkelos and Jonathan ben Uzziel on the Pentateuch. Translated and edited by J.W. Etheridge. 2 vols. London : Longmans and Co., 1862.

Unnik, William Cornelius van. "La conception paulinienne de la nouvelle alliance," *Littérature et théologie pauliniennes*. (Recherches Bibliques, vol. V.) 1960, 109-126.

Vawter, Bruce. "And He Shall Come Again with Glory : Paul and Christian Apocalyptic," *Analecta Biblica*. 2 vols. (Studiorum Paulinorum Congressus Internationalis Catholicus.) Rome : Pontificio Instituto Biblico, 1963, I, 143-150.

Vischer, Lukas. *Die Auslegungsgeschichte von I. Kor. 6, 1-11 Rechtsverzicht und Schlichtung* (Beiträge zur Geschichte der neutestamentlichen Exegese, vol, I.) Tübingen : J.C.B. Mohr (Paul Siebeck), 1955.

Volz, Paul. *Die Eschatologie der jüdischen Gemeinde im neutestamentlichen Zeitalter*. 2d ed. Tübingen: J.C.B. Mohr (Paul Siebeck), 1934.

Vriezen, Theodorus Christian. "Prophecy and Eschatology," *Supplements to Vetus Testament*, (1953), 199-229.

Weiss, Johannes. *Earliest Christianity*. Vol. II. Translated under the editorship of Frederick C. Grant. 2 vols. New York : Harper Torchbooks, 1959.

——. *Der erste Korintherbrief*. 10th ed. (Kritisch-exegetischer Kommentar über das Neue Testament, vol. V.) Göttingen : Vandenhoeck & Ruprecht, 1925.

Wernberg-Møller, Preben (ed. and trans.). *The Manual of Discipline*. Leiden : E.J. Brill, 1957.

Westermann, Claus. *Basic Forms of Prophetic Speech*. Translated by Hugh Clayton White. Philadelphia : The Westminster Press, 1967.

Whiteley, D.E.H. *The Theology of St. Paul*. Philadelphia : The Fortress Press, 1964.

Wikenhauser, Alfred. *Pauline Mysticism*. Translated by Joseph Cunningham. New York : Herder and Herder, Inc., 1960.

Williams, Charles Stephen Conway. "I & II Corinthians," *Peake's Commentary on the Bible*. Edited by Matthew Black and H.H. Rowley. New York : Thomas Nelson & Sons, Ltd., 1962, 954-972.

Wilson, Jack H. "The Corinthians Who Say There Is No Resurrection of the Dead," *Zeitschrift für die neutestamentliche Wissenschaft*, LIX (1968), 90-107.

Wrede, William. *Paul*. Translated by Edward Lummis. London : Philip Green, 1907.

Wright, George Ernest. "The Lawsuit of God," *Israel's Prophetic Heritage*. Edited by B.W. Anderson and W. Harrelson. New York : Harper and Brothers, 1962, 26-67.

Zimmerli, Walther. *Gottes Offenbarung*. (Theologische Bücherei, vol. XIX.) München : Christian Kaiser Verlag, 1963.

INDEX OF AUTHORS

Achtemeier, E. R., 68, 72, 73, 80
Albright, W. F. and C. F. Mann, 147, 148
Allo, E. B., 126, 138
Arndt, W. F. and F. W. Gingrich, 137
Barrett, C. K., 68, 100, 118, 135, 155, 157, 160, 161, 174

Barth, K., 80, 88, 99
Behm, J., 79, 142
Berger, K., 149-152
Bernard, J. H., 125
Betz, O., 116-117
Bornkamm, G., 145, 148, 155-156, 161-162, 174
Bousset, W., 8
Braun, H., 3-5, 8, 41, 49, 76, 93
Brichto, H. C., 156, 157
Brown, F., Samuel R. D., and C. A. Briggs, 131
Brownlee, W. H., 75, 164, 165
Brun, L., 143
Brunner, H. E., 87
Büchler, Adolf, 124
Bultmann, R., 17, 51, 55, 69-71, 78, 86-88, 94-96, 100-101, 138, 149, 174, 176
Burrows, M., 42

Campenhausen, H. F., von, 114, 155
Cerfaux, L., 176
Černý, Ladislav, 38
Charles, R. H., 9, 28, 30, 33, 54, 106
Cohen, A., 56, 58, 59
Collins, J. J., 152
Conzelmann, H., 69, 111, 119, 128, 148
Craig, C. T., 125
Cross, F. M., Jr., 41, 75
Cullmann, O., 95-96, 99, 101, 104
Dahl, N. A., 168
Dalman, G. H., 131
Danby, H., 52, 63
Daniélou, Jean, 43

Daube, D., 98
Davies, W. D., 9-12, 50, 59-60, 66, 101, 103, 106, 123-124
Deissmann, A., 122, 144, 145
Delcor, M., 127
Devor, R. C., 7, 51
Dibelius, M., 102, 145
Dietzfelbinger, C., 99-100
Dinkler, E., 126, 128-129
Döbschutz, E. von, 132
Dodd, C. H., 80, 105-106, 135
Dupont-Sommer, A., 41, 44, 47, 49-50, 74

Eichrodt, W., 15-19, 27, 33

Fascher, E., 156
Filson, F., 7-8, 133, 173
Fuchs, E., 149
Funk, R. W., 110-111, 163, 167

Galley, K., 99
Gaster, T. H., 143
Georgi, D., 126
Glatzer, N. N., 66
Goguel, M., 8, 96
Greeven, H., 155, 157
Grønbaek, J., 26
Güttgemanns, E., 158

Hamilton, N. Q., 106
Hammershaimb, E., 23
Hanson, A. T., 18
Hanson, R. P. C., 41
Harnack, A., 155
Heaton, E. W., 24
Herford, R. T., 56-57
Héring, J., 9, 163
Hirsch, E., 9
[Homer] *The Illiad*, 14
Hunter, A. M., 79
Hurd, J. C., Jr., 87, 116, 125-127, 138, 170

Jeremias, J., 94, 152
Johnson, S. E., 118
Johnston, G., 176

Kabisch, R., 9
Kapelrud, A. S., 19-20
Käsemann, E., 10, 17, 66, 69-72, 74, 78, 91, 94, 110-111, 118-119, 122-124, 129, 137-140, 148, 150, 152, 153, 156-158, 162, 173-174
Kee, H. C., F. W. Young, and K. Froelich, 10, 79, 94
Klassen, W., 88
Klein, G., 101
Kleinknecht, H., et al., 82
Koester, H., 74, 160, 174
Krodel, G., 163
Kuhn, K. G., 45, 87, 145, 162
Kümmel, W. G., 68, 96, 121 (revision of Feine and Behm book)

Lampe, G. W. H., 113, 116, 119-121, 137-139
Leenhardt, F. J., 80
Leisegang, I., 144
Levey, I., 143
Lietzmann, H., 9, 79, 124, 138, 145-146, 148-149, 158, 160, 172-173
Lindblom, J., 16, 17, 24-26
Lohmeyer, E., 9
Lohse, E., 124
Lyonnet, S., 2-3

MacGorman, J. W., 106
Manson, T. W., 29, 40, 65, 86, 102, 126
Manson, W., 107
Martyn, J. L., 96
Mattern, L., 1, 5-7, 39-40, 43, 48, 51, 68, 79, 80, 88-89, 140-141, 166-170, 175
Metzger, B. M., 176
Meyer, A., 54
Meyer, H. A. W., 125, 126
Michel, O., 79-80, 97, 144-145
Moffatt, J., 131
Mentefiore, C. J.G. and H. M. J. Lowe, 53-54, 59-61, 63, 84-85
Moore, A. L., 106
Moore, G. F., 31, 52, 54, 58-59

Moule, C. F. D., 113, 138-139, 141, 142, 147
Mowinckel, S. O. P., 19-20
Munck, J., 10, 12, 91, 153, 157
Müller, C., 100, 101

Neil, W., 132, 133
Nickle, K. F., 105
Noth, M., 53, 58, 60-61, 63
Nygren, A., 68, 69, 79, 86

Odeberg, H., 55, 57, 58

Pearson, B., 161
[Philo] 14
Plöger, O., 35
Plummer, A., 9, 133
Price, J. L., 71-72, 76, 79, 88, 97-99, 100

Rabin, C., 143
Rad, G. von, 26-27, 29, 38, 39
Rengstorf, K. H., 114
Rhys, H., 100
Ringren, H., 23-24, 26, 41
Robertson, A. and A. Plummer, 9, 119, 126, 128
Robinson, H. W., 31, 38
Robinson, J. M., 128, 129, 159
Rössler, D., 33, 66
Roetzel, C. J., 100
Russell, D. S., 28-31, 35-37, 66, 151

Sanday, W. and A. C. Headlam, 9, 100
Sasse, H., 110
Schechter, S., 52, 53
Schlatter, A., 9, 79, 161
Schlier, H., 9, 163
Schmithals, W., 105, 111, 156, 161, 174
Schneemelcher, W., 114
Schniewind, J., 129
Schoeps, H. J., 10, 12, 13, 53-54, 97, 107
Schoonhoven, C. R., 79
Schrage, W., 155
Schrenk, Gottlob, 77
Schubert, K., 41, 46, 56
Schubert, P., 87, 88, 104
Schulz, S., 76
Schürer, E., 117, 143, 144

INDEX OF AUTHORS

Schweitzer, A., 10-11, 59
Schweizer, E., 69, 96, 103-104, 109-110, 118, 123-124, 129, 155
Scroggs, R., 50, 87
Shedd, R. P., 10, 176
Smith, D. M., Jr., 78, 80
Smith, M., 57-58
Spicq, C., 159, 161
Stein, A., 126
Stendahl, K., 10, 66, 75, 91, 123
Stinespring, W. F., 15, 24
Strack, H. L., 58
Strack, H. L. and P. Billerbeck, 54, 65, 77, 89, 101-102, 121, 143
Strobel, A., 106

Stuhlmacher, P., 61-62, 73, 77, 79-80, 95, 97-98, 101, 105, 106

Talbert, C. H., 94
Tannehill, R. C., 88, 129, 147

Vischer, L., 126
Volz, P., 40

Weiss, J., 96, 111, 117, 119, 121, 123, 125, 156, 160, 163, 165, 172, 175-176
Wernberg-Møller, Preben 48
Westermann, C., 21-23, 91
Wilson, J. H., 126
Wright, G. E., 20

INDEX OF PASSAGES

OLD TESTAMENT

Genesis	
3	85
3:3	89
3:14	144
3:14-19	15
3:19	89
15:16	54, 98

Exodus	
2:1-7	158
4:14	64
4:22	100
16:10	100
22:27	162
24:16	100
25	27
27:26	27
40:34f	100

Leviticus	
20:11	116, 12
20:11-18	129
24:16	129, 162

Numbers	
5:8f	87
14:36-38	172
16:11-35, 41-49	172
21:2	142-143
21:1-9	172
21:5-9	172
25:9	172

Deuteronomy	
13:6	58
13:15, 17	142
14:1	100
20:17	143
33:21	61, 73

Joshua	
6:16f	142
6:18	151
6:22	143
7:13	142
7:15	151
7:16-21	124
7:25	151

Judges	
1:17	142, 143
2:16	16
5:11	17, 73

I Samuel	
8	15
8:20	16
10:6-13	157
12:7	17, 73

II Samuel	
12:13	124
15:4	15
15:6	16
24:10	124

I Kings	
8:33-39	124

II Kings	
19:11	143

II Chronicles	
20:24	151
34:24f	151

Ezra	
10:8	121, 143
37:27	154

Nehemiah	
8:6	154

Psalms	
5:8	73
7:7	19
9:4, 8	72
9:17f	19
11:5	19
28:4	19
31:1	73
32	98
35:24	73
36	73
48:10	73
50:6	72
56:8	19
71:2	73
79:6-8	19
82:1	20
88	73
94:2	19
96:13	72
98:3	72
99:4	72
143:1	73
143:11	73

Proverbs	
13:20	150

Isaiah	
1:2	18
1:2-3	20
1:9	153
1:10-17	18
3:13	17, 18
5:1	18
5:16	72
7:13	21
8:5-8	22

INDEX OF PASSAGES

8:14-15	153	4:4	18-19, 153	2:32	153
9:7-11	22	5:28	17-18	3	39
9:11	18-19	6:20	18		
10:12	17	6:24	154	*Amos*	
10:22	153	7:21-28	18	1:4, 7, 10,	
11:10	154	9:24	154	12, 14	18
13:8	154	9:25-26	153	2:1	18,22
17:10	18	11:1	18	2:5,9-11	18
22:8-14	22	11:20	72	2:5	26
22:13	154	17:4	18	3:2	18
22:16	21	18:6	153	3:9, 13	20
25:8	154	21:7	24	3:12	24
27:9	154	22:15-17	17, 21	4:6-11	19
28:7-13	22	28:13, 15	21	4:6-12	25
28:11-12	154	29:21-25	21	5:4	24
28:16	105, 153	30:13	17	5:15	24, 25
29:10	105, 154	31:1-3	18	5:18-20	19
29:13-14	22	31:31	18, 154	5:21-24	26
29:14	154	36:29	21	5:21-27	18
29:16	153			7:10-12	18
30:1-5	18	*Ezekiel*		7:16-17	21
30:12-14	22	5:13	18	9:8, 11-13	24
31:1-3	18	7:3	18		
37:23, 24, 29	21	16:4-14, 23	18	*Obadiah*	
40:13	154	20:8	18	9	27
45:9	153				
45:23	154			*Micah*	
45:25	73	*Daniel*		3	18
46:13	72	7:22	131	6:1, 3-5	20
47:1	27			7:7	27
49:8	154	*Hosea*			
51:5	72	1:10	153	*Habakkuk*	
52:5, 7, 11, 15	153-154	2:23	153	2:4	76, 153-154
53:1	153	5:10, 13	18		
54:1	154	6:6	18	*Zechariah*	
56:1	72	7:11	18	3:7	17
58:2	72	8:5	18	7:13	151
59:7-8	153	11:1-6, 8-9	18	12:1, 10	38-39
59:20-21	154	13:8	22	13:1	39
63:4, 5	38	13:14	154	14:11	142
64:4, 8	153-154	13:16	18		
65:1-2	105, 153			*Malachi*	
		Joel		1:2-3	154
Jeremiah		2:21	38	3:2	38
2:1-3, 35-37	18				

NEW TESTAMENT

Matthew		1:7	127	5:11	97
3:4-12	142, 154	1:13	77	5:12	85
5:19	148-149, 152	1:16	66, 77, 113	5:12-15, 16-22	88
5:23-24, 31-32	149	1:17	68, 70, 76, 78, 80-81, 96, 113, 153	5:12-21	87, 99
6:5	149			5:12-31	99
6:14	148			5:14	85
7:8	149	1:18-3:20	76, 79, 81-82	5:17	76
10:41	150			5:19	71
11:20-24	23	1:18	81, 93, 113, 173	5:21	87
15:5	149			6:3	87
18:15-17	149	1:18-31	80-81	6:4	103
23:16	149	1:21	86	6:5	86-87, 103
24:42-43	163	1:29	80, 86	6:6	103
25:12	159	1:32	85-86	6:7	87
25:13	163	2:3-5	81	6:8	103
		2:4-6	3	6:10	87
Mark		2:5	81, 83	6:13	76
4:24	148	2:5-12	173	6:16	76, 87
8:38	148	2:6-11	5	6:18	76
9:25	149	2:8	81	6:19	76, 97
10:10	149	2:9	77, 80	6:21	86, 97
		2:13	71	6:22	104
Luke		2:16	83	6:23	86-87
9:2	149	2:24-25	153	7:5	87
10:13-15	23	3:6	173	7:13	85-86
11	23	3:9	77, 80	8:1-13	171
11:10	149	3:15-17	153	8:1	97
12:18	148	3:20	71	8:2	87
14:11	150	3:21	153-154	8:4	103
16:18	149	3:24	87	8:6	86
17:3	149	3:25	80	8:13	85
		3:26	97	8:17	96, 102
John		3:29	153-154	8:18	97
4:25	97	4:2-8	98	8:19	107
8:44	119	4:3	76	8:21	103
		4:4	57	8:22	97
Acts of the Apostles		4:5-6,9, 11, 22	76	8:23	103, 107
5:1-11	138, 163	4:9-12, 13-17	98	8:24	102
18:24-19:6	111	4:15	81	8:26	96
		4:23-24	99	8:28	145
Romans		5:1-9	88	8:29	98
1:1	153	5:9	81-82, 97, 102	8:32	104
1:2	98, 153-154			9:3	144, 159
1:5	153	5:10	87, 88, 102	9:4	79

Reference	Page	Reference	Page	Reference	Page	Reference	Page
9:11	76	15:3	135, 171	3:18-23	128, 159		
9:13, 19-21	153	15:4	98, 171	3:19	141		
9:22	173	15:12	154	3:22	164		
9:24	77	15:18-24	156	4:1	166		
9:25-26	153-154	15:21	154	4:1-5	10, 167, 168		
9:27	102	15:26	127, 177	4:2	112, 135		
9:27-29	153	15:31	127	4:2-5	167		
9:33	105, 153-154	16:16	147	4:3	135		
10:1-22	171	16:20	119, 151	4:4	115		
10:3	70	16:25-26	154	4:5	115, 135		
10:9	102	16:26	153-154	4:6	112, 141, 159, 165-166		
10:11	153						
10:13	102, 153	*I Corinthians*		4:8	112, 128, 165		
10:15-16	153	1:2	127	4:11-13	128		
10:20	153-154	1:8	83-84	4:19	162		
10:21	105, 153	1:12-17	129	4:20	104		
11:2	100	1:17-2:16	159	4:21	162		
11:3	153	1:18	95, 102, 107, 141, 168, 173	5:1-13	115-125, 132-134		
11:5	97						
11:8	105, 154	1:18-2:16	128	5:1	118, 120, 125, 127		
11:12	128	1:19	141, 154				
11:17-24	101	1:20	102	5:1-8	10		
11:21	163	1:23	95, 107	5:1-10	174		
11:22	172	1:26-31	177	5:2	116, 118, 159		
11:25	153	1:31	154	5:3	114, 153		
11:26	102, 154	2:2	95	5:3-5	91, 118, 121		
11:27	79, 154	2:6	102, 119	5:4	113-114, 116, 122		
11:30-31	97	2:8	102				
11:34	154	2:9	145, 154	5:5	83-85, 102-103, 116, 123-124, 134, 141		
12:1	104	2:13-16	167				
12:6	155	2:16	154				
12:11	102	3:4-9	165, 166	5:6	118, 124, 151		
12:14	144	3:5, 10	156	5:6-13	118		
13:1-8	126	3:8	57	5:7	84, 116, 119, 125		
13:4	81	3:9	164, 166				
13:9	104	3:10-17	10, 112	5:9	125		
13:11	97, 106-107, 119	3:11	163-170, 172	5:9-13	115, 126		
			113, 164	5:11	121, 125		
13:11-14	106	3:13	166	5:11-12	116		
13:12	84, 104, 121	3:13-15	83	5:12	118, 119, 130		
14:1-23	134	3:14	57	5:13	119		
14:10	84, 104, 106, 113, 134-136	3:15	102, 166, 168	6:1-6	125, 127		
		3:16-17	92, 94, 112, 113, 168	6:1-11	10, 115, 125-132		
14:11	154, 173						
14:13	134	3:17	113, 148, 152, 162, 164, 166	6:2	130		
14:15	134, 136			6:2-3	115, 173		
14:17	104	3:18	102	6:5	133		
15:1-6	134	3:18-20	167	6:7	125		

6:7-8	125, 127	10:19	171	15:51	153, 157
6:8	129	10:20-23	160, 171	15:54-55	86, 154
6:9	102	10:23-33	170-171	15:57	103
6:9-10	5, 104, 129	10:24	170	16:13-14	160-161,
6:9-11	92, 125-126, 129	10:32	77		163, 172
		10:33	102	16:20	147, 161
6:11	125-126, 129	11:4	155	16:21	162
6:12	112, 121	11:17-34	92, 112	16:22	92, 114, 120,
7:1-5	127	11:20	137-138		122, 142-162
7:5	119, 173	11:21	92		
7:10	115	11:23	115	*II Corinthians*	
7:16	102	11:26	85, 95, 104,	1:9	85
7:25-31	104		139, 141, 147	1:14, 15	83-84
7:29	102	11:27	138-139,	1:22	103
8:1	128, 135, 159, 170-171		161-162	2:5	133
		11:27-32	10	2:5-11	120, 123-124
8:1-13	112, 170, 171-172	11:27-34	136	2:6	121, 130
		11:28	92, 139	2:6-11	133
8:2	159	11:29	93, 137, 139	2:10	130, 134
8:3	145, 159	11:30	116, 121, 138	2:11	119, 134, 173
8:4	170	11:32	139, 141	2:15	102, 173
8:8, 11-12	171	12:3	85, 161	2:16	173
8:12,13	136, 171	12:4, 10	155	3:4-8	79
9:1	112, 115, 157	12:13	77, 87	3:7	85
9:3	115, 167	12:28-31	155-156	3:14-18	154
9:4	170	13:1-13	155	4:1-18	174
9:14	115	13:4-13	160	4:3	173-174
9:15	85	13:10	162	4:4	119
9:16	4	13:12	103	4:6,7-11	174
9:17-18	57	14:1-9, 13-19, 22-39	155	4:10-11	153
9:22	102			4:11-12, 16	174
9:23	4	14:6, 18, 31	157	5:1-8	175
9:27	4, 168, 171	14:16, 21	154	5:1-10	106
10:1-10	92	14:19	135	5:4	175
10:1-12	10, 136, 138, 175	14:37	156	5:5	103
		14:37-40	160	5:9-10	173
10:1-13	92, 141, 170-172	14:38	148, 152, 156, 159-160	5:10	9-10, 57, 84, 113, 175
10:1-22	17, 160, 170-172	15:2	135	5:11	174-175
		15:3-5	111, 129	5:16-17	96
10:5	160	15:6, 20	87	6:1-10	174
10:6	160, 171	15:12	87, 129	6:2	83, 84
10:8	172	15:20	106		97, 154
10:11	119, 141, 171, 173	15:24	104	6:5-6	153
		15:24-26	86	6:8	174
10:12	116, 160, 169, 172	15:31	85	6:16-18	154
		15:32	85, 154	7:10	123, 173
10:13	175	15:50	104	7:10-12	120

INDEX OF PASSAGES

7:12-13	123	6:8	93, 173	4:13	106
7:11	133	6:12	95, 158	4:14	104
9:6	152	6:14	95	5:1	106, 119
10:16	156	6:17	158	5:1-11	106
10:17	154			5:2	83, 102
11:17	153	*Ephesians*		5:3	154
11:22	100	1:20	102	5:4	83
11:23	85			5:5, 8	84
11:24-33	153	*Philippians*		5:9	82
12:1-5	153	1:1	127	5:20	155
12:7	103	1:6	84	5:26	147
12:12	114, 153	1:10	83-84		
12:17	119	1:20	85, 107	*II Thessalonians*	
13:10	158	1:28	166, 173	1:5	104
13:12	147	2:10-11	154	1:5-10, 11	133
		2:12	106	1:5-12	113
Galatians		2:16	83	1:10	83
1:1	157	2:27, 30	85	2:1-12	10, 92
1:8-9	114, 120, 122, 163	3:5	100	2:1-15	93
		3:8-12	103	2:7	157
1:12-17	105	3:9	70	2:8, 12	93
1:15	153	3:10	87	2:9	119
1:16	71, 157	3:18	95, 166	3:1-16	132
1:19	148, 152	3:20	106	3:6	114, 127, 158
2:20	97	4:4	102	3:12-13	162
3:1	95	4:5	102, 107	3:13-14	127
3:6, 8	98			3:14	114, 120, 134, 158
3:10, 13	144	*I Thessalonians*		3:14-15	122, 124
3:11	154	1:10	81-82	3:15	120
3:16	97-99	2:10	102	6:7	127
3:24	71	2:12	104		
4:21-31	99	2:13-16	93	*I Timothy*	
4:24	79	2:15	113, 153-154	1:20	119, 122
4:27	154	2:16	81, 102,113		
5:4	172	2:18	103, 119	*Hebrews*	
5:5	106	3:4	153	2:14	117, 119
5:18-21	92	3:5	173		
5:21	104, 153	3:6, 12	132	*Revelation*	
5:22	16	4:3	121	3:10	173
6:7	106	4:3-8	92	22:18	148
6:7-10	92	4:6	113	22:20, 30	147

APOCRYPHA AND PSEUDEPIGRAPHA

I Maccabees		5:6	81	23:26-28	34
5:5	143	15:11, 15, 17, 18, 22, 26	32	24:8	54
				24:28-30	30, 82
Jubilees		15:33-34	32, 41	36:10	37, 81-82
2:27	34	23:19	32		

INDEX OF PASSAGES

I Enoch		98:10	84	44:15	35
1:1	84	98:12	131	48:14, 17	81
1:9	31	99:2	34	48:17	38
5:4	34, 37	100:7	37	48:40, 42, 47	34
5:6	81	102:2	32	51:3, 5, 7	34
5:9	37, 82	103:7	37, 81	59:6	81, 82
9:30, 33, 35		104:1	30, 32	64:4	38
91-104	30	104:13	31, 40	67:4	77
10:12	84	106:14	33, 34	68:5	30
16:1	84	108:1	34	68:5-8	38
22:4	84	108:3	37	77:1-4	34
27:3	77	108:13	36	78:5	36
38:1	39			83:4	102
38:5	131	*II Enoch*		84:4	33
45:6	39	30:16	89	84:8	32
47:3, 94	32	98:9-16	89	85:13-15	41
48:8	84				
48:9	131	*Psalms of Solomon*		*I Ezra*	
50:2-5	30	2:7-10	82	6:2, 6	36
50:4	36, 39	2:16-17	76	7:17, 32-34	36
55:3	84	2:36-40	36		
60:6	34, 77	3:3-4	36	*IV Ezra*	
61:8	31, 40	4:28-29	36	2:16-18	36
62:9-13	30	8:7-8	36, 39, 77	3:33	35
68:2-3	41	8:25, 30, 38-40	36	4:1-11	36
71:14	102	9:2-3	36, 39	4:11-27	102
80:8	41	9:17-18	32	4:12-32	36
84:1	37	15:13-15	39	4:23-30	35
84:4	37, 81, 82	17:12	36	6:20	102
84:6	37, 82	17:17, 32	30	6:55-59	35
90:18	30	18:3-6	30, 32	7:12-47	102
90:19	32			7:17	36
90:20-27	30	*II Baruch*		7:22	34
90:30	32	1:2	40	7:31-44	41
91:7	37, 81, 82	3:5	35	7:104	31
91:12, 14	30, 77	13:9-10	30	8:37-40	35-36
91:14-17	41	21:19	35	8:46-62	36
92:9	37, 81, 82	30:1-5	39, 41	8:53	89
93:5	77	32:1, 5	35	8:55-59	169
94:9	84	41:3-4	41	8:56	54
95:3	131	42:1-2	41	9:10, 31	34
97:1	84	42:2-3	169	50:112	102
98:3	37	44:7	34	81:52	102

QUMRAN LITERATURE

CD		1:20	46	4:6-9	47
1:4	46	1:31-32	47	4:9	46
1:5	47	2:6	46	5:11	46

6:2	46	5:6	43	7:12	45, 49, 144
6:14	47	5:8	46, 47	7:14	74
6:15	143	5:10, 18	144	7:20	46
7:9	47	5:11, 18, 19		7:28-30	175
7:20	43	20, 22	46	8:2	74
8:19	47	5:12	45, 49	9:9, 33	74
9:1	122, 143	6:8-9	130	9:14	73-74
9:11	144	6:15	46	11:7, 30	74
10:4-11	130	6:18, 22	47	12:31	74
10:14-18	48	6:24-7:25	130	13:17	73-74
14:6-12	130	6:25, 26,		14:15	74
15:7-9, 12	47	27-7:2	44	15:14	46
16:2, 5	47	6:25-27	121	16:9	74
16:15	143	7:3-25	44	16:11	73-74
19:1	47	7:5	49	17:17, 20	74
19:10	43	7:17	122		
20:12	46	7:18-21	124	*IQM*	
20:25	169	7:20, 24	133	1:1-2	44
20:30	45	8:15	48	2:1-14:16	48
		8:20-27	44	3:7	46
IQS		8:22	47	3:28	82
1:2-3	48	9:1-23	44	9:7	143
1:16, 18, 20, 24	46	9:9	47	14:4, 8	46
1:21	73	10:11-13	43	17:3	46
1:26	45, 49	10:16-21	49	18:5	143
2:4, 11	153	10:25	73		
2:10, 12	46	11:2, 5, 10-14	45		
2:15, 16	44	11:12	73	*IQp-Hab*	
2:18	122	11:14	74	1:11	47
3:14, 18	43			2:4	46
4:2-4	164	*IQH*		5:4	44-45
4:6-8	42-43	1:26	74	5:12	47
4:8-19	43	2:13	47	7:11	47
4:11-14	42-43	2:22	46	8:1	47
4:12	82	2:24	45	8:1-2	45
4:20	165	3:27	45	8:10	45
4:22	46	4:25	44	10:3	44
4:30	74	10:13	44, 49
5:1	144	4:30	74	10:13	44, 49
5:1-7:25	48	6:26, 29	44	12:4	47
5:3	46	7:6-25	45	12:14	44, 49
5:4-5	164	7:10	46	13:3	44, 49

EARLY CHRISTIAN LITERATURE

Didache					
10:1	145-146	10:6	145-147	14:1-3	146

INDEX OF PASSAGES

HELLENISTIC LITERATURE

Philo (Cohn Edition)	"On the Unchangeableness of God"	v, 429 144
"On Rewards and Punishment"		"Allegorical Interpretation"
VIII, 391ff 14	VIII, 21 14	I, 375-377 144
	"On Dreams"	

RABBINIC LITERATURE

Mishnah
Sanhedrin
6:2   124

Aboth
1:3   56
2:1   55
2:7   62
2:8   56, 58
2:14   57-58
3:12   65
3:14   67
3:16   56, 61
4:2   55
4:11   56, 57
5:3   62
5:18   61
5:23   57, 59

Keritoth
1:2   117

Babylonian Talmud
(page numbers in Soncino ed.)
Berakoth 109, 385   62

Shabbath
140   55
153-154   58
500   62
781   56

Erubin
125   52
129   62

Pesaḥim
180   52, 62

Yoma
11   52

48, 64   62
134   54

Rosh Hashanah
64   56, 59

Megillah
118, 148   52

Yebamoth
19-20, 486-487, 480, 711   62
527   52

Soṭah
22   65
184-185   62
252   64

Kiddushin
188, 209   52
329   54

Sanhedrin
402-403, 489, 618   62
601   59
718   64

Abodah Zarah
15   64

Zebaḥim
490   64

Bereshit
236   55

Tosefta
Sanhedrin
XIII, 2(Ps.ix,17)   59

Midrashim
Sifre
Dt, 12:23   55

Dt, 33:6   57
Dt, 'Ekeb para 45   53
Dt, 'Ekeb para 48   55

Genesis Rabbah
15:6   54

Exodus Rabbah
p. 353   52, 62
p. 427   53

Leviticus Rabbah
p. 400   52
p. 613   53

Numbers Rabbah
p. 112   53

Deuteronomy Rabbah
1:29   15
17:7   58
31:7   51

Pesikta Rabbati
102   53
187a   65

Targumim
(Etheridge trans.)
I, p. 47   62
I, p. 168   62
I, p. 171   62
I, p. 242   62, 63
I, p. 589   64

Mekilta
I, 238-239   59
II, 5   62
II, 236   60
II, 227-228   62
II, 278   59